England's Living Folklore

by
JERRY BIRD

GREEN MAGIC

England's Living Folklore © 2025 by Jerry Bird.
All rights reserved. No part of this book may be used or reproduced in any form without written permission of the author, except in the case of quotations in articles and reviews

Originally published as Landscape of Memory

Green Magic
53 Brooks Road
Street
Somerset BA16 0PP
England
www.greenmagicpublishing.com

Front cover photograph Catherine Tonge

ISBN 978 1 915580 34 4

GREEN MAGIC

CONTENTS

INTRODUCTION vii

1. South East England

Introduction	1
The Warrior Goddess of the Weald	3
Sussex Ablaze	15
Bedlam	27
The Chalk Giant	37
Piper at the Gates	49
A Cave and a Cauldron	59
The Witches of Eastbourne	67

2. Mercia

Introduction	77
The Horned God in Britain	79
Silken Threads	101
Hetty Pegler's Tump	109
Hunting the Wren	117
An Ancient Game	123
Magical Folk	131

3. Wessex

Introduction	143
The First Revival	145
Nine Stones	159
A Forgotten Pagan Writer	165
The Church in the Henge	177
Saints and Demons	185
Old Saresbyri	199
Evolution of a Sacred Site	205

4. South West England

Introduction	217
Poets and Lepers	219
The Wedding Party	229
The Sacrificial King	239
Ghosts Among the Stones	247
Tinners Hares	253
A Heathen Promontory	263
A Circle of Quartz	271
After the Deluge	

Landscape of Memory has been largely compiled from articles published over the last ten years or so in Merry Meet Magazine, an independent journal of Folklore and Paganism, edited by the author of this book. They have been largely rewritten and in some cases expanded, with many new illustrations from various sources. The author acknowledges the influence and scholarship of all those authors and experts whose works have been consulted, not least Laurence Keen OBE, who kindly agreed to act as archaeological consultant to Merry Meet in 2008, and has cast his expert eye over the relevant sections of this somewhat eclectic and sprawling tome. Thanks are also due to Graham King, who kindly allowed me to reproduce many images of items in the collection of the Museum of Witchcraft in Boscastle; John Hooper for allowing me to delve into his extensive photographic archive; Peter Woodward of the Dorset County Museum for permission to reproduce images of some artefacts in his care; Roma Harding for help with the chapter on Culbone, and many others who have provided invaluable information and/or inspiration.

Thanks are also due to my wife, Diane for her support, and to the many subscribers to Merry Meet Magazine who spurred me on to write in the first place, and encouraged me in the production of this volume. I would also like to thank Pete Gotto and the team at Green Magic for providing creative input and technical advice, and Peter Roe whose computer skills proved invaluable in the final stages of the creation of this book.

Jerry Bird
Dorchester 2009

Photographic & Image Reproduction Credits:

Alan Cheeseman (Wessex Morrismen) 192
Graham Higgins 241, 242, 244
John Hooper (Hoopix), 69, 71, 73, 74, 75, 196, 197
John Hooper/Museum of Witchcraft 51, 54, 57,83, 91, 94, 95, 99
Kerrian Godwin 141
Karen Cater 110
Laurence Keen (Dorset Engravings, William Barnes) 4, 209
Laurence Keen & Charlotte Lindgren (Somerset Engravings, William Barnes) 229, 236
Simon Meader 16, 17, 21, 23, 25
Harold Mockford 47
Caroline Munn (Old Glory Morris) 119,120,122
Catherine Tonge 19 & Cover photograph
Peter Woodward (Dorset County Museum) 85, 89

All other photographs and images are either by the author, in the public domain, or unattributed. Every effort has been made to contact copyright holders where necessary. If you think we have slipped up anywhere, please contact the publishers.

Front cover illustration: 'Gay Bogies' (left to right) Spencer Horne, Mick and Julia Bovee at Hastings Jack-in-the-Green celebrations, May 2008. Photograph by Catherine Tonge.

Back cover illustration: Boscastle sunset, Easter 2007.

INTRODUCTION

Britain, even though the vast majority of its population no longer attends church on a regular basis is still generally perceived to be one of the most traditionally Christian of countries. Yet lurking beneath a veneer of respectable and pious Christian culture lies an older, wilder, and more profoundly indigenous strand of religion.

There has been a tendency until recently to think of our history and ancestors in terms of epochs. Schoolbooks of the 1960s and 70s insisted that we were little more than savages until the civilized Romans came along; then the Romans became Christians and converted us too; then the Saxons arrived and we converted them; then the Vikings, and so-on up to the present day. History is, of course much more complicated than that model, and it is the survival against the odds of so much of our native pagan culture that has enabled the revival of Paganism as a thriving spiritual movement in modern times.

Paganism proved remarkably resilient in Britain. After the Roman administration collapsed in this country a large proportion of the populace who had become nominally Christian reverted to their former religious practices, and even after the Christian Church became well established and politically powerful the old religion survived in many ways: It survived in ancient philosophical texts and treatises; in the mythology and legends of our ancestors; in the folklore and customs of past and present ages. It survived in the romantic imaginations of poets, artists, musicians, storytellers and philosophers; in traditional witchcraft, healing and magic.

Philosophically speaking it survived in the hearts and minds of all those who were not too indoctrinated by established religion to notice the magic, beauty, mystery and divinity in nature.

It is not for nothing that Britain has been at the vanguard of a movement that seeks to reconnect with nature, a movement that brought about the founding of a new religion, Wicca, which has now spread worldwide. The landscape and traditions of Britain have inspired a whole new generation to look at their pagan ancestry and attempt to re-imagine and recreate the old religion.

Modern Paganism is often criticized for being a 'made-up' religion. Whilst that is perhaps true to a degree, nevertheless its roots lie deep in the soil of old Albion, whose inherent paganism has always lain just beneath the surface. Those pagan traditions, thanks in part to folklorists and archaeologists are now being uncovered and have provided the building blocks for the modern Pagan revival. This book takes the reader on a journey through the sacred landscape of England, visiting some of the lesser known sites of interest and exploring some of the stranger and often pagan aspects of folklore, music, tradition, literature, myth and legend that have survived in our hallowed land.

SOUTH EAST ENGLAND

The south east of England has much to offer the seeker after remnants of ancient paganism. Although the geology of the area, its intensively arable-farmed landscape and its large urban population means that stone circles and megaliths are few and far between, this once densely wooded part of Britain is rich in native folklore, music and tradition, and alive with stories of giants, faeries and witches. Sussex, where the sacred Samhain fires burn so strongly still was famously the last county in England to be converted to Christianity and much ancient lore lingers among the chalk hills and woodlands that stretch from the south coast to the banks of the Thames, where Kenneth Grahame introduced the Great God Pan into the English countryside in his novel The Wind in the Willows. Travelling through the region we encounter Mad Tom of Bedlam, a bogeyman from Tudor times whose insane rantings partly inspired Robert Graves to write about the White Goddess, a mysterious giant on the chalk downs, Andred the goddess of the Weald, a huge witch's cauldron in a Surrey church, and a story of modern Paganism triumphing over bigotry and discrimination in a south coast town.

England's Living Folklore

Oh, do not tell the Priest our plight,
Or he would call it a sin;
But we have been out in the woods all night,
A-conjuring Summer in!

Rudyard Kipling
Puck of Pook's Hill **1906**

THE WARRIOR GODDESS OF THE WEALD

It has often been stated that Sussex was the last county in England to be Christianized. It is probable that the sheer inaccessibility of the kingdom of the South Saxons was a significant factor in this curious historical fact. A major factor in its relative isolation was the vast and impenetrable forest known to its inhabitants as Andredsweald. In Roman times it was called Sylva Anderida and to the Belgae, the Celtic people who occupied the area in the 1st century BCE it was Coed Andred.

Andred was the name of a major Celtic deity, about which there is surprisingly little known. Andate, or Andraste, to give her her full, albeit Romanized name was a lunar mother-goddess figure associated with fertility and love. In her dark aspect she was associated principally with warfare and specifically with victory. She was the favoured deity of Boudica of the Iceni, or Queen Boadicea as she is more romantically referred to. She was venerated in woodland groves throughout Southern Britain.

Boudica's rebellion is well known. It occurred around 61 CE following the death of her client-king husband, Prasutagus, and the violent appropriation of his assets by the Roman authorities. The procurator Decianus Catus, in a remarkably insensitive example of Imperial high-handedness had her flogged, and her daughters raped after she declared herself the new leader of the Iceni. The resulting outraged rebellion nearly led to the complete loss of Roman control over the province of Britannia. Dio Cassius records that before setting out on her campaign, which was to lead to the sacking of Colchester, London and St Albans, the warrior-priestess performed a rite of invocation to Andraste involving the release of a live hare. It is unclear whether the hare was the sacred familiar of the goddess or whether it merely symbolized the start of the chase in which the Romans were to flee from their pursuers, the Britons. It could be that the hare's nocturnal foraging habits were thought to be appropriate to the dark, destructive aspect of the goddess.

After the sack of London, Boudica's female Roman prisoners were ritually mutilated before being sacrificed to Andraste by impaling, amid much feasting and abandonment by the victorious Britons at a place known as Andraste's Grove, thought to be somewhere in Epping Forest. Tacitus partially justifies the brutality involved as reflecting the expected consequences for the insurrectionists following the inevitable reinstatement of Roman rule.

Boudica as popularly imagined: An engraving by poet & antiquary William Barnes c1836

Boudica's name was derived from bouda, a Celtic word for victory. Queen Victoria, etymologically speaking, was to be her closest descendent. Dio Cassius states that Andraste was the Icenian word for victory, although it is quite probable that what he meant by this is that they used the name of the goddess as a battle cry. What is quite clear is that by invoking the dark aspect of the goddess Andraste, Boudica was demonstrating to both her tribe and to her Roman aversaries her power to enlist terrifying supernatural forces to wreak vengeful havoc on the occupiers. It is perhaps significant that when the Romans fortified the ancient British settlement at what is now the Sussex village of Pevensey to defend against the first Saxon raiders in the late 3rd century CE the association with the warrior goddess continued in the name: Anderida.

The first mention of Andred in Saxon times comes from the Anglo-Saxon Chronicle, for the year CE 477. It reads: "This year came Ella to Britain, with his three sons, Cymen, Wlenking and Cissa, in three ships: landing at a place that is called Cymenshore [near Selsey]. There they slew many of the Welsh; and some in flight they drove into the wood that is called Andred'sley." The next relevant entry comes in the year 490: "This year Ella and Cissa besieged the city of Andred, and slew all that were therein, nor was there one Briton left there afterwards". Pevensey was the name for the later Saxon settlement on this site, the name probably being derived from one of its first new inhabitants, a settler named Pefen. A Roman sword that was unearthed in 1940 just outside the castle walls during drainage work is now in the British Museum.

Roman masonry at the eastern entrance to Pevensey Castle

Virtually no Celtic-derived place names exist in Sussex, indicating perhaps the almost complete displacement of the Romano-Celtic population. The one possible exception to this is the ancient hill fort of Caburn, or 'Caer Bryn' [strong fort] near Lewes, perhaps indicating its use as a last refuge of Andred's Romano-Celtic followers against the Saxon invaders, a possibility which is supported by some archaeological evidence.

Friston Forest, Sussex, a remnant of Andredsweald

The Goddess Andred's name survived for some time after the Saxon invasion in the use of Andredes Leag, for the area to the north of the Downs, and Andredsweald for the great forest which still covered a large proportion of the area. This usage gradually declined

The Warrior Goddess of the Weald

after the South Saxons were converted to Christianity by St Wilfred who landed at Selsey in CE 681. Perhaps with the encouragement of the early Church, the largest area of uncleared forest south of the Trent gradually became known simply as The Weald. Chiddinglye Wood, near West Hoathly in Sussex was still being referred to as Andred's Wood as late as 1894.

The earliest known form of the Goddess' name is Ashtoreth, or Asherah, the supreme female deity of the Phoenician nations. In Babylonia and Assyria her counterpart was Ishtar. The name Astarte is first found in connection with a mother-goddess in Cyprus identified with Aphrodite and Cybele, goddesses of love, beauty and fertility, and the Greeks identified her with Selene and Artemis, representing the moon and the wildness of nature. The Greeks and Romans both emphasized her attributes of warfare and victory.

Much speculation has been made about the possible origins of druidic practises and belief. It is certain that the ancient Phoenicians along with the Chaldeans and Babylonians were learned in the arts of astronomy and mathematics, and that they were great navigators, with trade routes established as far north as Brittany and Cornwall. The Phoenicians recognized the divine in natural features of the landscape; trees, rocks, springs and wells. Single stones, pillars or trees were venerated in their sanctuaries, a practise which has obvious parallels with druidry. The spirit-guardian of such sacred sites was known as the Ba'al, whose consort was Asherah. According to the Old Testament one of their shrines was destroyed by Gideon, in one of the earliest examples of the Israelites' demonizing the gods of their predecessors [Judges 6]. Historians have theorized that there is a connection between Ba'al and the Celtic sun god Bel or Belinus.

It is certainly possible that a cult of Asherah or Andraste was brought to Britain by Phoenician traders long before the Roman invasion, and became assimilated into the Celtic pantheon as Andred. When recording that Boudica invoked this deity, so strongly associated with victory, the Roman chroniclers Cassius and Tacitus would naturally use the familiar Graeco-Roman name of the goddess in their histories.

It is even possible to draw the conclusion that the Mediterranean goddess had her origins in the pre-Celtic religion of Bronze Age Britain: The Greek historian Diodorus writing in the first century BCE tells of an ancient and continuing tradition where "certain sacred offerings wrapped up in wheat straw come from the Hyperboreans" (a Greek name, meaning the people from the island beyond the north wind, usually regarded by scholars as representing Britain). The offerings, which may have been first made around 2000 BCE were relayed to the tomb of the bearers of the original gifts, who had died on reaching their destination, the temple of Artemis on the Agean Island of Delos. He describes how it was common for the island girls to leave a lock of their hair on the tomb before they were married. Similar offerings of hair were a feature of the worship of Astarte on Cyprus. Diodorus also mentions that there was a great temple to Apollo [Stonehenge?] on the island of Hyperboria, and that Apollo's mother Leto had been born there but had fled to Delos to give birth to her child, with her daughter Artemis in attendance. These intriguing links between a Mediterranean moon-goddess Astarte/Artemis and the Hyperboreans seem to indicate that her cult may actually have been exported from the island of Britain, perhaps as the result of a sudden cultural change involving a shift of emphasis from moon to sun worship.

Andred's Legacy: Sites to visit

Pevensey Castle

Pevensey was the original settlement of Anderida which was fortified heavily by the Romans as a defence against the marauding Saxons about 290CE. Most of it still stands and the walls are indeed impressive, with only a short section having collapsed. The Roman masonry is still in good condition on the outer walls with finely worked ashlar blocks and decorative brick string-courses looking much as they must have looked when first erected, with large lengths of wall and some towers still standing to their original height. Once on a peninsula surrounded by sea and salt-marsh, due to shifting shorelines it is now situated about a mile inland from the coast between Pevensey village and Westham on the A259 between Hastings and Eastbourne. During the time of Alfred the Great it was referred to as Andredceaster.

Postcard of Pevensey Castle c 1900 (author's collection)

The Roman fort was repaired and refortified by Robert of Mortain (half brother to William the Conquerer), and the ruins of the Norman keep and moat are still impressive. It successfully withstood three sieges in 1088, 1147 and 1264, by William Rufus, King Stephen and Simon de Montfort's son respectively. By the sixteenth century it was derelict again, having been used as a state prison but it was briefly reinstated for defence purposes during the period of the threat of the Spanish Armada. Parts of the Roman walls were used as gun emplacements during the Second World War, which must make the fortress one of the most long-lived in the country in terms of its continuing strategic importance!

Now it is rather a sad place to visit, a bleak enclosure of grassy hillocks which are the only remnants of a once thriving Romano-British community. Entrance to the fort is free but there is a charge to enter the Norman castle ruins. Access is easy with a car-park outside the eastern entrance, and a rather good pub, the Royal Oak and Castle which stands just outside the walls. The castle is a short walk from Pevensey and Westham railway station.

Caburn

Caburn (Mount Caburn, as it is known locally), is still impressive, though the massive new bridge and earthworks on the A27 at Beddingham somewhat spoil the aspect of the site from the south these days. There is a mysterious enclosure on the north side known as Bible Bottom which has never been properly explained, and the difficulty of getting a water supply to the summit of such a high chalk hill must have been considerable. This has led some commentators to suggest that Caburn was more of a ritual site than a settlement or fortress. Deep shafts have been found on the summit that may have been used for sacrificial offerings to the gods. The small enclosure within the banks and ditches is only three and a half acres and little evidence has been found of buildings, though considerable quantities of both Iron Age and Bronze Age pottery have been found. Iron objects include a sword (250-100BCE), a dagger, a razor, some knife blades, a safety pin, a plough point, a piece of iron scale armour, an iron celt (axe blade) and a sickle. A lead weight, indicating there might have been trade through here was also found, the weight being similar to what is supposed to be the Celtic standard unit of measure. Coins found include a Phoenician coin from Carthage (c. 200BCE) depicting Persephone on one side and a horse on the other. Caburn may have been the site of the last stand of the Romano-British, Andred's people, against the Saxon invaders. There is certainly a local tradition that a great battle occurred here in the distant past.

There is much folklore surrounding Caburn: A Giant by the name of Gil is said to have walked its slopes, hurling his hammer from the summit. This aggressive image may be connected with the local tradition that the site was once a battle-ground. A nearby barrow that once stood on the site of the chalk quarry at nearby Glynde was called Gil's Grave and stood among other barrows which were found to contain iron knives and rough pottery. A Roman road has been traced crossing the stream at this point and once passed the barrow.

There are also two separate legends of buried treasure: A silver coffin and a knight in golden armour. The Caburn itself is said to be one of the clods of earth which the Devil flung across the landscape when digging the Devil's Dyke, a massive rift in the Sussex Downs north of Brighton; other fallen clods are said to have made Chanctonbury Ring, Cissbury, Rackham Hill and the Isle of Wight. The Devil is also said to be responsible for Bible Bottom, also known as the Devil's Book or The Bible on Ordnance Survey maps, so called because the rectangular banks are subdivided by a faint line and resemble a book.

The Iron Age fort of Mount Caburn, near Lewes, in East Sussex

Mount Caburn can be reached by taking the road through Glynde village off the A27 between Lewes and Eastbourne. A steep walk leads to the summit, which is often used by hang-gliders, and rewards the effort of the rambler with stunning views. Glynde railway station is just a short walk away and the adjacent pub, the Trevor Arms, is excellent for food and sells the full range of local Harvey's ales.

Cissbury Ring and Chanctonbury Ring

Further west, near the village of Findon is the massive (twenty-four hectare) hill fort known as Cissbury Ring. There is evidence of habitation here from the Neolithic, when the area was mined intensively for flints, to late Roman times when the fortifications were strengthened against the Saxon invaders. The fort itself dates from the Iron Age, contemporary with Mount Caburn, and has similar ritual deposition shafts at its summit. The ramparts are impressive still, and well worth a visit. Besides the legend that the Devil created the hill, there are also tales of hidden tunnels (probably as a result of the flint mines) and buried treasure guarded by serpents. The ramparts, though heavily silted up are still impressive. South west of Cissbury, Highdown Hill, is allegedly the burial place of the Saxon King Aella whom King Arthur defeated at the battle of Mount Badon.

An early postcard view: harvesting at the foot of Chanctonbury Ring (author's collection)

When visiting Cissbury it is worth walking north acrioss the Downs to Chanctonbury Ring. This is a smaller Bronze Age enclosure within whose ramparts two Romano-British temple buildings were constructed. There is much folklore connected with the Ring, the most famous being that if you run seven times (sometimes running backwards or anti-clockwise) around it on a dark or moonless night (midsummer's eve is said to be a favourite date) without stopping, the Devil will appear and offer you a bowl of milk, soup or porridge. If this is accepted, he will take your soul, and/or grant you your dearest wish. Some folklorists explain these tales as folk-memories of pagan rites carried out at the temple, with ritual dancing and feasting, memories that the Church was keen to associate with the Devil.

Wealden Forest

In Ashdown Forest

The once great expanse of forest is now shattered into fragments of woodland scattered across Kent, Sussex and Surrey, though there are still some relatively large areas of the precious wood that survive as vital habitats for wildlife, such as Ashdown Forest and Friston Forest. The Woodland Trust has been active in replanting in this area. Much of the forest was destroyed in the medieval period for shipbuilding, charcoal burning and the iron industry, of which the Weald was once an important centre. More modern development, farming and road-building have also taken their toll. Other large areas in Sussex and Kent were planted with conifers for use as pit-props in the local gypsum mines. With the decline of these activities the broadleaf forest is now making something of a come-back, though with climate change in the offing, many areas, especially where beech is prevalent are now showing signs of stress. The 'hurricane' of 1987 caused immense damage to woodland in the area, including the loss of most of the mature beech trees that once famously adorned Chanctonbury Ring.

The Weald and Downland Museum, near Singleton in West Sussex is certainly worth visiting with its reconstructed buildings rescued from around the south-east of England, many of them medieval. The café, in a reconstructed medieval hall, is particularly good. A new, award-winning building constructed in timber using ultra-modern techniques houses the museum's collections of artefacts and exhibitions on its conservation work.

Map References:

Ashdown Forest: TQ467310
Chanctonbury Ring: TQ139120
Chiddinglye Wood: TQ346323
Cissbury Ring: TQ139080
Friston Forest: TV537996
Highdown Hill: TQ092043
Mount Caburn: TQ444089
Pevensey Castle: TQ644047
Weald & Downland Museum: SU871127

SUSSEX ABLAZE

The bonfire tradition in Sussex is probably the county's most well-known contribution to English folk custom. A much revered tradition and a spectacular riot of celebration, its centrepiece is Bonfire Night on November the 5th in Lewes. The bonfire season in the county actually begins around the middle of September, and finishes around the end of November.

Bonfire does a very good job of dispelling the dark days of Winter, with torch-lit processions and firework displays. Bonfires were traditionally lit at the Celtic festival of Samhain, or Halloween, as the church referred to it, and originally may have been a form of sympathetic magic, using fire to propitiate the Gods so that the warmth of the sun would return once again after the dark days of winter. Having experienced the Lewes celebrations first around a decade ago, I can only describe it as breathtaking; a mix of equal parts chaotic noisy fun and awesome spectacle tempered with a sense of foreboding and echoes of dark religious and tribal significance.

The bonfire tradition in early modern times was revitalized as a result of the conspirators who sought to overthrow the Protestant King James 1st and establish a Catholic monarchy on the English throne. The conspirators, led by Catsby were almost successful in their attempt to blow up King and Parliament on November 5th 1605 using barrels of gunpowder stored in the cellar of the House of Commons. One of the conspirators, Guy Fawkes, was caught in the act and King and Parliament were saved. King James decreed that his fortuitous escape should be celebrated in perpetuity. The commonest form of celebration in those days involved the lighting of fires and fireworks, and Guy Fawkes has been ritually burned in effigy every November 5th since then.

Battle Bonfire procession, Nov 5 2005

After the Civil War the Commonwealth was established in 1647 with Oliver Cromwell as Lord Protector. One of his edicts banned public holidays of all kinds (even Christmas) as they were considered a waste of resources and ran contra to the Protestant work ethic. The one exception allowed was November 5th, being a celebration of deliverance from a potential Catholic monarchy, a celebration that the Protestant Cromwell felt to be the only important celebration of the year. As a result it became extremely popular, and continued to be so when most other popular holidays and customs were restored by Charles the Second. An extract from an old Lewes churchwarden's account-book from 1723 reads "Nov. ye 5th. Item: Pd ye Ringers being ye Day of Deliverance from ye powder plot..... 2/6."

Another reason for its popularity was that it could be adapted as the political climate changed. It could be pro Monarch, pro Parliament or anything else that seemed appropriate at the time. Bonfire always was and still is broadly political and patriotic, though in the sense that it has always been a custom of the common people and an expression of their will it could be said to be democratic and often anti-authoritarian in nature.

Battle Bonfire Nov 5 2005

The bonfires lit across England on November 5th were not the organized displays such as now occur on most town recreation grounds every year, but more spontaneous local affairs. These celebrations continued until around 1789 when revolution in France put the wind up the English aristocracy. The government suppressed any public gatherings for fear they would get out of hand. Bonfire celebrations were considered to be particularly likely to turn into anti-government riots. The French wars led to the establishment of a large military regime and local militia became commonplace across England, being used to maintain "public order" when not campaigning overseas. No doubt the 'Sussex Fencibles' as they were known, frequently clashed with the proto-Bonfire Boys of their day. This and the influence of the burgeoning industrial revolution, with rural communities dispersing to the towns and cities led to the decline of bonfire celebrations across much of the country.

However, in the southern counties from Sussex to Devon, the tradition lived obstinately on. People organised themselves into societies, generally known as Bonfire Boys to continue the custom, often in the face of stiff opposition from the authorities. Various costumes and blackened faces were used as disguise. Smugglers' attire was especially popular in Sussex, representing a fiercely anti-authoritarian past local tradition. The burning of unpopular figures and anti-bonfire objectors in effigy became commonplace in the early nineteenth century. Around this time torchlit processions and the style of celebration which continue today were established, although many seem to have been rather more drunken and rowdy affairs than now. The first 'official' Bonfire Society in Lewes was established in 1847 in response to the Riot Act being read in the town, and there are now seven rival societies all vying to put on the most spectacular display. The emphasis of the event in Lewes is more specifically sectarian than the others, commemorating the burning of seventeen Protestant martyrs in Lewes High Street from 1555 to 1557 under the reign of Mary Tudor, the Gunpowder Plot of 1605, and the landing of William of Orange on 5th November 1688 to restore a Protestant monarchy. Nowadays the sectarian content is played down by the Lewes Bonfire Council, although burning crosses are prominent in the procession and the Pope is still burned in effigy along with Guy Fawkes and more recent 'folk-devils' such as Osama Bin Laden or Sarah Palin.

The Lewes celebrations have always enjoyed a reputation as being the most riotous and spectacular. Since 1829 when burning tar barrels were first dragged through the streets in response to a ban on the lighting of fires in the street the authorities have sought to suppress the activities of the Lewes Bonfire Boys in one way or another. Cautions were issued in 1832 but the celebrations were carried on with greater determination than ever and fighting between the boys and special constables were reported in 1838 and 1841. On the latter occasion one Superintendent Flanigan was knocked to the ground with a boulder, and bludgeoned and trampled upon. This resulted in some twenty jail sentences and the following year the tar barrels were reduced to two, the Bonfire Boys compensating themselves with the introduction of a band of musicians into the procession. In 1846 the boys protested once again against the attempted suppression of their pyrotechnic activities, and hundreds of men carrying sticks and wearing disguise dragged flaming barrels to the house of a magistrate named Blackman, attempted to set the building alight, and knocked him out cold when he attempted to remonstrate with the mob. The following year there was more fighting in the streets of Lewes and the riot act was read once again. After this there was a relative truce, due in part, no doubt to the growing uneasiness about the violence among the townsfolk, and the establishment of the first of the 'official' bonfire societies. However, when in 1850 the Pope re-established the Catholic Church hierarchy in England, anti-Popish sentiment was so high in the town that the Bonfire Boys in Lewes were allowed free reign and the 'fifth' of 1850 became legendary in the annals of Sussex bonfiredom.

Lewes Bonfire Procession 1853 (from a contemporary painting reproduced by Beckett)

The establishment of the bonfire societies brought a slightly different flavour to the celebrations, with different societies wearing their own distinctive costumes and disguises. More importantly perhaps, the authorities now had organized groups to deal with instead of unruly ad-hoc bands of individuals, and the processions became a more important part of the proceedings. The more organized bonfire societies could also carry out fundraising activities to make their events more spectacular, which is largely how the celebrations are funded today.

Lewes High St. November 5th 2008

On the coast the St Leonards Society was formed in 1859 and in 1860 the larger Hastings Borough Bonfire Society was formed. In contrast to Lewes there is no mention of any anti-Catholicism in Hastings, even in 1850. In 1884 it was commented that both "Romanists and non-Romanists" were members of the Hastings bonfire societies. When the new Catholic church was built in Hastings Old Town the Bonfire Boys were encouraged to riot by the anti Catholic Tories. Constables surrounded the church, but nobody turned up, the Bonfire Boys having decided instead to protest against the Salvation Army, who being pro-temperance, were considered a more considerable threat!

The late nineteenth century saw another concerted effort to suppress the bonfire tradition across England; the banning of fires and fireworks in the street in 1906 more or less ended the custom in most towns and villages. However, it still survives strongly in Sussex and just a handful of other places, such as Ottery St Mary in Devon and Allandale in Northumbria because of the strength of local organized societies, most of whom continued in good natured defiance of the law. Even now in many places it is still only barely tolerated by the authorities. Every year the Lewes police object to the celebrations and warn outsiders not to enter the town on 'the fifth'. Many societies were re-established towards the end of the twentieth century as part of an upsurge in revived folk customs generally.

Battle Bonfire procession, Nov 5 2005

In Sussex tar barrels have their own special significance. They began in Lewes as an ingenious way of getting round the law: Flaming casks were rolled through the streets, and allowed to cause spontaneous bonfires where they burst, presumably so that no one individual could be held responsible. Similar activities still take place today, though the barrels are now represented somewhat symbolically by metal oil drums on wheels. Tar Barrels have become absorbed into Sussex bonfire tradition as a symbol of Sussex stubbornness and defiance, and on a practical level provide a useful receptacle for spent torches and create a deafening roar of iron against road at the back of a procession that adds to the noisy spectacle.

The processions themselves have become a huge spectacle in their own right with fancy dress and burning torches being the order of the day. Nowadays many bonfire societies, wearing their own 'colours' join in the processions of other societies, which is one reason why the Sussex celebrations are spread between mid September and late November. An account of the Eastbourne Bonfire procession from 1906 gives a flavour of the celebrations of around 100 years ago, and interestingly, seems to include an account of a 'Jack-in-the-Green' in attendance. The article in the Eastbourne Gazette of Wednesday November 6th 1906 lists an eclectic army of eccentrically outfitted characters who attended the bonfire celebrations in that year, including many people dressed as "darkeys" (whether this describes guisers with black faces, or people dressed as Red Indians and/or African natives is not revealed – either is possible given that political correctness had yet to be invented!). There was also a quack doctor, a man in an enormous white hat and chequer-board trousers, a man in a black and gold spangled robe and tall conical hat, footballers, schoolgirls, pierettes and assorted cross-dressers. It states:

"Of the dresses worn perhaps the most notable was that of "the man in green". He had completely enveloped himself in evergreens which formed an arch over his head and descended to his feet. On a large card he had inscribed the words 'a part of the New Park'." (Presumably the then recently created Hampden Park north of the town centre).

The Eastbourne Bonfire Society was revived in 2001 after a break of thirty-five years and achieved a seafront procession in 2005, but has been hampered by the obfuscation and discouragement of local authorities and police.

Sussex Ablaze

Battle Bonfire procession, Nov 5 2005

Battle is looked upon by many as the true home of bonfire, 'Battel Bonfire Boyes' being the oldest bonfire society in the country. There are records of it going back almost continuously to 1646. One of the earliest references to Battle's bonfire celebrations so far discovered is in the churchwardens' accounts of the parish church where it is recorded that in 1686, seventeen shillings and six pence was "Expended at Gunpowder Treason" for "Rejoycing". Among the signatures which appear on this document are Thomas Longley and John Hammond. The former's descendants are still active in the Bonfire Society, showing continued association with Battle's Bonfire celebrations for three hundred years. Ten years earlier John Hammond had converted the watermill at Pepperingeye for the manufacture of gunpowder, an industry which was to continue at Battle until 1874.

It was probably the easy availability of this, the "Finest Powder in Europe", according to Daniel Defoe, that gave Battle its reputation for pyrotechnic excellence. The art of firework making, although widespread locally, was never considered acceptable by the authorities, which threatened severe penalties for those caught setting them off. In 1781 the town crier of Hastings warned that those who let off fireworks in the town "to the great terror of the inhabitants" would face being "pressed on board a Man of War". These draconian measures appear to have had little effect, as even with the establishment of a regular County Police Force in the 1840s, the bonfire celebrations proved so popular that the authorities were forced to accept defeat.

Battle's own great terror was the notorious Battle 'rouser'. Up to the 1950s gunpowder could be purchased over the counter from the local ironmongers and during the autumn months rouser making was a local cottage industry, as it was in Lewes and many other Sussex towns. Probably the greatest and most prolific firework maker of all was William Longley of Battle. He advertized his services locally as "Hairdresser and Pyrotechnist" and manufactured his "celebrated squib" commercially from a building in Vale Road.

The nineteenth century celebrations, while generally good-natured, were not for the faint-hearted. About five o'clock all buildings were shuttered and hoardings were erected as if the town was preparing for a siege. At 7.30 p.m. the Bonfire Boys would muster at The George Hotel and then proceed to the Abbey Green from where the procession began. The route covered was much the same as the present one, although the numbers involved were generally smaller. Ninety Boys in fancy dress with the local drum and fife band leading was considered to be a good turn out. However, the progress was much slower with frequent calls at local hostelries. When at length the parade returned to the Abbey Green the bonfire, already ablaze, received the Boys' flaming torches. Throughout the day, from six in the morning when the church bells were rung, until midnight, the incessant the rouser was heard. However, this orgy of fire and gunpowder was not to last; the bacchanalian style of the celebrations was out of step with Victorian notions of order and respectability.

The 1906 byelaw was, for a while at least, to wipe out scores of bonfire celebrations virtually overnight throughout the county and all but destroyed the Battle bonfire. The authorities drafted in extra police to ensure the new law was observed, but they were not needed.

The Battle Boys along with most other bonfire societies in Sussex obeyed the law. Around seven in the evening the revellers assembled on the Abbey Green and with the drum and fife band leading, processed along the traditional route, ending this time in the Wellington Fields to the north of the town where a legal fire was lit. For the first time almost since the Gunpowder Plot the Great Gatehouse of Battle Abbey stood dark and silent. Battle's celebrations had been well and truly tamed and rather than continue with a travesty of the old 'fifth' the Battel Bonfire Boys disbanded.

Hunters Moon Morris, Battle Bonfire procession, Nov 5 2005

This would perhaps have been the end of the story had it not been for a few enterprising young men from Battle Hill. They formed an offshoot society to be called the Battle Hill Bonfire Boys. And so in 1907 the Battle Hill Bonfire Boys held their first celebrations. The route of the procession was unaltered save for the bonfire site, which was in Old Lane off Harold Terrace. The new society grew in stature during the following five years or so, and perhaps with a sense of hurt pride certain elements of the old Bonfire Boys began to plan a rival celebration. From 1909 onwards, ever larger quantities of combustible materials began to be heaped onto the annual fire on the Green and once more the "Rouser" was heard in the streets of the town. This good-natured defiance of the law continued until the First World War, which effectively enforced a sabbatical on such activities.

The armistice bonfire of 1919 was for some fortuitous reason, once again held on the Green and this reprieve has lasted until the present day, in one form or another. Indeed, even during the blackouts of World War Two, a candle was left burning on the ring of cobbles, which was laid down for the bonfire when the Green was tarmacadamed in the 1930s. With the victory celebrations of 1945 the Battle and Battle Hill Bonfire Boys could look forward to a secure future for their festivities safe in the knowledge that only in theirs, of all the towns in Sussex, does a Bonfire celebration take place on its original site.

The Sussex bonfire tradition is now as strong as ever, and is supported strongly by the local Pagan community, who are not known for passing up an opportunity to dress up and party. Lewes Bonfire Council now organizes a competition for the best costume. Along with the bonfire societies and their effigies, assorted morris dance sides and carnival drummers now process through Sussex streets in a gloriously noisy and anarchic display. The celebrations in various towns and villages throughout the county take place from September to December. While this is partly for pragmatic reasons, so that each bonfire society has a chance to join in the others' celebrations, one cannot but help the feeling that the modern bonfire tradition in Sussex has far less to do with Guy Fawkes and his Gunpowder Plot than with welcoming in the dark time of the year and celebrating local community spirit. The sacred fires of Samhain, at least in this part of England, have been well and truly rekindled.

BEDLAM

For to see Mad Tom of Bedlam,
Ten thousand miles I've travelled.
Mad Maudlin goes on dirty toes,
For to save her shoes from gravel

Chorus:
Still I sing bonny boys, Bonny mad boys,
Bedlam boys are bonny,
For they all go bare, and they live by the air,
And they want no drink nor money.

I now repent that ever
Poor Tom was so disdained
My wits are lost since him I crossed
Which makes me thus go chained

I went down to Satan's Kitchen
For to get me food one morning
And there I got souls piping hot
All on the spit a-turning

There I took up a cauldron
Where boiled ten thousand harlots
Though full of flame I drank the same
To the health of all such varlets

My staff has murdered giants
My bag a long knife carries
To cut mince pies from children's thighs,
And feed them to the faeries

The spirits white as lightening
Will on my travels guide me
The stars would shake and the moon would quake
Whenever they espied me

No gypsy, slut or doxy
Shall win my mad Tom from me
I'll weep all night, with stars I'll fight
The fray shall well become me

And when that I'll be murdering
The man in the moon to a powder
His staff I'll break and his dog I'll shake
And there'll howl no demon louder

So drink to Tom of Bedlam
Go fill the seas in barrels
I'll drink it all, well brewed with gall
And maudlin drunk I'll quarrel

For to see Mad Tom of Bedlam,
Ten thousand miles I've travelled.
Mad Maudlin goes on dirty toes,
For to save her shoes from gravel

This, as far as I can tell, is roughly how the song known as Mad Tom of Bedlam is still sung today. The ballad is one of a group of anonymous compositions that first appear in early seventeenth century manuscripts and popular anthologies that reflect the Elizabethan and Jacobean fascination with madness. There are actually a great many versions, which together comprise far too many verses to reproduce here. Suffice to say that most are variations on the same theme or themes, either Mad Maudlin's search for her Tom, or Mad Tom's search for his Maud, Maudlin or sometimes Bess.

"The Interior of Bedlam," from A Rake's Progress by William Hogarth, 1763

The lyrics reflect, as you might expect, popular notions of the time of the causes of insanity: drunkenness, sexual inconstancy or lunacy (literally, affected by the moon); many also share a common lexicon of classical imagery. Tom, or Tomfool first emerges as a term for the insane (as opposed to 'acting the fool, or jester') in the mid sixteenth century, with Maudlin as the female equivalent. Maudlin may be conflated with Magdalen, and hence associated with both prostitution (by popular tradition Mary Magdalen was a prostitute reformed by Christ) and the name for the famous mental asylum commonly known as Bedlam – St Mary of Bethlehem (though in this case the St Mary was the mother of Christ). At least one verse from an older version of the song hints heavily that Tom's madness is a result of a sexual disease:

**With a thought I took for Maudlin
and a cruse of cockle pottage,
With a thing thus tall, skie blesse you all,
I befell into this dotage.
I slept not since the Conquest,
'Till then I never waked,
'Till the roguish boy of love where I lay
Me found and stript me naked.**

16th-17th century English usage:

Maudlin = prostitute
Cockle = term for female genitalia
Dotage = derangement (excessive fondness was a much later usage of the word).

The song is a compendium of the ravings of the insane, as imagined by the balladeer. Some lines are very striking, and trawling through a few different versions one can find spirits, ghosts, faeries, giants, Satan, cauldrons, flaming spears, cannibalism, infanticide, goblins, hags, Classical gods and goddesses, the morning star, the moon [frequently], the 'man in the moon', a heavenly farrier, bloody war, plague and the end of the World, no less. Even a rhinoceros makes an appearance, though few of the singers of the time may have known what one was. A veritable panoply of nightmarish imagery – perhaps the song was the Tudor equivalent of a 'video nasty', which might explain its popularity of course!

The song was published in different anthologies: In Wit and Drollery (1656), and Pills to Purge Melancholy (1700), the latter being more or less in the form printed above. According to William Chappell in Old English Popular Music (1859) the song's popularity was boosted by Henry VIII's dissolution of the great monastic establishments which resulted in thousands of the "infirm in mind" wandering the countryside who had formerly been cared for in convents and monasteries. It is probably from around this time that the slightly sinister old nursery rhyme was composed:

Hark, hark, the dogs do bark,
The beggars are coming to town.
Some in rags and some in jags
And one in a velvet gown.

Jags, in this instance are slits in clothing that allow material of a different colour to show through; a popular fashion of the time.

A class of professional beggars, called variously 'Tom's flock of wild geese', 'Poor Toms', and 'Abraham Men' were described in London in 1616. Brewer's Dictionary of Phrase and Fable quotes: The Abraham Ward, in Bedlam, had for its inmates begging lunatics, who used to array themselves "with party-coloured ribbons, tape in their hats, a fox-tail hanging down, a long stick with streamers," and beg alms; but "for all their seeming madness, they had wit enough to steal as they went along." This reference may suggest a connection with the Bedlam Morris tradition, a wild and vigorous form of the dance in which the tatter clad dancers used sticks, rather than hankies in the dancing and is now more commonly known as 'Border' Morris, after the counties in which it survived most strongly in the nineteenth century.

The Abraham Beggars, or 'Abraham Coves' as they became known became a distinctive sight on the streets of London and elsewhere, and developed into a public nuisance. It was even felt necessary in 1675 for the hospital to issue a disclaimer distancing the institution from those who took on the persona of the Bedlam Beggar as a "false pretence to colour their wandering and begging, and to deceive the people".

If these characters, as seems likely had adopted the ballad as their own anthem, it would certainly explain the many verses that exist portraying 'Poor Tom' as starving. There was also an alternative chorus:

While I do sing, any food
Feeding drink or clothing?
Come dame or maid, be not afraid,
Poor Tom will injure nothing

The persona of the Bedlam beggar, is the same as the 'Tom o' Bedlam' character that Edgar assumes in King Lear, as described by Shakespeare in Act Two of the play:

"The country gives me proof and precedent
Of Bedlam beggars, who, with roaring voices,
Strike in their numb'd and mortified bare arms
Pins, wooden pricks, nails, sprigs of rosemary;
And with this horrible object, from low farms,
Poor pelting villages, sheep-cotes, and mills,
Sometime with lunatic bans, sometime with prayers,
Enforce their charity... poor Tom!"

Design for the new hospital 1815

Bedlam itself was a convent founded in 1247 on the site of a Roman burial ground just outside the London Wall for the order of St. Mary of Bethlehem. By 1330 it had become the General Hospital of St. Mary of Bethlehem, ready to treat the full gamut of common ailments. However, by 1403, the institution had developed into a hospital for the mentally ill, the first such in England. In 1547 King Henry VIII granted the hospital, popularly known by now as Bedlam, to the City of London as an asylum for the mentally deranged. It was a popular pastime of the day to gawp at the inmates, on payment of one penny, a fee which went some way towards paying for the patients' upkeep. It was sometimes even possible to hire out some inmates as entertainers at weddings and banquets.

The site of the original asylum now lies beneath part of the Liverpool Street Station complex, while the surrounding area, known as Spitalfields, still commemorates the famous 'hospital'. It was moved in 1676 to Moorfields and again in 1815, to the building in Southwark, a part of which is now the Imperial War Museum. In 1930 the hospital was transferred to Eden Park, near Beckenham in Kent. One of its most illustrious inmates was the Victorian painter Richard Dadd, who was committed there in 1844 after murdering his father. He became famous for his masterly paintings of spirits and faeries. As he based some of his paintings on traditional folk ballads it is not unlikely that Tom of Bedlam influenced at least some of his art. A case of art following life following art following life, perhaps? Other artistic inmates included the cartoonist Louis Wain and the architect Nicholas Pugin, who designed the current Houses of Parliament.

The Painter Richard Dadd

Perhaps the most important reason that Tom of Bedlam is often considered to be a pagan song is that the writer Robert Graves, who wrote the hugely influential (on modern Paganism) book The White Goddess, considered it to be so. In 1927, Graves received a visit from the Australian writer Jack Lindsay who asked him if he would write the introduction to a collection of versions of the song for the Fanfrolico Press. Graves apparently agreed with some enthusiasm, as he "already had ideas" about the ballad.

Graves' essay duly appeared as the foreword to Loving Mad Tom: Bedlamite Verses of the XVI & XVIIth Centuries. He concluded his essay on a dramatic note by suggesting that Tom o' Bedlam's Song, far from being a mere inspiration for Edgar's subterfuge in King Lear, was in itself an unattributed Shakespearean text, no less.

Provenance aside, the ballad was a preoccupation of Graves for years to come. He came to regard it as "the most 'purely poetic' of all anonymous English compositions" and a "perfect compendium" of Moon Goddess worship. As he writes in The White Goddess: "Anonymous English balladists constantly celebrate the Goddess's beauty and terrible power. Tom o' Bedlam's Song is directly inspired by her". The following year Graves reprinted his introduction to Loving Mad Tom in the first collection of his writings on poetry, The Common Asphodel.

It is clear that Graves regarded Tom of Bedlam as quintessential 'White Goddess poetry', with high literary merit and associations with 'primitive religion', but how far does Graves' assessment stand up to close scrutiny?

The ballad is certainly technically accomplished in rhyme and metre and does contain references to planetary deities: Apollo, Venus, Mars, and the Moon, but not only does it lack a sense of religious invocation, but references to religious ritual or ceremony of any kind are also absent. The one possible exception is the line 'The Moon's my constant mistress', but this is just as likely to be simply a reflection of the folk-belief that lunatics are ruled by the moon. Precisely which elements of pagan goddess worship Graves sees in the ballad he does not make clear. It is likely, given this and other writings that he regarded popular traditions about the moon in sixteenth and seventeenth century England to be a survival of 'primitive' religion but unfortunately, he does not elucidate more on the ballad's lyrics.

Interestingly the proposition that Moon-Goddess poetry could have been written during the English Renaissance is not at all far fetched. There exists a whole sub-genre of English poetry from the period that was generated by the cult of Queen Elizabeth I as Goddess of the Moon.

This literary 'cult' eulogised the Queen under various names - Cynthia, Diana, Belphoebe - and was instituted by Sir Walter Raleigh, the ageing Queen's favourite in the 1580s. What Raleigh began as a personal and private tribute, his friend Edmund Spenser introduced to the Elizabethan public and the mythical Moon Goddess became the most popular of all the symbols used by the poets and painters who allegorised the Virgin Queen in the late 16th Century. In drama, several plays were written specifically to glorify the Queen: Lyly's Endymion (1588) personifies Elizabeth as Cynthia, chaste and unattainable goddess of the moon. This, however is not an area that Graves chooses to explore in his analysis.

It is not surprising that Tom of Bedlam is often (despite, or perhaps because of its weirdness!) regarded as a 'Pagan' song, given the tendency to eagerness which many Pagan writers exhibit in claiming some of the stranger elements of British folk tradition as their own. However, it is to be noted that the song is not featured in the most comprehensive of published works on English folksong and its pagan origins, Bob Stewart's Where is St George, which itself has also been subject to much criticism by more orthodox experts on English ballads and folklore.

The ballad was an important inspiration for Igor Stravinsky's opera The Rakes Progress in which the chief protagonist of the story, Tom Rakewell, after a series of misadventures ends up bankrupt and insane in the notorious Bedlam asylum. In more recent years the song has become a firm favourite with many folksingers and their audiences (it has a great chorus for session singing), and has been recorded by Nic Jones (as part of the group

Halliard), Steeleye Span, Maddy Prior, Tom Gilfellon (of The High Level Ranters), The Morrigan, and more recently American singer Jolie Holland.

Maddy Prior has referred to traditional songs as "a magic lantern on the past". In the sense of a 'magic lantern' providing an entertainment, which while based on reality is a theatrical phenomenon intended to shock and wow an audience with its outlandish inventiveness this is certainly true of Tom of Bedlam.

Map References:

Eden Park: TQ369691
Imperial War Museum: TQ313791
Spitalfields: TQ333818

THE CHALK GIANT

The Long Man of Wilmington, the mysterious and dignified silent guardian of the South Downs, has baffled archaeologists and historians for hundreds of years. At 226 feet long (or tall) he is Europe's largest representation of the human form, cut into the turf on the steep (28°) northern flank of Windover Hill in East Sussex. He appears as a naked and featureless outline, carrying two staves a little taller than himself. He is designed so that from a distance he appears to be well proportioned though from the air he is much elongated.

His origins are lost in the mists of time, and the subject of much controversy. Until recently the earliest known record was a drawing made by William Burrell in 1776 when he visited Wilmington Priory, which nestles under the steep slopes of Windover Hill at the foot of the giant. This shows him carrying a rake in one hand and a scythe in the other, and includes facial features and what looks like some sort of headscarf. In 1993 however a previously unknown drawing of the Long Man was discovered in the archives of Chatsworth House, made by surveyor John Rowley in 1710. This drawing suggests that the original figure was a shadow or indentation in the grass rather than a solid line; there were facial features that are no longer visible; the staves being held were not a rake and a scythe as previously described and the head had a distinctively helmeted appearance, giving some credence to the idea of the figure as having once been a war-god.

By the 19th century the Long Man was only visible in certain light conditions, or after light snowfall, being merely an indentation in the hillside – "a mere phantom like appearance, to be seen only when the dew or hoar frost were on the turf", as described in a local newspaper at the time. In 1874, it was marked out in yellow bricks at the behest of the landowner, the Duke of Devonshire who wished to preserve the giant for posterity. Evidence from the aforementioned drawings and from recorded contemporary eyewitness accounts would appear to suggest that during this restoration the feet were incorrectly positioned, having previously pointed in different directions. It could be that this part of the giant was so indistinct by then that the Reverend De Croix, who oversaw the operation decided that the best course of action was to mimic the Cerne Abbas giant in Dorset, whose feet both point to his right side. There is, however no evidence, historical or archaeological, to suggest that the prudish Victorians deprived the Giant of his manhood as has occasionally been suggested!

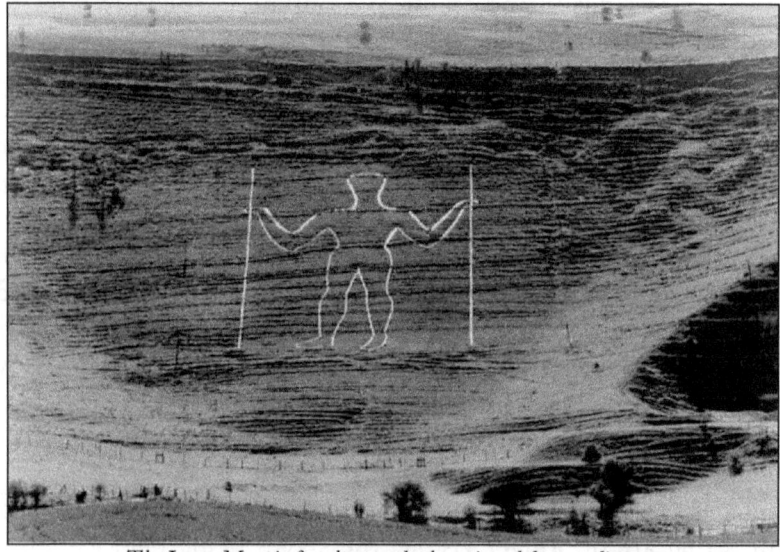

The Long Man is foreshortened when viewed from a distance

The figure has certainly changed over the years though, as natural soil creepage and erosion has led to the outline shifting, and today some of the 770 concrete blocks that replaced the bricks in 1969 have become distinctly displaced near his feet. Some of the original bricks have been found to exist alongside the newer blocks suggesting that each time the giant has been 'restored' his outline has changed a little. Since 1925 the site has been in the hands of the Sussex Archaeological Trust and the outline is regularly painted by the Long Man Morris dance side, based in nearby Eastbourne. During World War Two the figure was given a coat of green paint to prevent him being used as a landmark by enemy aviators.

The lack of firm historical evidence means that theories abound about his history. Many Sussex people are convinced that he is prehistoric, others believe that he is the work of an artistic monk from the nearby Priory, which dates from 1215. Roman coins bearing the image of a standard bearer in a similar pose suggest he may have originated in the fourth century CE and there may be parallels with a helmeted figure found on Anglo-Saxon ornaments. More recently many have argued that the giant only dates from the eighteenth century at the earliest, citing a lack of written evidence, but then the same could be said for the Cerne Abbas Giant, which is generally regarded as ancient, while the first written reference to the three thousand year old Uffington White Horse dates from 1190. An excavation carried out in 1969 shows that the giant was created by cutting a shallow trench, which was backfilled with chalk. This trench is considerably wider than the concrete blocks, so the giant would have appeared at one time as a much bolder feature in the landscape. According to the Eastbourne Herald of April 1874 "Roman brick" was cleared from the figure during the Duke of Devonshire's restoration. This would at first appear to prove the giant to be pre-Roman, but any such assertion is unreliable as the action of soil creep could have carried such material into the trench during any post-Roman period. There was some Roman activity at the top of the hill above the giant with at least two track-ways dating from this period, and an Iron Age farmstead existed nearby with strip lynchets still visible today. Thus the brick or tile material could have originated at the top of the hill and been carried down the slope at any subsequent time. The 1969 excavation also found quantities of fired clay which is also probably

Roman mixed with the infill in one of the staves, but as this had been deliberately crushed this only adds to the mystery.

The giant as seen from Wilmington Priory

There may well be some features that have been lost. In the latter part of the 19th century, so it was said, it was sometimes possible to see lines on either side of the giant, parallel to his staves. Whether these features were a shallow bank or ditch is uncertain, though the lines apparently ran from the base of the hill to the summit and were therefore possibly the remnants of ancient field boundaries. It was also generally thought in the local area from time to time that the figure of a cockerel could be seen to the west of the giant near the top of one of his staves. Although the giant doesn't seem ever to have been clothed there are several accounts of facial features, with pits for eyes and a raised nose and lips. Features around the top ends of the staves and above the head are also plausible: A resistivity survey has shown up a possible plume above the giant's head suggesting that he may have been helmeted, and also significant disturbance around the tops of both staves. It has been suggested that the items the giant is holding are variously spears, or a rake and scythe, or a club and a bow.

The Long Man, by Kerry Tanner 1950-2002 (author's collection)

The purpose and symbolism of the giant remain as much of a mystery as his age. Many theories have been put forward. One of the first was that the giant was cut for amusement by the monks from the local priory. To support this theory, there is the fact that the other well known giant hill figure in this country at Cerne Abbas also had a religious house at its base and the founder of Cerne Abbey was the great grandfather of Earl Godwin, one of whose Sussex manors was at Wilmington. Other than amusement, it has been suggested that the monks constructed the giant either because they were part of a secret occult society(!) or were inscribing the image of a pilgrim.

Going further back in time, another theory suggests the giant represents Beowulf, fighting Grendel with a spear in each hand, the cockerel that has sometimes been seen next to him a misinterpreted image of Grendel. Given that recent scholarship has re-located the site of Beowulf's legendary battle to Kent, this is perhaps not quite as far-fetched as it sounds. Arthur Beckett in his book Spirit of the Downs (1909) gives a vivid imaginary account of the Saxon conquest of Windover Hill, and the cutting of the giant heroic figure to commemorate their victory. He bases his thesis on the seventh century Torslunda plaque found on a Swedish island in 1870.

Arthur Beckett's drawing of the Torslunda Plaque

There are a host of other theories making the Giant out to be

The Chalk Giant

some sort of god or hero. Morris Marples lists Baldur the Beautiful, Beowulf, Woden, Thor, Varuna, Bootes, Apollo, Orion, Mercury, the Prophet Mohammed, or even St Paul as possible subjects. Bel, Pol, Solomon, Samson and a green man are also to be found among other more mundane figures such as a pilgrim, a haymaker or a Roman standard bearer. Sir Flinders Petrie suggested that the Long man was a representation of the Hindu god Varuna. He pointed out that the figure faces north, the quarter of the compass that is associated with the god, and that for ten months of the year, the period of 'gestation' controlled by the god, the Downs cast their shadow across him. He suggested that a Hindu cult could have migrated to Britain with travelling bronze-smiths in the second century BCE.

Postcard view c 1920s (author's collection)

A slightly more convincing theory is that he represents the Saxon warrior-hero Waendel. Wilmington is currently in the Longbridge hundred which today comprises the parishes of Berwick, Arlington, Wilmington and Folkington. At the time of the Domesday Book the area was occupied by two separate hundreds, that of Wandelmestrei and Avronehelle. Jacqueline Simpson once pointed out in Folklore Magazine that the name of the ancient hundred of Wandelmestrei has a link with the Anglo-Saxon Waendel as at Wandlebury where T. C. Lethbridge allegedly discovered a collection of ancient gods and goddesses inscribed on a hill in the same manner as the Long Man. Unfortunately, leaving aside the innate unreliability of place-name etymology the giant actually resides in what was then Avronehelle rather than Wandelmestrei.

A Saxon origin for the giant is also at least plausible due to the similarity of the figure to a warrior or war god depicted on a belt buckle discovered in a Saxon grave at Finglesham, Kent, who is depicted naked apart from a buckled belt and a horned helmet and with a long spear in either hand. It is possible that the monks of Wilmington may have allowed the helmet and belt to become grassed over and the spears to become staves so that the giant took on a less warlike (or pagan) appearance. As Sussex was the last county in England to be Christianized it is entirely possible that a pagan figure could have survived into the early Middle Ages, especially given the example of the Cerne Abbas giant whose most notable attribute was not expunged until it offended Victorian sensibilities in the nineteenth century. It is also possible that the priory was sited close to the Long Man as a kind of exorcism, or to put a halt to perceived pagan activity connected with him.

The cautious say the giant is some sort of idol or fertility symbol created some time between the Neolithic and late Medieval period. Before his first restoration in 1874 he was occasionally known by name as the Green Man, being entirely grassed over, and sometimes as the Lanky Man or the Lone Man. The earliest known mention of his name as the Long Man is in a 1765 lease agreement for Wilmington Court Farm that refers to a field strip by the name of the Longman Laine. Some have interpreted the staves as a gate, which the giant is holding open or passing through either to heaven or the underworld, or as the 'gates of dawn'. Interestingly, the ancient parish church at Wilmington is dedicated to St Mary and St Peter, the latter being the guardian of the famous pearly gates of heaven. Rodney Castleden, in his book The Wilmington Giant (1983) concluded that the giant was a Neolithic sun-god "arriving to bring high summer through the ritual gateway to the world of men"

– a kind of embodiment of the spirit of John Barleycorn.

An alternative symbolism was suggested by Alfred Watkins in The Old Straight Track (1925) in which he suggests that the Long Man represents a "dodman" or "ley-man" using his staves to survey spirit paths or ley lines in the landscape. This is also how Dion Fortune regards him in her novel The Goat Foot God (1936). The late lamented Ronald Millar developed a similar theme with a wonderful short story in his book the Green Man Companion and Gazeteer (1997) in which the monks of Wilmington employ a Wind Smith with his long ash staves to determine the location of their new mill. This theme re-emerges in Kevan Manwaring's recent novel The Windsmith (2006).

There is a great deal of local folklore attached to the giant, as might be expected with such a prominent and unusual landmark. Legend has it that the figure is either a memorial to a giant who lived on Windover Hill or the actual outline drawn around his body where he fell dead. In one version of the tale the giant tripped down the hillside and broke his neck, but in another he was killed by pilgrims on their way to the priory. This version may contain a fragment of folk-memory of the giant being objected to or mutilated by the medieval Church. There is also a rather silly story that the giant expired after a shepherd threw his dinner at him! The commonest tale, however is that there were two giants, one of whom lived on Windover Hill and the other on Firle Beacon, three miles away across the Cuckmere Valley. The pair quarrelled and threw boulders at each other, with the Firle giant being the victor. Some say the Windover giant lies buried in the nearby long barrow known as Hunter's Burgh, while the many depressions on the top of the hill caused by ancient flint and chalk mining are supposedly the marks left when the boulders rained down during the battle. Given that both hilltops are adorned with large ancient burial mounds it is entirely possible that the folklore commemorates the tribal feuding between rival chieftains in prehistory; there is also a frequently encountered legend of treasure buried nearby, which probably relates to the ancient tumuli. There is also persistent folklore that there was at least one other giant nearby. When T.C.

Lethbridge was a schoolboy an old shepherd apparently told him that the giant had had a companion and that they were known as Adam and Eve. In 1905 the folklorist J P Emslie records that there was a tradition of a chalk figure cut into Hindover Hill above Alfriston in the form of a "man thrown from a horse" that was said to have commemorated the site of a Saxon victory over the Normans. Emslie also recorded a local tale that treasure was buried within the giant's outline. According to J. H. Allcroft "Men who were schoolboys in the 1860s recollect it well enough, though it is now so vanished that learned folks refuse to believe them." The current figure on Hindover Hill, at a place called High and Over across the valley from the Long Man, is the now slightly scruffy horse that dates from 1838, but there is no reason to suppose that older figures did not precede it. Also the fact that the horse is so close to the top of the slope may account for the 'thrown rider' legend, if the human figure, as is entirely possible, appeared below the horse on the same steep hillside.

Druids Greg Draven and Damh the Bard share a joke at the foot of the Long man

In recent years the Long Man has been the centre of much modern Pagan activity. The flattened spoil heap from a chalk pit which lies at his feet makes the perfect place for an out-door ceremony, and several Sussex Pagan groups use it as such, including the Anderida Gorsedd grove of Druids which holds regular open rituals. The Long Man was a favourite site of Doreen Valiente and many a Wiccan initiation has been held there over the years. A quarry-pit at the summit of the hill frequently bears the marks of ritual fires and at night is a very evocative place, surrounded by ancient earthworks on all sides and a clear starry sky overhead. A few years ago the original Eastbourne Pagan Circle held a memorable Imbolc celebration here that was followed by storytelling and music in the village hall.

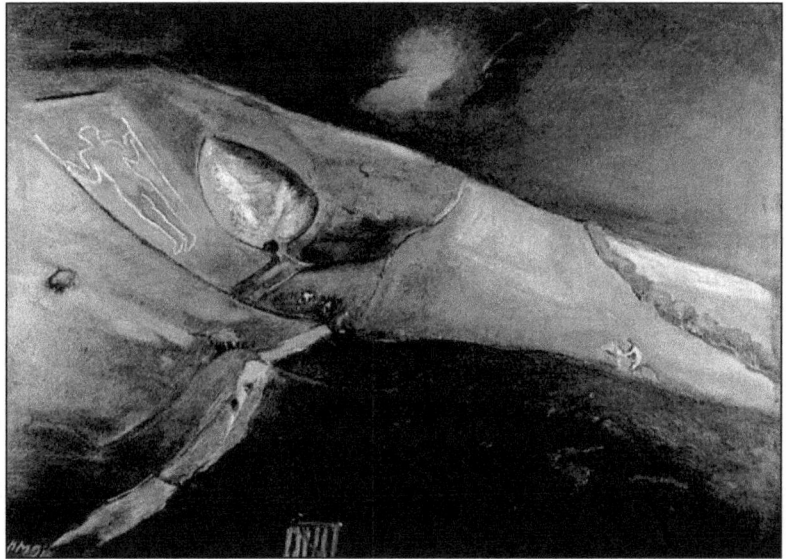

The Long man on the Downs, by Harold Mockford (b 1932)

The Long Man, almost as much as the Cerne Abbas Giant, has become something of a popular icon in the twentieth century. Doreen Valiente wrote a poem about him, and he has been represented in art many times. The great water-colourist and wood-engraver Eric Ravilious depicted him several times including a view as seen from the window of a passing train, while more recently he has appeared in Harold Mockford's wonderfully evocative paintings as a sort of spiritual guardian of the landscape. He is also celebrated in Ashley Hutchings' song Along the Downs with the lines:

**At Wilmington there stands a man
A chalky stave in either hand
A memory of times gone by
When giants strode beneath the sky**

Fertility symbol? Sun God? Ancient Warrior? Ecclesiastical joke? We will probably never know. Until definitive dating evidence is unearthed, if it ever is, we shall have to content ourselves with the words of the Rev A A Evans who said "The Giant keeps his secret and from his hills he flings out a perpetual challenge."

The Long Man of Wilmington is situated six miles northwest of Eastbourne It is signposted from the A27, two miles west of the junction with the A22 at Polegate and ten miles east of Lewes and located south of the village of Wilmington. Buses serve the A27, and the nearest railway station is at Berwick, about three miles away.

The giant is close to the South Downs Way long distance footpath which at this point follows the ancient ridgeway track at the summit of the chalk scarp. From the car park at Wilmington Priory the giant is a relatively easy walk of about ten minutes. The priory is now owned by the Landmark Trust and is sadly no longer normally open to the public but the church is well worth a visit with its thirteenth century chapel containing the beautiful 'bee and butterfly window' depicting St Peter among the insects. The massive yew tree in the churchyard must be one of the oldest in the country and probably pre-dates the church itself. While in the village have a look for the Celtic-style stone head that adorns one of the cottages in the main street. The Giant's Rest pub is worth a visit too!

Map References:

Firle Beacon: TQ485059
High and Over: TQ510009
Hunter's Burgh: TQ549036
Long Man of Wilmington: TQ542034
Wilmington Church: TQ544042
Wilmington Priory: TQ543041

THE PIPER AT THE GATES

The goat-footed, priapic, horned god Pan is perhaps the most popular manifestation of the male aspect of deity honoured by modern Pagans, especially Wiccans. Given the choice of several such deities which could have been adapted to modern Paganism, including the (perhaps) more native Cernunnos, why did the relatively minor Greek God become so important to today's Pagan movement?

Pan's origins lie in Arcadia, the remote rural area of ancient Greece, regarded as primitive by more sophisticated Greeks. Probably for this reason, he was never really counted as one of the pantheon of Olympean Gods. In his role as patron of hunters and farmers, the goatherds, shepherds and beekeepers, he was a god of the rural poor. A rather touching piece of anonymous ancient classical verse shows how he could be propitiated by even the lowliest offering, and was therefore open to the prayers of everyman without the need for grand temples and high priests. Thus he was truly a god of the common people:

Alcimenes, an ancient man
Though poor and humble ne'er forgot
To offer little gifts to Pan:
Spring water in an earthen pot,

A fig, an apple, nothing more,
And standing made his lowly prayer.

**Thou giv'st me from thy plenteous store
All that my trees and seedlings bear,**

**So take this water from the spring,
The fruits that thou hast made to thrive;
Take not too close a reckoning,
But give me more than I can give.**

His sexual exploits were celebrated in legend. He was the only god to whom the formidably virginal Artemis ever yielded. His tastes were eclectic and he often pursued male partners and sometimes animals. His principle lovers were the forest nymphs and the Maenads, wild women who took part in the orgies of Dionysus. Dionysus himself, as the horned child, has many similarities to Pan. To the Romans he was Faunus, or Sylvanus, and is therefore linked to the image of the Green Man, as the god of the forest peering through the woodland glade. With the spread of the Roman Empire his cult spread far and wide, and no doubt merged with many local deities and genus loci of sacred sites throughout Europe.

Pan is one of the few gods whose worshippers practised their rites naked, or sometimes wearing only goat-skins. Ritual nudity was something quite uncommon in the ancient world, and Ovid, perhaps tongue-in-cheek, gives an amusing explanation for this anomaly, which also emphasizes the god's role in mythology as both sexual predator and trickster:

One day Pan, or Faunus, found Hercules and Omphale, the Queen of Lydia, enjoying a post-coital snooze in a grotto. He intended to take advantage of the young woman as she slept. However, unknown to Pan the lovers had exchanged clothes in their sexual playfulness. In the darkness of the grotto Pan was deceived by the skin of the lion which Omphale now wore and slipped into bed next to Hercules who was wearing the Queen's soft robes. He was, unsurprisingly, rudely repulsed and flung unceremoniously from the bed, and so to avoid any similar embarrassing incidents in the future, Pan decreed that all his priests and priestesses should be naked when they celebrated his festivals!

The Piper at the Gates

In the Roman world, as Faunus, Pan's great festival was the Lupercalia, held on February 15th up until 494CE at which time the feast was consecrated by Bishop Gelasius as a Christian festival of purification and moved to February 2nd. Formerly goats and dogs had been sacrificed to Pan, after which their skins were cut into thongs and then formed into whips. The priests of the festival, the Luperci would then run through the streets of Rome striking all whom they encountered. Married women particularly would stand in their way, as a strike from the hallowed thongs was said to aid fertility and ease the pain of childbirth.

Pan indulging in his favourite activity (Ralph Harvey's collection)

This aspect of Pan and his festivities would have been very attractive to Gerald Gardner when he was formulating the earliest books of shadows in the 1940s. Gardner was well known both for his naturism and for some unusual sexual proclivities, and it is likely that the whips of the Luperci were the inspiration behind (or possibly justification for) his introduction of the scourge into Wiccan rites. Ritual nudity also fitted well with Margaret Murray's thesis of historical witchcraft being a relic of ancient pagan rites, with witches dancing naked before a mysterious horned figure. Pan was also very important to Crowley, who managed posthumously to scandalise the residents and burghers of Brighton when his Hymn to Pan was read at his funeral in the town in 1947.

Carved oak plaque showing Pan in goat form playing the pipes (author's collection)

Another of the Classical myths explains the origins of the Pan-pipes, and is perhaps an interesting comment on the relationship between music and sexual desire, in which the frustrated god finds solace in the ethereal sound of the pipes:

In the snowy mountains of Arcadia lived a well-known hamadryad (tree-nymph), called Syrinx. All the gods of the forest, smitten by her beauty had attempted to court her, but to no avail, as she was adept at avoiding their advances, wishing to stay single and free, hunting in the forest like her mentor Artemis. Finally, the ardently priapic Pan met the nymph on one of his expeditions into the forest, whereupon he approached and courted her passionately.

The virgin nymph treated him with disdain and fled through impassable terrain until she found herself on the bank of a slow running silted river called Ladon, whose banks were far enough apart to prevent her from crossing. Here she invoked Artemis, to have mercy upon her and to transform her before she fell into the hands of the goat-footed god. Meanwhile Pan had caught her up and in his passion he embraced the hesitant nymph as she stood on the shore. He was both surprised and enraged when instead of the lithe body of the nymphet, he found himself embracing a reed in his arms. Frustrated in his desire, his heavy breathing resonated through the reed resulting in a sweet, musical sound. The magic from this pleasant sound consoled the deceived god. "Alas, you are transformed", he cried, "nevertheless our bond shall be eternal!" From the reed he cut seven pipes of different lengths, bound them together with wax and named his lovely sounding flute after the elusive hamadryad. The shepherd's pipe has ever since been known as the syrinx, and is commemorated by Macedonius' poem from the sixth century CE:

Daphnis, I that piped so rarely,
I that guarded well the fold,
'Tis my trembling hand that fails me;
I am weary, I am old.

Here my well-worn crook I offer
Unto Pan the shepherd's friend;
Know ye, I am old and weary;
Of my toil I make an end!

Yet I still can pipe it rarely,
Still my voice is clear and strong;
Very tremulous in body,
Nothing tremulous in song.

**Only let no envious goatherd
Tell the wolves upon the hill
That my ancient strength is wasted,
Lest they do me grievous ill.**

Pan once competed with his flute against Apollo's lyre, but the syrinx was judged by Tmolus to be inferior. Everyone agreed with this judgement except King Midas, who called it unjust. For this Midas unfortunately acquired by the will of Apollo the ears of an ass, which thereafter he tried in vain to conceal under a turban.

Bronze figurine (Museum of Witchcraft collection)

Music, dancing, and especially laughter were all important facets of the rites of Pan, while his sensual, all-encompassing nature shows

The Piper at the Gates

also a gentler side, which appealed very much to the romantic revival of classical pagan imagery in early modern literature and art, which in turn influenced the post-WW2 Pagan movement. One of the most beautiful evocations of Pan as the horned God in modern literature comes from the pen of Kenneth Grahame writing in Wind in the Willows, in the chapter entitled The Piper at the Gates of Dawn:

"This is the place of my song-dream, the place the music played to me,' whispered the Rat, as if in a trance. `Here, in this holy place, here if anywhere, surely we shall find Him!'

Then suddenly the Mole felt a great awe fall upon him, an awe that turned his muscles to water, bowed his head, and rooted his feet to the ground. It was no panic terror--indeed he felt wonderfully at peace and happy--but it was an awe that smote and held him and, without seeing, he knew it could only mean that some august presence was very, very near. With difficulty he turned to look for his friend, and saw him at his side cowed, stricken, and trembling violently. And still there was utter silence in the populous bird-haunted branches around them; and still the light grew and grew.

Perhaps he would never have dared to raise his eyes, but that though the piping was now hushed, the call and the summons seemed still dominant and imperious. He might not refuse, were Death himself waiting to strike him instantly, once he had looked with mortal eye on things rightly kept hidden. Trembling he obeyed, and raised his humble head; and then, in that utter clearness of the imminent dawn, while Nature, flushed with fullness of incredible colour, seemed to hold her breath for the event, he looked in the very eyes of the Friend and Helper; saw the backward sweep of the curved horns, gleaming in the growing daylight; saw the stern, hooked nose between the kindly eyes that were looking down on them humorously, while the bearded mouth broke into a half-smile at the corners; saw the rippling muscles on the arm that lay across the broad chest, the long supple hand still holding the pan-pipes only just fallen away from the parted lips; saw the splendid curves of the shaggy limbs disposed in majestic ease on the sward; saw, last of all, nestling between his very hooves, sleeping soundly in entire peace and contentment, the little, round, podgy, childish form of the baby otter. All this he saw, for one moment breathless and intense, vivid on the morning sky; and still, as he looked, he lived; and still, as he lived, he wondered.

'Rat!' he found breath to whisper, shaking. `Are you afraid?'

`Afraid?' murmured the Rat, his eyes shining with unutterable love. `Afraid! Of him? O, never, never! And yet, and yet, O, Mole, I am afraid!'

Then the two animals, crouching to the earth, bowed their heads and did worship.

Sudden and magnificent, the sun's broad golden disc showed itself over the horizon facing them; and the first rays, shooting across the level water-meadows, took the animals full in the eyes and dazzled them. When they were able to look once more, the Vision had vanished, and the air was full of the carol of birds that hailed the dawn."

It is interesting to note how Grahame brings Pan into his story as an archetypal woodland guardian deity. The god was even featured on the cover of the first edition of the novel, which is ironic considering how often the above quoted passage has been expunged from later (usually 'children's') editions. Born in Scotland, Grahame was brought up in the village of Cookham Dean, and the nearby Quarry Wood on the south bank of the River Thames is said to be the original 'Wild Wood' of the novel. Grahame wrote the book in 1908, after retreating from his life as secretary of the Bank of England in London following an incident in which he was shot at by a lunatic. He returned to the Mount, a large house owned by his grandmother (now a prep school), where he had spent many happy years of his childhood. In the book the 'wild wood' is a threatening place in which mole sees the trees "all fixing on him glances of malice and hatred: all hard-eyed and evil and sharp". Grahame's Pan is the gentle guardian of the wood and protector of the animals, a role which does not appear in Classical literature, and yet seems to suit him well in the context of modern Paganism. Grahame, as far as anyone knows would not have called himself a Pagan, though his

The Piper at the Gates

first book, published in 1893 was called Pagan Papers; it was a collection of essays and stories on the general theme of bucolic escapism, extolling the pleasures of long walks in the country and pints of beer sipped in picturesque wayside taverns, while railing fashionably against the harshness of the modern machine age. Paganism today owes a great debt of gratitude to this gentle, neurotic, unworldly man who not only recast Pan in the role of a generic horned God, but introduced him as such to millions of children and adults over the last century.

There is a permanent exhibition to Grahame's Wind in the Willows at the River and Rowing Museum, Henley on Thames, which is well worth a visit.

Pan in the form of an oil lamp (Museum of Witchcraft collection)

In more recent literature, Pan crops up in Dion Fortune's classic occult tale The Goat Foot God, and in Tom Robbins' poignant and hilarious novel Jitterbug Perfume, both of which ought to be on the shelves of any well-read Pagan. Arthur Machen's The Great God Pan is a classic of its time though remains perhaps something of an acquired taste to the modern reader.

The word pan means literally 'all; everything'. Doreen Valiente wrote that "the various representations of Pan show him as *the* (my italics) positive Life Force of the world", no less. It is this manifestation as the spirit of all nature that perhaps hints at Pan having once been far more important in the ancient world than his Demi-God status in Graeco-Roman mythology would have us believe. Madame Blavatsky wrote that "Pan was at one time Absolute Nature, the One and Great All; but when history catches a first glimpse of him, Pan has already tumbled down into a godling of the fields, a rural god; history will not recognize him, while theology makes him the Devil". Fortunately modern Paganism has seen fit to honour the Arcadian, goat-footed god, and restore some of his erstwhile importance. His cult lives on, and due to the remarkable spread of modern Pagan ideas, partly, it has to be said due to the 'pan-global' phenomenon of the internet, it can now be truly said to be 'of the World'.

Map References:

Quarry Wood: SU860853
River and Rowing Museum: SU767820
The Mount, Cookham Dean: SU871842

A CAVE AND A CAULDRON

Surrey is a county not generally noted for witchcraft in its folklore, compared with say, Sussex, Devon or Cornwall, and yet there are many fascinating, if little known sites, some with strange stories attached. One such particularly rich in legend is Mother Ludlam's Hole, a cave near Frensham, between Farnham and Hindhead.

In the year 1216 the spring which had supplied Waverley Abbey since its foundation in 1128 suddenly dried up. The spring was called Ludewell in the Abbey's Annals, according to which the problem was solved by a monk named Symon. He discovered a "living spring", and with "much difficulty and invention... labour and sweating" he enlarged it and brought the water to the Abbey by means of a system of underground channels. The new spring was named St. Mary's Well (also the dedication of nearby Frensham Church). It seems likely that the two springs were close together, and that Symon dug into the hillside nearby to find water. The cave which is still accessible today is the result of this early feat of hydraulic engineering, now somewhat overgrown but still with a moderately sized entrance. It rapidly contracts down to an extremely low arch through which flows a small stream. There is a slightly daft piece of local folklore that says, apropos of nothing else in particular, that geese would enter the cave at Frensham and re-emerge at Guildford without their feathers!

In 1673 antiquarian John Aubrey visited Frensham to collect information for his book on the county of Surrey, which was published in 1718. He was told that Ludwell was named after King Lud of the South Saxons, who went there to bathe his wounds after a battle. He adds that the monks of Waverley "made it their Helicon, where they met their Muses".

Some of the present-day remains of Waverley Abbey

Mother Ludlam was supposed to have lived in the cave, which by the 1680s fell within the landscaped grounds of Moor Park, the home of Sir William Temple, the horticultural enthusiast who introduced the tulip to the gardens of England. The cave had probably been turned into an ornamental grotto by 1724, when extensions to the formal gardens were completed. In 1782 A visitor, John Byng, describes "a great cavity in a sandy rock, thro' which runs a little stream; it is paved, has several stone benches in it, and is by much the best place I ever saw for a cold collation on a summer's day: never was place more adapted for quiet meditation . . . Mother Ludlam is reported to have been a witch of benevolent temper, who benefited, instead of injuring, her poor neighbours."

Sadly even as early as 1820 the well had become derelict, as described in William Cobbett's Rural Rides: "From Waverley we went to Moor Park. . . Here, I showed Richard 'Mother Ludlum's Hole'; but alas! It is not the enchanting place that I knew it, nor that which

Grose describes in his Antiquities! The semicircular paling is gone; the basins to catch the never ceasing little stream are gone; the iron cups fastened by chains for people to drink out of, are gone; the pavement all broken to pieces; the seats, for people to sit on, on both sides of the cave, torn up and gone; the stream that ran down a clean paved channel, now making a dirty gutter; and the ground opposite, which was a grove, chiefly of laurels, intersected by closely mowed grass walks, now become a poor ragged-looking Alder coppice".

Engraving of 1785 showing the cave and gardens (author's collection)

Aubrey is the first author to mention "an extraordinary great kettle or cauldron", which can still be seen in Frensham Church. There was a belief that it had been conveyed there by the fairies long ago. The fairies had apparently carried the cauldron to Frensham from a place called Borough Hill, which Aubrey tells us was a mile distant. "On this Borough Hill, in the tything of Cherte [now Churt], in the parish of Frensham is a great stone lying along, of the length of about six feet; they went to this stone and knocked at it, and declared what they would borrow, and when they would repay, and a voice would answer, when they should come, and that they should find what they desir'd to borrow at that stone. This caldron, with the trivet, was borrow'd here after the manner aforesaid, but not return'd according to promise; and though the caldron was afterwards carried to the stone it could not be receiv'd and ever since that time no borrowing there". Aubrey adds the intriguing remark that "the people saw a great fire that night", but apart from emphasising it was not a heath fire, he provides no explanation for this phenomenon.

Aubrey was dismissive of the legend, and believed that the cauldron was an ancient utensil used by the villagers in 'love feasts'. It is mentioned again in 1736 in Salmon's History of Surrey. This writer relates the fairy legend and is of the opinion that it had come originally from Waverley Abbey, being, he thought, of a type commonly used for the entertainment of parishioners at the weddings of poor maids.

Mother Ludlam's Cauldron

Grose (1785) confuses the issue. In his account Mother Ludlam and the cauldron are linked with Ludwell. She performed much the same duties as the fairies of Borough Hill, by lending utensils, but in

A Cave and a Cauldron

this account the cave must be visited at midnight, and the borrower must turn around three times and repeat their requirement with each turn. They must also promise to return it within two days, far less generous terms than the fairies in the earlier legend. Seasoned earth-mystery enthusiasts will note that in this version the cave has taken on aspects more usually associated with standing stones and megalithic circles. In another version first written down in 1869 the cauldron originally stood in Mother Ludlam's cave. Anyone in need had only to drop a coin into the cauldron and Mother Ludlam would grant their desire. All was well until one night the Devil stole the cauldron. He made off with it towards the Devil's Jumps but dropped it as he leaped from hill to hill. It fell onto Kettlebury Hill where it was found later, which is how the hill got its name. No doubt this account reflects the natural tendency for wells to become 'wishing wells' over time, attracting visitors whose coins cast into the water for luck would be collected by the landowner to maintain the site.

The Devil's Jumps. A postcard from around 1915 (author's collection)

Over the years the tale has gained even more variations, many of which were current at the same time. The original story concerning the fairies that lived in Borough Hill seems to have become muddled with a later story concerning the 'white' witch Mother Ludlam. The location of Borough Hill is not certain. However, the name 'borough' can denote an earthwork or tumulus, and there are many accounts in folklore of fairies living in mounds or tumuli, sometimes entered by moving aside a great rock; just under a mile to the east a cluster of tumuli stand on a ridge across Frensham Common.

A story which links the witch, the cauldron and another possible site for Borough Hill was recorded from an elderly lady who died in 1937. Mother Ludlam was both witch and herbalist. People came to her for potions that she prepared in a large cauldron. One day the Devil came in disguise and asked if he might borrow the vessel, but Mother Ludlam saw his cloven hoof marks in the sand and refused. At this he seized the cauldron and made off, with Mother Ludlam in hot pursuit on her broomstick. The Devil took seven great leaps, and wherever his boots touched the ground a hill arose, forming the Devil's Jumps, a series of conical hills just over a mile from Frensham, near Churt village, the highest of which is known as Stony Jump. He dropped the cauldron on the last, Kettlebury Hill (which interestingly is on Pot Common), and disappeared into the ground, forming the Devil's Punchbowl at nearby Hindhead as he did so. Mother Ludlam then took her cauldron and placed it in Frensham Church for safety.

In an even weirder tale, published by the Farnham Herald in 1985 one Reg Baker recounted a version of the legend current during his boyhood in Frensham in the 1920s. The cauldron could be borrowed by climbing the hill south of the village (Stony Jump again), and whispering to the faeries who lived there through a hole in the huge outcrop of rock on the summit. All went well until once again the cauldron was not returned on time. The faeries refused to take it back and condemned the unfortunate borrower to have it follow him wherever he went. Eventually, tormented by the presence of his unlikely three-legged pursuer, he sought sanctuary in the village church. There he collapsed and died, leaving the cauldron trapped inside. Another legend has the Devil leaping from hill to hill when he is seen by the god Thor. Thor, as was his custom, threw an enormous stone at the Devil, which became embedded in the hilltop. There is little doubt that the rock on Stony Jump was a prominent natural outcrop. Being on a hilltop, it would have been a natural candidate for a place sacred to the pre-Christian populace. Unfortunately it has now been destroyed and a house occupies the summit.

St Mary's Church, Frensham

It is possible, or perhaps even likely that these legends contain folk memories of ancient ritual practice. Intriguingly, in 1799 the Gentleman's Magazine reported that "The Devil's Three Jumps [whether the tumuli on the common, or the hills is not made clear] were regarded with awe, and that formerly, on Whit Tuesday, the country people used to gather to dance and make merry on the easternmost and highest". This tempts some interesting and amusing speculations. Could it be perhaps that in early medieval times when the Church still did not quite reign supreme the cauldron was used in these revenant Pagan celebrations? One interpretation of the 'borrowing' legends might be that whoever looked after the cauldron between rituals once failed to turn up in time for an important annual rite and was shunned by the local populace, or maybe they converted to Christianity and denied the Pagans the focus of their ceremony by handing the cauldron over to the priest, or perhaps someone sought sanctuary in the church having stolen it from the enraged Pagans. A more likely scenario of course is simply that at some point it was confiscated and locked away in the church by a local clergyman outraged at such blatantly 'ungodly' behaviour going on in his parish.

Whatever its true origin and history, Mother Ludlam's enormous cauldron, or 'kettle' still stands in the church at Frensham, resting on its trivet. It is made of hammered copper, three feet in diameter, and nineteen inches deep. According to the church guidebook it is said to have contained ale drunk at festivities in the Middle Ages. Whatever its true origin and use, it has spawned a fascinatingly rich tapestry of legends into which are woven strands of folklore, written literature, archaeology and the sacred landscape.

Most of the places mentioned in this chapter can be visited. The ruins of Waverley Abbey stand in a meander of the River Wey two miles south east of Farnham. The abbey was, of course, both the inspiration and the setting for Walter Scott's famous novel, and it is rather sad to see the ruins so neglected and vandalised. Moor Park, once also the home of mystical philosopher and novelist Alice Bailey, is now a private adult education centre. Temple's original 17th century walled gardens at Moor Park survive and are Grade II listed, but are not normally open to the public. Mother Ludlam's Hole, with an iron grating across its gothic arched entrance is near the drive, about a third of the way up the hillside. Just below, and a little to the north of a much smaller cave which can only be entered by crawling and which ends after a short passage. This is said to be the original Ludwell. The Devil's Jumps are now part of a nature reserve open to the public provided visitors keep to the paths, and Kettlebury Hill is on land used by the army but on which the public may walk. Frensham church is three miles south west of Waverley Abbey.

Map References:

Frensham church: SU841414
Kettlebury Hill: SU908439
Moor Park: SU861464
Mother Ludlam's Hole: SU871459
The Devil's Jumps: SU866395
Waverley Abbey: SU867452

THE WITCHES OF EASTBOURNE

Shortly before Yule 2000 somebody suggested holding a small folk festival the following August, to celebrate the fiftieth anniversary of the repeal of the Witchcraft Act. It kind of made sense as there were several good folk musicians in the Eastbourne Pagan Circle willing to lend their services, and those morris dance stalwarts of the Pagan scene, Wolf's Head & Vixen, and the Wild Hunt were both within easy travelling distance.

The Lammas Fayre as it became known took shape rapidly over the next few months. The plan was to use the attractive lawns on the seafront close to the 'Wish Tower', an old Napoleonic fortification now used as a puppet museum. The proceedings were to start with morris dancing, and a parade along the seafront involving giants and people in fancy dress, with musical acts performing on a stage in the afternoon followed by an open ritual at dusk. As festival organiser I submitted a plan to the local council and we duly awaited a reply.

We waited... and waited... and after several more letters, eventually a reply came from Tourism Director Ron Cussons that permission was refused as there was already "a full programme of events for the seafront this summer". The eastbourne.org web site actually revealed a grand total of five planned events between May and October – hardly a crowded schedule. When this was pointed out to the council leader, the reply came that there was "a need to balance events with the tranquillity of the seafront", whatever that meant. Further protests to councillors and officials met with a flat refusal to negotiate.

That would probably have been that, had not a reporter from PIE (People in Eastbourne) Magazine telephoned the council posing as a company representative wishing to hold a "corporate promotional event" on the seafront on August 4th (the date we had requested). He was immediately told "no problem, there's nothing on that weekend". The magazine then ran a full page article accusing the council of blatant prejudice, with the headline of "Pagans May Sue Council Over Religious Discrimination", mentioning the new Human Rights Act. This created a certain amount of interest locally, and some surprising supporters emerged, including Liberal Democrat councillor Ron Parsons, a devout Christian, who tabled a motion mentioning the Lammas Fayre and proposing that:

"Where members of the community are prepared to organize and promote suitable events, presenting little or no cost to the town, it is the view of the council that such community activities should be encouraged and positively supported by the council undertaking an enabling role".

This apparently prompted an extraordinary, and rather comical spectacle in which the controlling Tory members of the council felt the need to stand up and declare their Christian faith in the council chamber, before voting the motion down, effectively declaring themselves to be against all local community events. It later emerged that the decision-making cabinet of the council contained several members of the local, evangelical King's Church.

July arrived and we effectively had a festival but no site on which to hold it. However a saviour emerged in the person of Mel Myland, the puppet museum proprietor who was making our giants. The Wish Tower has a small dry moat (now gardens) where he had previously held some puppet performances, and he saw no reason not to let us use this area. Mel (who is not a Pagan) was keen to support the event. Close scrutiny of the correspondence with the council revealed no mention at all of the Wish Tower moat. A revised plan was sent to Mr Cussons, whose reply stated that "the council would not look favourably upon the proposal", but did not categorically say "no". The Lammas Fayre was back on!

The Witches of Eastbourne

Events at the Green Man Bookshop had raised money for essentials like public liability insurance and beer for the morris dancers(!), and a local studio company had promised a professional sound system and an engineer. Local performers, singer-songwriter Maria Cunningham, English ceilidh band Rattlebone, Irish band Ruff Micks, Mark Ye Morris and award-winning guitarist Terry Lees all agreed to perform free of charge, while the headline act, Vikki Clayton was paid for by sponsorship. Three morris sides: Wolf's Head & Vixen, Wild Hunt, and Eastbourne's own Old Star had agreed to dance, and storyteller Derek Legg (one of our Christian friends) was to be on hand to entertain the crowd between the musical performances. Leaflets were printed, and advertisements placed in local publications and the tourist office. The seafront café owner was delighted to be warned to expect several hundred extra customers on the Saturday, and the pier manager was keen to have the dancers perform outside his bar. The RNLI were more than happy for us to have their collecting boxes on hand to raise a bit of money during the parade.

Dancers from Wolfs Head & Vixen Morris outside the Wish Tower

A few days before the event, a press release was sent out, and as a matter of courtesy the council's tourism department was sent a copy. That's when the 'proverbial stuff' hit the 'what's-it'! Mel Myland received a furious telephone call from Mr Cussons threatening to withdraw his lease on the Wish Tower should the event take place, and saying that furthermore any performers who appeared on the seafront that day would be arrested on sight (quite what for was not made clear – can morris dancers be arrested for morris dancing?). With his livelihood under threat Mel understandably felt compelled to withdraw permission and cancelled his planned puppetry performance. We decided, however, to carry on as intended but make it quite clear that we were at the Wish Tower without permission! A quick ring round the performers elicited unanimous support. The press now became interested and I was interviewed live on BBC Southern Counties Radio. The council fortunately did not help their case at all by failing to provide an interviewee, relying instead on a prepared statement written in stodgy legal jargon. The August edition of PIE magazine duly appeared, featuring an article entitled "Pagans Will Defy Council Ban to Stage Charity Seafront Festival", and the Eastbourne Evening Argus ran with the headline "Pagans to Defy Seafront Order". By and large the reporting was both sympathetic and factual.

The council seemed incredulous that we would not back down. One or two hapless council officers called at the Green Man Bookshop nervously fishing for information only to be told that leaflets were available from their own Tourist Information Centre. One council employee described their reaction as "like headless chickens". Another was hauled in front of her superiors and grilled for half an hour when it became known that she had once attended one of our evening lectures!

Letters from the council's legal executive duly arrived hand-delivered stating that we were breaking health and safety guidelines and that myself and Mel Myland would be held personally responsible for any trouble or damage. They protested feebly that the event would have an adverse effect on seafront businesses (the café owner disagreed and actually stayed open late on the day). They were obviously desperate to find some justification for the ban to mask their blatant prejudice.

My solicitor's advice was not all reassuring - while the council had clearly broken the law by discriminating against the Eastbourne Pagan Circle, they were still the 'de facto' law-making body until challenged in a court of law, and it would take at least four weeks to prepare such a challenge (she actually expressed an interest in doing so on a point of principle). In the meantime the police were unlikely to intervene unless a 'breach of the peace' seemed imminent. Her advice was to be careful, and she gave me her duty solicitor's mobile phone number "just in case".

Mel Myland's interpretation of Herne the Hunter on parade.

Saturday dawned bright and clear, and there was no sign of police or council officers as the stage was set up (borrowed from the local municipal art gallery). Musicians, dancers and helpers began to arrive at the shop, and the tea urn was well patronised. One hitch soon became apparent – an exhausted Mel had failed to complete both the giants on time despite having worked all through the night. Willing volunteers were immediately dispatched to his workshop to help.

Eventually with some trepidation, a small group of us left with the giant Herne and most of the morris dancers in tow. The Goddess Andred was still being dressed and would join us later. We arrived at the Wish Tower to find the stage and generator set up with Dougie the sound engineer tinkering with the equipment. The morris dancing started outside the café where a small crowd had already gathered, including our friendly councillor who had supported us. The crowd grew rapidly and press photographers were out in force. After the dances we proceeded along the promenade, led by Eastbourne's town crier, Anthony Chamberlain-Brothers, noisily clanging his bell and proclaiming a "celebration of the Goddess and religious freedom". The colourful parade included drummers, morris dancers, the giants (the Goddess Andred had now arrived) and various people dressed as faeries and wearing flowers or straw. There was a feeling of exhilaration as we marched along, publicly declaring our Paganism. The public's reaction was initially one of startled surprise, and then of sheer delight, as a multitude of cameras and camcorders followed us the full length of the seafront to the pier where more dancing took place. Hundreds of leaflets were handed out explaining who we were and what we were celebrating. There seemed to be much genuine interest from the public.

On our return, the performers were ready to mount the stage, but before the music started I read the following prepared statement, directed at the Council:

"You question our right to be here; we are here to take part in a celebration of the ancient festival of Lammas, one of the most important of the seasonal rites observed by Pagans (and some Christians), and to commemorate the fiftieth anniversary of the repeal of the Witchcraft Act. Some councillors and council officers have seen fit to oppose the right of Pagans to celebrate their faith in public. We believe you are actively discriminating on the grounds of our religion. By doing so you are clearly acting against the letter and spirit of the Human Rights Act which states:

'Everyone has the right to freedom of thought, conscience and religion; this right includes freedom to change his religion or belief, and freedom, either alone or in community with others and in public or private, to manifest his religion or belief in teaching, practice, worship and observance'.

We also intend to raise money for the RNLI, by collecting from the audience who are here to be entertained by the performers. By obstructing us in this aim you would be harming the community of Eastbourne and would be publicly doing a great discredit to your profession which is surely to support the community as a whole, without regard to religious or other persuasion."

Folksinger Vikki Clayton

That said, the music began and we were treated to a superb and varied programme of entertainment which lasted into the early evening with Vikki Clayton's set at the end. The weather grew rather cold and the first spots of rain began to fall as the giants led us to the seafront car-park where a ritual dance took place, performed by a newly formed Pagan Morris side who were later to become known as Hunters Moon. The dance re-enacted the death and rebirth of John Barleycorn, while Maria Cunningham sang the well-known traditional song.

The first Lammas ritual on the beach at Eastbourne

The open ritual took place on the beach, attended by around a hundred people. A police inspector made a brief appearance when the torches were lit, but kept a respectful distance and disappeared quietly when he realised that the situation was orderly and under control. We called the quarters in the gentle rain, with the sound of the sea constantly in the background. It was all very beautiful and moving, and the little crowd of observers watched from the promenade in silence; at no time were we shown any hostility or disrespect by the public. Looking back afterwards from the promenade, there was a perfect circle of pale dry pebbles where we had stood, which faded gradually as the soft rain continued to fall. The Lammas Fayre had exceeded all our expectations and had gone off with scarcely a hitch.

The outcome of the foregoing has been very positive. The Eastbourne Pagan Circle is a much more confident group than hitherto and has dispelled some of the misconceptions about who we are and what we do. We are taken fairly seriously by the press and the council treat us as another community group, rather than a sinister threat. At least one of the King's Church councillors' resigned from the cabinet, which is now controlled by the Lib-Dems anyway. More importantly the Tourism Department have let 'bygones be bygones' and are co-operating with us fully on this year's festival which will be held on Saturday August 3rd. Oh, and the Lifeboat fund received an extra £460.

Sometimes a little direct action can go a long way!

The Lammas ritual Eastbourne 2008

England's Living Folklore

This chapter appeared as an article in the Lammas 2002 edition of Pagan Dawn magazine. Since then the event, now known as the Eastbourne Lammas festival has continued to be run annually on the seafront by the local Pagan community and has raised thousands of pounds for the RNLI.

For more details of the festival see www.lammasfest.org

MERCIA

Travelling through the ancient and fiercely independent Saxon kingdom of Mercia we find echoes of ancient pagan practice such as Hunting the Wren, and the Abbots Bromley Horn dance - two ancient traditions that survive from the times when communities came together to work magic for the fertility of the land. Mercia was also home to William Shakespeare, who recorded much folklore and legend in his writing. Without him the Legend of Herne the Hunter might not have survived, Puck and Robin Goodfellow would not be household names and we might not have appreciated that Nine Mens Morris was a game once played on turf at certain important times of the year. In Oxfordshire Cropredy is home to Fairport Convention's annual folk-rock festival, and we discover some close parallels between the folk music revival and the post-war Pagan revival. Ritual, history and mythology mingle in the story of Fair Rosamund, who is commemorated at Blenheim Palace, Woodstock, while the Cotswold Hills are studded with the barrows and megaliths that our pagan ancestors constructed.

And this, our life, exempt from public haunt,
finds tongues in trees, books in the running brooks,
sermons in stones, and good in everything.

William Shakespeare
As You Like It 1599

THE HORNED GOD IN BRITAIN:

The Horned God has been around for a very long time. He appears in cave-paintings and carvings from the Bronze Age pre-Aryan cities of the Indus Valley, and further east in the ancient art of Nepal and Tibet. In some strands of Bhuddism Yamantaka, an ancient bull-horned deity survives as the 'terminator of death', representing the goal of the Mahayana practitioner's journey to enlightenment.

In Pheonicia, Baal was worshipped as the Carthaginian ram's-horned deity of the sky and vegetation. Interestingly, the word Baal actually means 'Lord' and was originally used by the Jews as a generic word for a deity, but as Yahweh became more powerful, and the priests of the Pheonician Baal clashed with Hebrew hierophants such as Elijah it became more associated with the opposition, and was therefore demonised in Biblical texts. Beelzebub is a derivation of Baal. In ancient Egypt, Osiris the god of fertility, and also of death and resurrection was often depicted with the horns of a bull, while in the hills of Arcady, Pan, the half-goat, half-man horned deity was a popular if minor member of the Greek pantheon, though he has since played a more prominent part in our history.

The oldest known depiction of a horned god figure in Western Europe is a wall painting in the Pyrenean caves known as 'Les Trois Freres' discovered in Southern France in 1914. The image is known as 'Le Sorcier', a strange man/god/shaman/deer/bison figure, depicted along with realistic renderings of a reindeer, an Ibex, ten horses and more than thirty bison.

Abbe Breuil's famous drawing of 'Le Sorcier'

The 13,000 year-old figure is unclear in many respects, and there is no general agreement about what he truly represents. His legs appear human, but the body and forelimbs are rather leonine. The ears are certainly not human. The face could be a lion or other feline, or it could of course be a depiction of a man in mask. The genitals seem to be human, but are certainly not positioned so. The tail and antlers could be a depiction of some sort of animal costume. The famous drawing commonly reproduced in history books (drawn by Abbe Breuil, who was present when the images were first discovered) is certainly somewhat stylized and exaggerated when compared to photographs of the original, although it is possible, of course that time may have taken its toll on the latter. Other figures, including what appears to be a bison-headed creature playing a flute are similarly vague.

Modern Paganism is often criticized for a somewhat simplistic adoption of the Horned God and Mother Goddess, the Lord and

Lady of Wicca, as the dual deities of nature. Part of that criticism is based on the use made of the 'Trois Freres' figure as somehow proving an early antecedent of Cernunnos, Herne, and various other European horned gods who are now so popular in the movement. Great emphasis was placed on 'Le Sorcier' by such writers as Margaret Murray, Gerald Gardner and Doreen Valiente, who found evidence in accounts of the European witch-trials of a horned god figure who was enthroned at the sabbats while the witches danced around the ritual bonfire, and conflated the two images.

Of course, there can be no proof that the 'sorcerer' really represents a god. In her book The God of the Witches, Margaret Murray asserted that most of our knowledge about Cernunnos, the horned/antlered god of the Celts comes from the records written by monks and priests as the ordinary people who worshipped him were illiterate and left no records. This position, taken up by many other writers on the subject presupposes that Cernunnos was an important deity throughout the Celtic world rather than, as evidence suggests, a local deity worshipped by the Parisii, the late iron-age tribe of the Seine valley in the vicinity of modern Paris. However, since then more persuasive evidence for a cult of a Horned God in pre-Christian Europe, and indeed in Britain has come to light.

The primordial nature of the horned-god archetype is obvious. The fundamental need for sexual energy to maintain a population is a basic element of any fertility cult or religion. Early religious and shamanic practices involving the ritual use of animal hides and skulls would have reflected the perceived qualities of the animals themselves, and the stag, goat, ram and bull are all 'horny' animals in both their physical attributes and in the more modern, colloquial sense of the word. The earliest known British anthropomorphic figure is a Stone Age engraving on bone found in Pin Hole Cave, Derbyshire. The figure is too crudely executed to be described as definitively horned and masked but its appearance, including its large penis does suggest kinship with its French counterparts. Several deer antlers excavated at Star Carr in Yorkshire, and dated to the Mesolithic era were interpreted as having been adapted to fit some kind of head-dress or cap for human use. Unfortunately in

Britain the process of glaciation meant that Palaeolithic art in general, and cave paintings in particular did not survive as they did on the continent.

Deer antlers, with their regenerative qualities are intrinsically significant to fertility ritual and are frequently to be found in a funerary context, perhaps as a form of sympathetic magic to encourage re-growth in the next world. In some Neolithic deposits phalluses carved from antlers have been found. Many ritual deposits at Bronze and Iron Age sites in this country have contained antlers, and their use continued well into the Roman era. In one case in Warwickshire two pairs of antlers were arranged in a square around burnt remains and inscribed simply with the word "feliciter" ("for luck") – perhaps an echo of a religious rite of former times which had by then degenerated into a superstitious/magical practice, much as leaving offerings to deities at springs and water-sources metamorphosed into the modern 'wishing-well'.

The Celtic deity most associated with the stag is of course Cernunnos. It should be mentioned here that Cernunnos' name is found only once in archaeology, and the word is simply a generic term meaning 'The Horned One' in Gaulish Latin. The famous depiction interpreted as Cernunnos on the Danish Gundestrup Cauldron has him sitting cross-legged with an impressive pair of antlers on his head and with a snake in one hand. This image probably dates from around 100BCE. While there are no such elaborate depictions to be found in Britain, there are plenty of cruder images of horned gods engraved on stones in the Iron Age and early Roman periods, and in some cases we know their names from the dedications on tablets associated with the sites.

One thing to remember about Celtic deities is that they tended to be very site-specific. Just as the Romans had numerous gods and goddesses for almost every conceivable purpose, it seems that the Celts had one for almost every conceivable sacred site, be it a river, spring, mountain, cave, grove or almost any notable physical feature of the landscape. It seems genius loci were the dominant form of deity in the Celtic world, and this explains why such similarly attributed gods have multifarious names throughout the Gaelic or

Brythonic speaking areas of the Roman Empire.

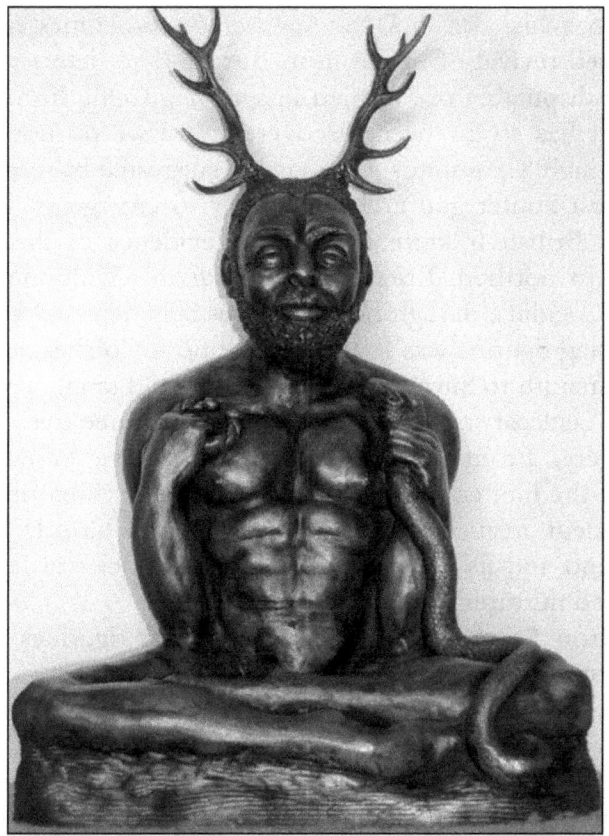

A modern statue of Cernunnos (Museum of Witchcraft collection)

Perhaps the most striking image of a Celtic horned deity is that found on a silver coin found in Petersfield in Hampshire and dated to c20CE. It features a bearded and moustachioed face with a prominent set of antler-like horns and a wheel above his head. The wheel/wheeled cross was probably a symbol of the sun and is common throughout the Celtic world, often found stamped in gold artefacts, which would tend to confirm that interpretation. There is a similar wheel depicted on the Gundestrup cauldron. Some of the more plausible Roman accounts of Celtic religious practices also mention Sun-worship. The medieval wheeled 'Celtic cross' common throughout the western or Celtic fringe of Britain is often seen as a form of solar symbolism with connotations of paganism and Pelagianism, which was a Dark Age heresy sometimes regarded as an attempted revival of druidism in Britain. The Petersfield coin is the only indisputably pre-Roman image of a Celtic horned god in Britain that has so far been discovered, and we do not know his name, although 'Cernunnos' is inevitably suggested by many writers.

The forest-hunter god archetype, later to emerge as 'Herne the Hunter' in British folklore is much in evidence in the Romano-Celtic era. In northern Britain, along Hadrian's Wall one such was known as Cocidius, though he was not usually depicted with horns. A bronze stag figurine was found in a shrine at Colchester dedicated by a coppersmith to Silvanus Callirus (woodland king), while a relief carving at Castlecary in Scotland of a stag with three trees reinforces such imagery. From European iconography we know that the concept of the hunter and his prey, locked in a symbiotic, dualistic, interdependent relationship was at this period already associated with the land and its prosperity – the genius loci writ large as the guardian and nurturer of communal prosperity.

In late Iron Age and Roman Britain, bronze figurines of horned animals, notably bulls are often found at temple sites. Occasionally some truly enigmatic hybrid animal iconography appears, such as the bronze bull's heads surmounted by eagles' heads found at Thealby in Lincolnshire. A particular feature of British bull iconography is the fact that their horns are often knobbed, which may be a sign of the animals' domestication. The horns of oxen were often given knobbed adornments to prevent damage to other animals and to gateposts when being used for ploughing up until the mid-twentieth century. While it is certainly true to say that not all the gods of the Celts were horned, the number of horned animal figurines found at ritual sites of this period does indicate a continuing connection with Celtic deity.

In the late Roman period the mystery cult of Mithras was popular especially with the military. Several shrines have been found in Britain, and a Mithraic altar, complete with a depiction of a bull-sacrifice, may be found hidden away, seemingly reluctantly preserved behind a discreet curtain in the church of St Mary the Virgin at Stone-in Oxney in Kent.

DORCM 1939.55 - The tinned-bronze figurine of the three-horned bull, Maiden Castle, Winterborne St Martin.Dorset County Museum

The late-flowering of paganism in the dying days of the Roman occupation of Britain saw new shrines and temples being constructed in the re-occupied pre-Roman hill forts as the indigenous Britons reverted to their former strongholds and, it would seem, their former gods in a time of uncertainty. One extraordinary cult-object from this period is the unique bronze three-horned bull figurine exhumed from the temple site at Maiden Castle in Dorset, which has three female feathered figures atop its back (one of which, unfortunately has lost its head). While the three-horned bull is more frequently found in Gaulish France, at least five other examples have been found in Roman Britain, including examples in Colchester and Cirencester. Miranda Green writes that: "The tripling of the horn may have several purposes: triplism was important both for 'threeness' itself, as a powerful sacred number and for simple intensification. Horns were potent Celtic fertility symbols and thus the multiplication of the essence of a creature, its power, vigour and virility is a natural way of increasing the symbolism". As an aside, in archaic religion the number of horns sported by a god could often indicate the importance of the deity, hence the seven horns of the 'Divine Lamb' in the Bible's Book of Revelations represents the absolute acme of divinity. Incidentally the Gundestrup cauldron's Cernunnos has seven tines on his antlers. A 'stag of seven tines' is mentioned in the opening line of a poem attributed to the Irish Bard Amergin, written down in the early Middle Ages.

Ronald Hutton, in The Pagan Religions of the Ancient British Isles points out that while native male deities in the Roman provinces were often officially given additional names relating to Roman gods, the goddesses retained only their Celtic names (Sulis/Minerva in Bath being the only known exception), perhaps because the goddesses were inseparable from the land. It is also true to say that horned deities did not feature in the Roman pantheon, although such Greek imports as Pan and the (sometimes) horned Dionysus were often honoured as cult-figures in Roman society. Thus it is fair to say that the horned gods that we know about which were worshipped in Roman Britain were almost certainly indigenous. In a few places their names have survived, but in many cases have been attached to Mars or Mercury, showing how far the Romanization of local populations had progressed, particularly in the military occupied zones. Thus we have Mars Corotiacus in Suffolk and Mars Toutatis in Essex. The most frequently depicted horned deity, especially in the north of England is Belatucadrus, a warrior-god depicted with horns, a spear, a shield and a large penis. While the druids, the priestly caste of the Iron Age Celts were ruthlessly crushed for their relentless opposition to Roman rule, far from suppressing the religious practices of the iron-age, the occupying Romans allowed the indigenous population to carry on their ritual observances at local shrines, groves and springs. Indeed there is much evidence that many shrines to local deities were constructed during this period, with well-constructed stone temples serving local communities and their gods. The variety of funerary practices from this period also attest to variations in religious rites in different regions of Britain. Clearly, apart from their temple architecture, and a reduction in the political influence of their priests, little changed for the old gods during the period of Roman rule.

From early on in the third century CE, Christianity became more and more influential in Roman Imperial life. At first, all faiths were tolerated, although Christianity was favoured. A few pagan holy centres were closed down before 357 when a general suppression of paganism took place, but by 361 Julian the Apostate had restored the status quo, and it was not until 394 when Theodosius took control that a complete closure of temples and the abolition of sacrifices was decreed. By this time, Britain was already slipping out of Imperial control, and so it is likely that the process was much slower here than in continental Europe, though the absence of literary sources from the province at this time makes any definitive statement on this matter impossible. While the major temple at Bath seems to have been abandoned by the end of the fourth century, smaller cult centres such as those at Lydney and Maiden Castle were certainly more long-lived.

It can be said with some certainty that Celtic Britain south of Hadrian's Wall, by the efforts of missionaries had become Christian by the middle of the sixth century, by which time even the Irish had abandoned the old gods. The remote Scottish lands to the north took a little longer to fall, lasting probably another century or so. In the meantime another wave of invaders, also pagan, were busy settling the southern half of the country.

The Germanic tribes brought with them their own pagan gods, but while there were some similarities with the Celtic pantheon, such as Lugh/Wotan and Taranis/Thunor, being horned was not a noticeable trait among any of them. This seems slightly odd, given the image of the Viking and Saxon warriors with their horned helmets, beloved of school history books and Hollywood movies, and what may be described as the cult of the drinking horn which is so prevalent in the sagas. However, even given that this image is probably a romantic exaggeration, few horned helmets ever having been found, it seems as though horns represented the manly, warlike attributes of the animal kingdom rather than any notion of sacred fertility, which was the likelihood in the case of Celtic imagery. In fact no image of any deity from the Saxon/Nordic pantheon in Britain survives at all from the pre-Christian era, probably because the Christian missionaries made bonfires of all of them. While the remains of sacrificed oxen have been found at ceremonial sites from this period, such practice was common to all European pagan people whether their gods were horned or not. In any case, by the early eleventh century, the Scandinavian kingdoms were themselves Christian. It would, on the face of it, seem that the horned god had completely deserted the western isles of the Celts.

However, the old gods proved to be tenacious. There are many examples of pagan shrines and temples being re-used by the new religion, and occasionally the iconography survived as well. The famous Virgin of Chartres Cathedral is a figure from a fourth-century pagan altar, and the various black Madonnas in southern Europe tend to appear on churches built on former shrines to Ceres. An actual statue of Ceres and her daughter Proserpina masqueraded as the Madonna and Child in a church in Italy up to the nineteenth century, when they were placed in a museum on the order of Pope Pius IX. In Britain and Ireland, many of the gods and goddesses became saints of greater or lesser significance. St Brighid is almost certainly the Celtic goddess Bride while numerous Cornish and Welsh Saints owe their existence to the former guardian spirits of the holy wells over which they now preside. Some imagery, such as Christ's halo, was borrowed from pagan Roman usage, but horns as a sign of virility and fertility were probably just too pantheistic to be taken up by the followers of the cult of Christ.

The Horned God in Britain

Where the horned god appears in medieval architecture, unlike his distant cousin, the green man, examples are few and far between. The fine carving in the Dorset County Museum is a rare survival from a secular building. While it is described as medieval it could easily be earlier, perhaps incorporated into a medieval wall having been found among remains from the Roman period in what was an important Roman town. Such carvings are notoriously difficult to date.

DORCM 2008.38.2 - Colliton Arch keystone, one of two.
Dorchester. Dorset County Museum

Where horned figures appear in church architecture, they are almost always demonstrably the Christian Devil, often grotesquely humorous with pointy tails and grinning countenances, such as the curiously endearing Lincoln Imp, in the cathedral of that city. Whilst many Green Man carvings are grotesque, many more are simply foliate faces, benign and with a certain dignity. There are also examples of lewd exhibitionist carvings in British church architecture such as the sheela-na-gigs and their much rarer male counterparts, but at least when it comes to the male depictions they almost certainly depict the sins of the flesh and are often accompanied by horned demons as a warning.

Where the horned god did survive, he did so by becoming a part of folk and magical lore. One aspect of Germanic religion which does appear to have influenced the folkloric survival of the horned god was the Wild Hunt. This was the terrifying rush to Valhalla of the spirits of dead warriors lead by their leader Odin, astride his eight-legged steed Sleipnir. The Wild Hunt is now almost universally associated with Herne the Hunter, that shadowy figure of somewhat dubious provenance who appears to have taken on all the attributes of the antlered god of the Celts, Cernunnos the Horned One, the wild nocturnal huntsman riding through the night to the baying of his hounds of Hell, in search of lost souls to carry away.

In one version of the famous legend of the Berkshire forest the story goes that Herne was one of the Royal keepers in the time of King Richard II (1367-1400). He had two large black hounds and was hated by the other keepers who were jealous of his great skill. One day when King Richard was hunting a stag, it turned on him and he would have been killed had not Herne stood between him and the enraged animal. Unfortunately in rescuing the King, Herne himself was wounded and fell to the ground, apparently mortally wounded. At this point a strange dark figure appeared and told the King he was a magician named Philip Urwick, and could cure his keeper with his magic. Richard assented and Urwick cut off the stag's antlers and placed them on Herne's head. He then took Herne to his hut on Bagshot Heath some miles away, to complete the cure. The King swore that if Herne recovered he would make him his chief keeper. As a result the others hated Herne even more and wished him dead. Urwick returned and offered them a bargain – if they would grant him the first request he made, although Herne would recover, he would lose his woodsman's skills. They agreed and everything the wizard had foretold took place. Herne

The Horned God in Britain

recovered, albeit now with the antlers a permanent fixture on his head, but he was so devastated by the loss of his skill that he hanged himself from a mighty oak, whereupon his body disappeared.

The other keepers soon discovered that they too had lost their woodcraft. They sought out Urwick and asked him to help. He told them to meet at the oak the following night, where the spirit of Herne appeared, telling them to fetch hounds and horses for a chase. This they did and when they returned Herne took them to a Beech tree. The magician appeared in a shower of sparks and flame. His first request was that they form a hunting party for Herne and swear an oath of allegiance. Bound by their oath, night after night, the unfortunate keepers were forced to hunt through the forest.

Herne the Hunter (Museum of Witchcraft collection)

While Herne first appears in literary form from the pen of William Shakespeare, no less, his name is celebrated in many place names throughout Britain. Herne Bay, for example in Kent. Others include Herne on the Thames Estuary and Herne Hill in London. If one accepts as many do, that Herne and Cerne have the same etymological derivation then Cerne Abbas in Dorset is an obvious commemoration of the horned god, although the famous chalk giant in the village, while certainly horny, does not appear ever to have had horns or antlers attached to his head. Even the name of Cornwall (Kernow) could arguably be from the same source. Cerne place-names seem to occur most in Wiltshire and Dorset with a few Cerneys in Gloucestershire, while Herne tends to be found more in the south-east, although a place called Hurn does exist near Bournemouth.

Herne, probably thanks to Shakespeare's Merry Wives of Windsor (1597), in which the writer has him impersonated by Falstaff, is inextricably linked with the great Berkshire forest, and also with royalty. It is said the ghostly hunting party appeared on the eve of Henry IV's death (1413), and several times during the reign of Henry VIII (1509-1547) when the bluff king imposed his will at the expense of those around him. He walked again before Charles I's execution (1649). In more modern times, he was seen just before the two World Wars (1914 & 1939), at the outset of the Great Depression (1931), and before Edward VIII's abdication (1936) and George VI's death (1952). While the timing of such appearances on the face of it have little relevance to an ancient god of fertility, they do have some resonance when one considers the aspect of a fertility god as being intrinsically connected not only with the fertility of the land, but with the well-being of 'The Land' and its people.

There is an old tale goes that Herne the hunter,
Sometime a keeper here in Windsor forest,
Doth all the winter-time, at still midnight,
Walk round about an oak, with great ragg'd horns;
And there he blasts the tree and takes the cattle
And makes milch-kine yield blood and shakes a chain

The Horned God in Britain

In a most hideous and dreadful manner:
You have heard of such a spirit, and well you know
The superstitious idle-headed eld
Received and did deliver to our age
This tale of Herne the hunter for a truth.
[W. Shakespeare The Merry Wives of Windsor]

Herne's oak was a much venerated landmark. The original, from Shakespeare's time was in the grounds of Frogmore House, next to Windsor Great Forest, It was felled in 1796 and replaced in Queen Victoria's time by another, which was planted in the wrong place, a mistake corrected by King Edward VII who planted the current tree that bears the name in 1906.

A more shadowy version of a horned god in English folklore is Robin Goodfellow. Once again Shakespeare provides us with a description of this mischievous woodland sprite:

..that shrude and knavish sprite
Call'd Robin Goodfellow; are you not he
That frights the maidens of the villagery;
Skim milk, and sometimes labour in the quern
And bootless make the breathless housewife churn;
And sometime make the drink to bear no barm;
Mislead night wanderers, laughing at their harm ?
Those that Hobgoblin call you, and sweet Puck,
You do their work, and they should have good luck.
[W. Shakespeare, A Midsummer Night's Dream]

While the old gods tended to be portrayed as the Devil in later medieval Christian writings, and linked with Biblical demons such as Beelzebub and Lucifer (themselves derived from the gods of the Hebrews' enemies), in the popular imagination they often degenerated into the realm of faerie. Shakespeare's use of contemporary folklore here links together Robin Goodfellow, Puck and hobgoblins.

England's Living Folklore

Engraving of Puck, 1639 (Museum of Witchcraft collection).

Puck was also the Pookie or Pook in Irish lore, or the piskie in Cornwall and Devon - a magical creature who could either help or harm, according to their whim, or in some folktales with a more moralistic tone, dependent upon the good or bad behaviour of those with whom they made contact. He was, of course, much later celebrated in Kipling's famous work Puck of Pook's Hill. There is a much reproduced engraving of Robin Goodfellow from 1639 in which he is shown in an obvious state of arousal leading a group of dancers, his head adorned with horns and carrying a broomstick in one hand and a very phallic wand or staff in the other. He also has cloven hooves. The image appears to associate him with witchcraft, which is something that Shakespeare managed to avoid.

Folk traditions also appear to have continued to celebrate the old horned one, with frequent disapproving grumblings from the Church. The Abbots Bromley Horn Dance is a rare and interesting survival into modern times of a form of processional dance which involves the use of reindeer antlers. It is claimed that it was recorded as early as 1226 and certainly the actual antlers involved have recently been radio-carbon dated to around that time. Its significance is now lost but it is likely that similar communal and ritual events to this one at one time had the fertility of the land and the community at the heart of their purpose. At Killorglin in Ireland, a goat is dressed and paraded around the town in the annual Puck Fair, held every August.

Abbots Broml;ey Horn Dancers c1970s (Museum of Witchcraft collection)

Such folk rituals were still relatively common in Tudor times, and once again Shakespeare makes use of such rites in As You Like It, in which the clown Jaques sings:

What shall he have that killed the deer?
His leather skin and horns to wear
Then sing him home:
Take no scorn to wear the horn
It was the crest ere you were born
Thy father's father wore it

**And thy father bore it
The horn, the horn, the lusty horn
Is not a thing to laugh and scorn.**
[W. Shakespeare, As You Like It]

Curiously, the words can be, and sometimes are sung to the tune of the Abbots Bromley Horn Dance, which while it was first collected in 1857 is regarded as being genuinely old, probably medieval. The celebrated Dorset Oozer, a ceremonial horned mask, may have been a surviving artefact from a similar ritual. Sadly the original rotted away in a loft in Crewkerne around 1900 but it had survived long enough to be photographed, and a modern replica is now on display in the Dorset County Museum.

"The Ooser on loan from the Wessex Morris -The original of this model was lost. It was last seen in Crewkerne in c.1905.".

By Shakespeare's time there had been something of a resurgence of interest in the old pagan gods, at least of the Classical pantheons, and the old horned god of Arcadia, the goat-footed Pan made something of a come-back. John Fletcher (1579-1625) wrote his Hymn To Pan [published in the Oxford Book of English Verse], and in art and literature at least his popularity remained undimmed into the twentieth century – long enough to become an important icon in the revival of Paganism as a religion of relevance to the modern world.

Cast of a carving from a church in southern France (author's collection)

The idea of a romantic pagan past had become common currency among poets, writers and composers by the eighteenth century, possibly as the concept of the 'noble savage' became more and more familiar as the 'new' world slowly became more accessible to the 'old'. With the onset of the modern age with its wars, urbanisation and racing technological advance such a romantic mythical Arcadian past began to feel more and more attractive. In the twentieth century writers such as Rudyard Kipling and Kenneth Grahame produced work romanticising paganism to the extent that extracts from some of their writings have commonly found their way into modern Pagan liturgy. Kipling's Puck of Pook's Hill and Grahame's Piper at the Gates of Dawn (in The Wind in the

Willows) are both highly sympathetically drawn pagan archetypes, while Arthur Machen's Great God Pan and Dion Fortune's The Goat Foot God both have the old hairy-legged deity at their heart. Aleister Crowley's rhapsodic and erotically charged Hymn To Pan (1929) was a very different work to John Fletcher's pastoral poem, but still managed to portray a romantic vision of the pagan past by incorporating fauns, nymphs and satyrs within its imagery. Such romanticism also influenced some historians, folklorists and archaeologists who began to use such evidence as existed to 'play up' the importance of paganism in Britain's more recent past. In 1930 the 'Hal-an-Tow' was revived by the Helston Old Cornwall Society as part of the Flora Day festivities, and the words "Take no scorn to wear the horn it was the crest when you were born, your father's father wore it and your father's father too" were once again to be heard sung in the streets of a British town. The horned god was on his way back!

In 1921, Margaret Murray, folklorist and Egyptologist published her now notorious work The Witch Cult in Western Europe, which stated explicitly that witchcraft was a survival of an ancient fertility religion. In her later book The God of the Witches (1933) she proposed that the 'Devil' so frequently mentioned in the transcripts of witch-trials was actually a priest of the witch-cult, in other words a man, wearing a horned mask, rather than a supernatural being. Her evidence for this was largely the existence of the aforementioned Dorset Oozer which she firmly believed was an example of such a mask. Murray starts with the Trois Freres cave painting and draws on the work of previous writers such as the occultist Montague Summers, the anthropologist James Frazer and other writers on the occult such as Karl Pearson and Jules Michelet. At the heart of Murray's mystery religion was the horned god, who was also the sacrificial king, a theory she expanded in The Divine King in England (1954). In several of her writings however, she also stressed the importance of the goddess to the cult, and was obviously influenced by Leland's classic text on Dianic witchcraft Aradia. Thus, for the first time, the ancient horned god of the British Celts was paired with his consort, the moon goddess, and virtually ever since they have been venerated together by modern-day Pagans.

Doreen Valiente's altar figure, carved by Bel Bucca

Gerald Gardner was, alongside Margaret Murray a prominent member of the Folklore Society and Murray wrote an enthusiastic introduction to Gardner's Witchcraft Today (1954). By now the witchcraft act had been repealed in English law and such books, much to the chagrin of academic historians who derided such 'suspect' interpretations of folklore and history, started to find a huge popular audience. The 20th century revival of Paganism and the foundations of a new religion, Wicca, were under way, and by the end of the millennium the Horned God was definitively back, with a new-found importance at the very heart of a popular and growing spiritual movement.

Modern images of the Horned God tend to make him a benign and dignified looking Pan/Herne Cernunnos hybrid, and he is no worse off for this combination. Bel Bucca's beautiful carving which was owned by Doreen Valiente has him as an antlered, lordly bearded figure, cross legged and with an obvious erection, cradling two rams-horned figures in his outstretched arms. Perhaps one of the most significant portrayals in the twentieth century was the character Herne, in Richard Carpenter's television series Robin of Sherwood, in which he is both god and shaman, the magickal woodland guardian who chooses Robin as his son. This mystical element made the series enduringly popular among the Pagan population and introduced the Horned God to a wide audience.

The Pantheism which is at the heart of the Pagan revival has found a figurehead which represents both nature 'red in tooth and claw' and the gentle giant, spirit of the woodland, the green man with whom we need to re-acquaint ourselves in order to regain our mystical connection with nature and the land, and to heal the rift between man and nature that threatens to destroy us all. With the advent of the World Wide Web his significance is assured. Typing 'Horned God' into Google currently turns up 260,000 English pages. Cernunnos, Pan, Herne, welcome back, mankind has need of you once again.

Map References:

Abbots Bromley: SK079245
Bath, Roman Baths museum: ST749647
Dorchester, Dorset County Museum: SY692907
Maiden Castle: SY671884
Pin Hole Cave: SK533741
Star Carr: TA028812
Stone-in-Oxney, Mithraic altar: TQ940273
Windsor Great Park, Herne's Oak: SU951717

SILKEN THREADS

George Collins walked out one May morning
When May was all in bloom.
There he espied a fair pretty maid
A-washing her marble stone.

She whooped, she holloed, she highered her voice,
She held up her lilywhite hand.
"Come hither to me, George Collins," she said,
"For your life shall not last you long."

He put his foot on the broad waterside,
And over the lea sprung he.
He embraced her around the middle so small,
And kissed her red rosy cheeks.

George Collins rode home to his father's own gate.
"Rise, mother, and make my bed,
And I will trouble my dear sister
For a napkin to tie around my head."

"And if I should chance to die this night,
As I suppose I shall,
Bury me under that marble stone
That's against fair Elanor's hall."

Fair Elanor sat in her room so fine,
Working her silken skein.
She saw the fairest corpse a-coming
That ever the sun shone on.

She said unto her Irish maid:
"Whose corpse is this so fine?"
"This is George Collins' corpse a-coming,
That once was a true lover of thine."

"Come put him down, my six pretty lads,
And open his coffin so fine,
That I may kiss his lilywhite lips,
For ten thousand times he has kissed mine."

"You go upstairs and fetch me the sheet
That's wove with the silver twine,
And hang that over George Collins' head.
Tomorrow it shall hang over mine."

The news was carried to London town,
And wrote on London gate,
That six pretty maids died all of one night,
And all for George Collins' sake.

G B Gardiner noted down this version of the song George Collins from the singing of Henry Stansbridge in Lyndhurst, Hampshire, in 1906, while Bob Copper collected an almost identical version, also from Hampshire, in 1954. It appears to combine two Child ballads (no 42 Clerk Colvill and 85 Lady Alice), and seems to be a more complete version of either. There are many other variants, some of which go by the name of Giles Collins, including several American versions of the song, which tend to have a more homely and less dreamlike quality to them. It is likely that William Blake was familiar with at least one version, as his somewhat gloomy poem Fair Elanor appears to have been inspired at least in part by this mysterious tale.

One of the ways in which paganism survived after Christianity was in the spontaneous recurrence of certain references to pagan symbolism and ritual activity in folk practices and sung ballads, such as this one. The points to note in this song are that in this case, the hero who is also ultimately the victim comes to the heroine of his own accord; she is washing a marble stone, a type of activity that crops up frequently in the more magical traditional songs of these isles; it is also the month of May - a time of the year associated significantly with fertility and sacrifice. Despite her warning that "your life shall not last you long" he crosses water to embrace the girl and accepts his fate, asking only that he be buried beneath the marble stone, and that he be properly shrouded in death. Fair Elanor, on seeing the corpse does not recognize her former lover, but when her maid points out its identity she insists on the finest sheet "that's wove with the silver twine" to be hung above his head, hinting as she does so that she also may be about to die, though interestingly not necessarily through grief as other more conventional versions would have it. Silver, or silken thread is another highly charged piece of pagan symbolism, most obviously lunar, but also frequently found to be the means of navigating a maze - often a metaphor for a journey through the mortal world to the afterlife or a journey through initiation into the 'mysteries'. The heroine in such songs as this is often a capricious creature and this is not the only occasion in folklore in which she murders her lover having taken pleasure in him. In this particular case she shows herself in various aspects – maiden, mistress, mother, sister, murderess and finally mourner.

One possible explanation of the song's mysterious storyline is that the girl by the stream is a water-nymph or fairy of some kind. In later versions of the related ballad Clerk Colvill she is a mermaid, while in Scandinavian ballads she is a witch. The young man has been in the habit of visiting her but he is about to marry a mortal, and the fairy takes her revenge with a poisoned kiss. Robert Graves' interpretation was that the girl was a witch and that the young man was a part of her cult group or coven who betrayed her. She then puts a 'death spell' on him. The story is one of the great archetypal romances of European mythology. Its roots and branches reach into Scandinavia, Germany, Italy, France, Spain and elsewhere. The medieval German poem of the Knight of Staufenberg (c. 1310) is an early literary form of the tale. Elanor may possibly be a version of Elen in Welsh mythology, the virgin princess dreamed of by Macsen Wledig. The word elen means nymph in the Welsh language, while the closely related eilun means image, or idol.

Sometimes myths and legends are embellishments of historical stories, or at least are formed when such embellishments become attached to historical figures. The larger-than-life Queen Eleanor of Aquitaine (1122 – 1204) would be the obvious candidate here. In this context it is worth mentioning the medieval romance which grew up surrounding the Queen and the historical figure of Rosamund Clifford, known in legend as Fair Rosamund.

The entrance to Blenheim Palace, Woodstock

In the legend the renowned beauty was the mistress of Henry II, who installed her in his palace at Woodstock, Oxfordshire. He, however, subsequently married the formidable Eleanor. For

Rosamund's own safety she was hidden in a bower in Woodstock, surrounded by a labyrinth and guarded by the King's knight, Sir Thomas. The maze was impenetrable save for a silken thread which indicated the way through. When Henry was called away to war in France Queen Eleanor had Sir Thomas killed and having learned of the silk thread, penetrated the maze, confronted Rosamund and forced her to take a lethal poison.

Fair Rosamund, by Waterhouse

The truth is a little more prosaic: At some time after Henry's marriage his mistress Rosamund Clifford withdrew from the house he had built for her near Woodstock to a convent at Godstow, beside the River Thames at Oxford, where she eventually died peaceably in 1177.

The more romantic version of the tale started to appear in the fourteenth century and is a good example of how history can become legend with embellishments gleaned from ancient folklore and mythology. Whether or not a medieval ballad writer had Eleanor in mind when setting out the story of George Collins no one can tell. Certainly Ranulph Higden, the chronicler of Chester who first set down the legend of Fair Rosamund around 1330CE, would have known the storyline found in the ballad. Interestingly, history relates that after her death Rosamund Clifford was buried in a place of high honour before the altar at Godstow. In 1192 Bishop Hugh of Lincoln, visiting the convent enquired whose was the tomb "covered with a pall of silk and set about with lights of wax", and on being told it was Rosamund's he ordered the nuns to "Take out of this place the harlot and bury her outside the church." She was then buried in the cloisters. Sadly, the convent did not survive the reformation and the medieval ruins are scant. A well in the gardens at the eighteenth century Blenheim Palace at Woodstock supposedly marks the site of Rosamund's bower; the association between sacred wells and labyrinths is well known.

Bob Stewart has pointed out that in the above quoted form the ballad is closely related to the tale told of the Daghda in Irish legend. The Daghda (the good god) was one of the leaders of the Tuatha De Danann. He met a woman on the ancient feast day of Samhain who was standing astride a river, washing herself. He made love to her and she revealed herself to be the Morrigan (meaning 'phantom' or 'dark queen') - the Goddess of fate, death and warfare. After their lovemaking she formed an alliance with him to help the Tuatha De Danann to overcome their enemies, the Formorians. As the 'Washer at the Ford' in Celtic lore she is supposed to have appeared before a battle washing the bloodstained clothes of those doomed to die, in this form she appears throughout the British Isles. In 1896 William Sharp, writing as Fiona McLeod Christianised her in his pseudo-mythology The Washer of the Ford making her out to be Mary Magdalene standing in a stream washing souls who crave eternity. In Welsh mythology Modron, or Morgan plays the same role as the Morrigan at the ford.

The Goddess is similarly found in the traditional song The Bells of Paradise, otherwise known as Lullay Lullay, or the Corpus Christi Carol, in which she is conflated with the Virgin Mary. Here she is found kneeling on a stone beneath which there runs a flood "one half water, the other half blood". The Morrigan is also closely associated with the cauldron, a transformative magical object which appears in a great many tales in Celtic myth and legend, and which is of course one form of the Grail. It has been suggested that the flood of blood and water also refers to the red and white springs that flow beneath Glastonbury Tor, further cementing an association with the Grail.

The Morrigan by Karen Cater

While many later ballads tell of murderous lovers, often involving innocent or pregnant girls, these, including some other versions of

George (or Giles) Collins are really no more than melodramatic tales of blood and gore, usually with a strong moral tone. In the older more magical tradition of which this is an example, the ballad has more than a whiff of ritual murder and magic about it and it is that which makes it such an intriguing part of the folk tradition.

Many folksingers have recorded versions of the song and its variants including Shirley Collins (on the classic album Sweet Primroses), The Copper Family, Sandra and Nancy Kerr, and the New Lost City Ramblers.

Map References:

Blenheim Palace: SP440161
Fair Rosamund's Well: SP436165
Godstow Abbey: SP486090

HETTY PEGLER'S TUMP

The succinct information board on the gated entrance to this site reads:

"A prehistoric burial mound about 180ft in length containing a stone built central passage with two chambers on either side and another at the end: the earthen mound is surrounded by a dry-stone revetment. The barrow was excavated in 1821 and again in 1854 when several skeletons were found in the passage and in the chambers; it was probably built before 3,000BCE."

Hetty Pegler's Tump

A region well known for its chambered tombs and long barrows is the area of the Cotswold Hills, especially along the steep escarpment on the western edge overlooking the River Severn where several are set on jutting headlands with spectacular views across the valley to the Welsh Hills beyond. The Severn-Cotswold group, as they are known to archaeologists are distinctive both in their construction and usage from those in Wessex and Sussex. The local oolitic limestone of which the hills consist is ideal for building such structures, with large megaliths supporting slabs held in place with extensive dry-stone walling and revetments. This allowed the tombs to be re-used over a long period of time as opposed to the simple earthen mounds which form the commonest types on the southern chalk uplands, in which the bodies were all interned simultaneously. The Severn Cotswold tombs were probably the equivalent of modern-day family vaults, in which deceased members of a family or tribe would be successively buried, with ritual activity carried on in the forecourt.

The entrance to the Tump with its massive portal stone

Hetty Pegler's Tump has to be one of the finest and best-preserved megalithic tombs in the country. Situated near the pretty

Cotswold village of Uley, it is a splendid site to visit. Once barred to the public, English Heritage now allows visitors to enter the tomb on hands and knees beneath the massive portal stone supported on stone blocks. Once inside the gallery it is possible to stand almost upright and inspect the chambers on either side.

The view of the entrance from inside the barrow

Jaquetta Hawkes writes:

"And these few steps carry one from the familiar, brightly lit Cotswold scene into a strange cave world, with dark, shadowy entrances and a lingering ghostly presence in the air that may be felt only by the imagination but is none the less potent for that. Indeed, he would be a stone who in such an atmosphere is not tempted to materialize before him the men who once moved about in the cave of their own making, who cannot see a party of them coming through the low portal, staggering a little beneath the weight of the corpse they are bearing to its sepulchre. Lifting it into one of the side-chambers, they must move aside the bones of earlier ancestors before they can deposit the body of their tribesman lying on its side with knees drawn up to the chin. After celebrating the last rites and leaving with the body a few ornaments, and perhaps a bow and arrow and some pots holding food and drink, they withdraw, and carefully seal up the entrance behind them. So it will lie until the day of the next funeral, but the site of the entrance remains a centre for ritual, where offerings may be laid and the ancestral spirits be propitiated or invoked."

The name of the barrow derives from Hester Pegler, the wife of Captain Pegler of Wresden. He was the alleged owner of the land. She died in 1694, as recorded on a monument in the local church. The barrow was also known to local people as the 'Giant's Chamber. One Doctor Bird, who had been present at the opening of the Nympsfield barrow stated around 1870 that an old friend of his had told him many a time he and other boys had gone to Uley tumulus and had a fight with the "giants' bones" in the chambers. The clergyman of the parish, some time afterwards, had all the human bones collected and buried in the corner of the churchyard. Some, however were recorded later as having been preserved at Guy's Hospital.

The following is a curious extract from an article in Folklore called Cotswold Place Lore and Customs, published in 1912, which records the making of a suet plumb pudding which is referred to as 'Heg-Peg Dump' on St Margaret's Day (20th July):

"Village Feasts. Many Cotswold parishes keep their annual Feast in the autumn, usually on the Sunday after the church dedication festival, which is sometimes observed on the date according to Old Style. There are family gatherings, a special dish for the occasion, and often open house, especially at the smaller public houses...
...at Nympsfield, puddings or dumplings are made of wild plums or "heg-pegs." There is a local rhyme, twitting the Nympsfield folks,

who are very sensitive on the point:

**Nympsfield is a pretty place, Built upon a tump,
And what the people live upon Is heg-peg dump.**

Nympsfield lies between "Hetty Pegler's tump," - *i.e.* Uley Bury tumulus, --and Lynch Field; but there is a Barrow field, of which only the name remains, in the village itself."

It is intriguing to find that a local delicacy may be connected in some way to the folklore of an ancient sacred site – but then of course plum puddings are still very much associated with ritual feasting on at least one sacred occasion of the year!

The easiest place to park for a visit is probably the small lay-by at the entrance to the local water company's compound across the road from the sign. Incidentally, most of the local signs and some map references refer to the site as Uley Long Barrow or Uley Tumulus, which can be a bit confusing. The site, easily visible from the road is reached by a short walk along the edge of a field.

Inside, on the occasion of my last visit, there was mercifully little vandalism or litter in evidence, though in the past this has not been the case, and the end wall has now been blocked off by a wire cage, presumably to prevent further damage by stupid idiots with tea-lights. Someone had poked a stalk of corn through the wire, which had sprouted green shoots. This is the most womb-like of structures, and inside I felt an overwhelming sense of safety and peacefulness, and on a cold December day it was much warmer inside than out. Colonies of large spiders also seem to find the interior most congenial – arachnophobes, you have been warned!

For those claustrophobically inclined, the layout of nearby Nympsfield chambered long barrow is very similar, but the twenty-seven by eighteen metre mound has long disappeared and the capstones were used for road-building, so it is possible to inspect the interior without crawling around in the dark with a torch.

It is located in Coaley Park picnic area, on the edge of the scarp looking over the River Severn and the Bristol channel to the Welsh

Hills. There is plenty of parking and picnic tables abound. It is quite hard to find if you don't know where to look. It is to the right of the car-park entrance as you drive in. The ordnance survey map is particularly vague on its exact location and is no use at all for this site! Look towards the stand of trees on the edge of the scarp towards the north of the site and you will see a low mound, almost indistinguishable from the surrounding landscape. As you get closer you will see the stones of the exposed interior. English Heritage have done a good job presenting the barrow in its opened state and it is certainly worth visiting out of archaeological interest, though it obviously lacks the atmosphere and feeling of sacredness that Hetty Pegler's Tump retains. At least you don't have to get your knees dirty to appreciate the architecture here!

The remains of Nympsfield Barrow

When the barrow was excavated in 1862 and 1937 the remains of at least thirteen human skeletons as well as Neolithic pottery were found. Other interesting objects interred were 'a piece of bone carved perhaps in the shape of a human figure', three shiny quartz pebbles, and a perforated dog whelk shell. Red ochre was also found, which must have been brought from a least a dozen miles away - the use of this bright pigment in burials is known from around the world, presumably for its symbolic association with blood. Local folklore had it that Nympsfield was originally built as a shelter for lepers, and locals avoided it. Obviously those who robbed the site of its mound and capstones for building materials had no qualms about its previous usage.

It has been suggested that the name Nympsfield may be derived from 'nyfed' – old Welsh for a shrine or holy place, but this can only ever be pure speculation. There is certainly archaeological evidence for a Romano-British shrine in the area, between Hetty Peglar's Tump and nearby Uley Bury hill fort at West Hill. Here a Neolithic burial feature similar to Hetty Peglar's Tump was reused and extended in the late Iron Age with a square wooden building and enclosure. This was the basis for a second century CE temple building constructed sumptuously in stone with glazed windows, as part of a complex of buildings on the site. This appears to have been in use throughout the Roman period until the early fifth century when it seems to have become ruinous. In a rare instance of the continuity of a sacred site there are signs of an early Christian church and baptistery dating from the early sixth century which probably lasted until the eighth. The head of a classically-styled cult statue of Mercury from the temple was found buried outside the building, as if it had been carefully interred. It is now in the British Museum.

During extensive excavations the remains of votive offerings were unearthed, including weapons from the pre-Roman period. The cult deity seems to have become associated with Mercury in the Roman era, and a second century statue was carved from local stone which included a goat and a cockerel, his cult animals. A great many stone and lead tablets were discovered, though many had been partially destroyed by later development and ploughing. They are mostly dedicated to Mercury and concern instances of theft. One example from the late second or early third centuries reads:

"Honoratus to the holy god Mercury. I complain to your divinity that I have lost two wheels and four cows and many small belongings from my house. I would ask the genius of your divinity that you do not allow health to the person who has done me wrong, nor allow him to lie or sit or drink or eat, whether he is man or woman, whether boy or girl, whether slave or free, unless he brings my property to me and is reconciled with me. With renewed prayers I ask your divinity that my petition may immediately make me vindicated by your majesty."

It is worth spending some time here strolling around the park taking in the spectacular views across Gloucestershire, the River Severn and Wales. There is a large metal panoramic map at the south end of the area at Coaley Peak which is a help when spotting the various landmarks.

Map References:

Hetty Pegler's Tump: SO789000
Nympsfield Long barrow: SO793013
Uley Bury Hill Fort: ST784989
West Hill Roman Shrine: ST789995
Coaley Peak: SO793010

HUNTING THE WREN

O where are you going? said Milder to Mulder,
O we may not tell you said Festle to Fose
We're off to the woods said John the Red Nose,
We're off to the woods said John the Red Nose

What will you do there? said Milder to Mulder,
O we may not tell you said Festle to Fose
We'll hunt the Cutty Wren said John the Red Nose,
We'll hunt the Cutty Wren said John the Red Nose

How will you shoot her? said Milder to Mulder,
O we may not tell you said Festle to Fose
With bows and with arrows said John the Red Nose,
With bows and with arrows said John the Red Nose

That will not do then said Milder to Mulder,
O what will do then? said Festle to Fose
Big guns and big cannons said John the Red Nose,
Big guns and big cannons said John the Red Nose

How will you bring her home? said Milder to Mulder,
O we may not tell you said Festle to Fose
On four strong men's shoulders said John the Red Nose,
On four strong men's shoulders said John the Red Nose

That will not do then said Milder to Mulder,
O what will do then? said Festle to Fose
Big carts and big waggons said John the Red Nose,
Big carts and big waggons said John the Red Nose

How will you cut her up? said Milder to Mulder,
O we may not tell you said Festle to Fose
With knives and with forks said John the Red Nose,
With knives and with forks said John the Red Nose

That will not do then said Milder to Mulder,
O what will do then? said Festle to Fose
Big hatchets and cleavers said John the Red Nose,
Big hatchets and cleavers said John the Red Nose

How will you cook her? said Milder to Mulder,
O we may not tell you said Festle to Fose
With pots and with pans said John the Red Nose,
With pots and with pans said John the Red Nose

That will not do then said Milder to Mulder,
O what will do then? said Festle to Fose
In a bloody great brass cauldron said John the Red Nose,
In a bloody great brass said John the Red Nose

Who'll get the spare ribs? said Milder to Mulder,
O we may not tell you said Festle to Fose
We'll give them all to the poor said John the Red Nose,
We'll give them all to the poor said John the Red Nose

Thus goes the mysterious Cutty Wren song, as collected from a group of men in Adderbury, Oxfordshire in the early 1900s, although a version had actually been published as far back as 1744. While it sounds a little like a children's question-and-answer song, akin to the Who Killed Cock Robin nursery rhyme, the song was actually part of a serious traditional ritual custom which had survived against the odds in at least fifteen counties in England, and is also known to have taken place in similar form in Scandinavian countries, while Irish, Scots, Welsh and Manx versions of the song have since been collected.

The Oxfordshire wren hunters had no idea why they performed such a rite, only that it "had always been done", and were unaware of similar goings on in other parts of the country. The hunting of a wren, and occasionally its crucifixion, was at one time a common occurrence on St Stephen's day. This blatantly bizarre custom, and its song with lyrics which exaggerate the gravity of the act into the realms of the fantastical at first sight seem to be completely nonsensical, and yet both the form of the song's music, with its hypnotic rhythm and insistent beat, along with its (almost liturgical style) call-and-response lyrics hint that something altogether more serious is going on.

Cutty Wren ceremony, Middleton, Suffolk 2006

In societies where the written word was the privilege of the chosen few, chants and songs were, and in some cases still are, a useful mnemonic device for imparting important lyrical content for significant ritual occasions. The call-and-response pattern of the song recalls the magical rituals of both 'primitive' and sophisticated peoples, from aboriginal hunting rites to the Catholic mass. Bob Stewart, in his seminal work on British folksong *Where is St*

George, hints that the song may actually be a survival of a formal liturgical song from pre-Christian days. Certainly, the imagery of the song's perceived nonsensical lyrics might well have passed over the heads of the religious censors of the middle ages, even if no Christian interpretation of their content could satisfactorily be provided.

Cutty Wren ceremony, Middleton, Suffolk 2006

The protagonists in the song challenge and respond to each other's call, and their claims appear to be judged by the character John the Red Nose, the final arbiter. The hunting of the wren, the smallest of birds seems to require enormous effort – bows and arrows are not sufficient, there must be big guns and cannon; four strong men cannot bear the weight of the prey – carts and wagons are needed, and so on. Thus the cutty (little) wren is something small and yet at the same time very great. This may be an echo of the old folktale in which the wren becomes the king of all the birds by stealth – simultaneously the smallest and yet the most important of creatures. This is a common enough motif in the western mystery tradition, with hints of 'as above, so below'.

The slaying of the sacrificial King, for which Frazer claims the wren to be a symbolic substitute is a well known if academically disputed part of ancient pagan religion, in which the King and the Land are one, and the King must be sacrificed in order that the land can be renewed each year. Thus the wren may well be a substitute for a blood sacrifice which will bring prosperity and fertility to the land, and good luck to the villagers. Perhaps the exaggerated lyrics once served as a reminder that while the symbolic slaying of a tiny bird might seem a trivial thing, the actual import of the ritual had a massive significance – the survival of the local community no less. It is also worth noting that at any other time apart from the wren hunt, it was considered extremely bad luck to kill a wren, and thus the timing of the ritual, usually around the winter solstice, was crucial to its efficacy.

The brass cauldron has obvious connections with the death and rebirth cycle of Celtic mythology concerning the goddess Kerridwen the ancient mother, the source of divine wisdom and immortality. Thus the fertility aspect of the custom, the renewal of the land, is inextricably linked with not just the physical, but the spiritual survival of the soul. The wren is also sacred to Taliesin in Celtic mythology

If this seems like reading rather too much into what is ostensibly a nonsense song, then listen to it sung in a folk club or pub song session and join in. The insistent rhythm and repetitive lyrics certainly evoke something atavistic deep within the psyche, which comes from the heart rather than the head, the soul rather than the intellect. Despite the probable corruption of the lyrics down through the years no other British folk song feels so inherently Pagan as this one.

Probably the best recording of the song, and to my mind the most stirring and evocative is by Steeleye Span on their album Time with Maddy Prior taking the lead vocal against a rich tapestry of instrumentation underpinned by an almost shamanic drum beat. Hunting the Wren on John Kirkpatrick's Wassail! Album is also worth a listen. Four Scottish and Irish wren tunes appear on the CD Boys of the Lough - The Day Dawn. A selection of traditional Cutty Wren recordings of Wales, Ireland and the Isle of Man can be found on A Celtic Christmas. 'String Whistle' have a whole section of their CD Spirits of the Past devoted to the Cutty Wren.

The Cutty Wren ceremony is performed on the evening of St Stephen's day by the Old Glory molly dancers in the village of Middleton, Suffolk who revived the custom in 1994. A man dressed in Victorian agricultural clothes leads a procession of corduroy clad men in hats and overcoats and hobnail boots; he has a blackened face and wields a broom, sweeping a path for the 'Lord and Lady' (both male) who follow behind him, and a man carrying a carved effigy of the wren, hidden in a bush of ivy on a garlanded pole. The procession moves slowly to a drum beat, followed by the musicians and the villagers carrying lanterns in eager anticipation of the rite, which takes place outside the local pub after molly dancing displays from 'Old Glory'.

Cutty Wren ceremony, Middleton, Suffolk 2006

Pete Jennings, author of Pagan Paths and Northern Traditions and former president of the Pagan Federation was instrumental in the revival of this custom, and subsequently succeeded in enticing the old Glory molly dancers to the 1999 Pagan Federation national conference. Doubtless there are now other revivalists around the country, and the song itself is well known in song sessions across the land. There is also a much loved and hilarious comic send-up of the song, almost inevitably by Les Barker

AN ANCIENT GAME

Ask most people to name an ancient traditional board game and they will come up with chess, draughts or perhaps backgammon, these being still popular today. However, in the days before we all became obsessed with the little box of electronics in our living rooms, board games were common and exceedingly numerous, and some of them were, and are, exceedingly ancient in origin.

One of the most venerable of our traditional board games is Nine Men's Morris, also known as Nine Man's Morris, Mill, The Siege of Troy, Merels, Merrils, or sometimes just plain Morris. It was widely played in England by the fourteenth century, and visitors to Norwich, Chester, Canterbury, Salisbury and Winchester can see gaming boards cut into the cloister seats or stonework of the cathedrals by the monks. A board cut into a stone found in Dublin has been dated to the thirteenth century, while a wooden carving was discovered in the Oseburg Viking ship burial, so it is possible that the game was played in Britain from Roman Times and all through the Dark Ages. A markedly similar game, Fidchell is mentioned in the Mabinogion in the story The Dream of Rhonabwy, in which King Arthur plays against Owain. This game is also mentioned in ancient Irish texts from the seventh century, and there is one extant board that dates from the tenth century.

The origins of the game are uncertain, but certainly go back much further than the Middle Ages. It is related to both Tic-tac-toe and Noughts and Crosses, though without the diagonals. It is likely that the game was played in China as early as 500BCE and was mentioned by the Roman poet Ovid (43BCE – 17CE). Roman boards were made of wood or stone, though the very rich apparently had them made from more exotic materials such as ivory, proving that the game was popular in all classes of society. The pattern of the board also seems to have been used as a decorative or possibly protective symbol, and may be very ancient indeed, being carved into an Egyptian temple at Kurna (c 1400BCE), and in the Acropolis in Athens. Further back still, it may be found in prehistoric rock carvings in France, Austria and Afghanistan, and also in the Bronze Age burial mound at Cr Bri Chualann in Ireland. In Britain decorative (or at least, non-practical from the gaming point of view) versions of the pattern are found carved on gravestones in Yorkshire, and the Isle of Man, and inscribed (along with other seventeenth century graffiti) onto the chancel arch of Singleton Church in Sussex.

Seventeenth century graffiti in Singleton church, West Sussex

The remnants of a board were actually found in the remains of the ancient city of Troy; the name 'The Siege of Troy' probably reflects the game's ancient origins generally, and folklore connecting mazes with Troy in particular. In France it is called Marelle, and Janet and Colin Bord, in their book Ancient Mysteries of Britain suggest that the game may be related to Hopscotch, the old French name for the latter being 'Jeu de Merelles', which is similar to Merrils, the name

An Ancient Game

which the game was usually referred to in England in the Middle Ages. It has also been suggested that, along with the dance, the word Morris is derived from 'Moorish', suggesting that the game may have had its origins in the middle-east, though as it was played in Britain long before the Crusades, this is unlikely. In fact in this instance the known antiquity of the game could be used to disprove this much mentioned and much disputed piece of speculative etymology.

A fine example of a Nine Men's Morris board carved into stone was found recently in Creswell Crags, a cave in Nottinghamshire which was occupied from the Ice Age to the Middle Ages, and so far remains undated. A far more easily dated board was found in the wreck of the Tudor battleship The Mary Rose, carved into the lid of a barrel. It is now on display in Portsmouth's Historic Dockyard Museum, along with many other fascinating finds.

From the eighteenth century, a board survives carved into the side of one of the tea chests which were cast into the sea during the infamous Boston Tea Party in 1773 of which only two are extant (preserved in the Boston Ship & Tea Party Museum in America).

Illustration from a book on games commissioned by Alfonso the Wise, King of Castile and Leon, in 1283

The Reverend Thiselton Dyer in his Folk-Lore of Shakespeare (1883) writes that:

"This rustic game, which is still extant in some parts of England, was sometimes called "the nine men's merrils, from merelles, or mereaux, an ancient French word for the jettons or counters with which it was played. The other term 'morris' is probably a corruption suggested by the sort of dance, which in the progress of the game the counters performed."

He also describes an open-air version of the game played on turf:

"In that part of Warwickshire where Shakespeare was educated, the shepherds and other boys dig up the turf with their knives to represent a sort of imperfect chessboard. It consists of a square, sometimes only a foot diameter, sometimes three or four yards. Within this is another square, every side of which is parallel to the external square; and these squares are joined by lines drawn from each corner of both squares, and the middle of each line. One party or player has wooden pegs, the other stones, which they move in such a manner as to take up each other's men, as they are called, and the area of the inner square is called the pound, in which the men taken up are impounded. These figures are by the country people called nine men's morris, or merrils; and are so called because each party has nine men. These figures are always cut upon the green turf or leys, as they are called, or upon the grass at the end of ploughed lands, and in rainy seasons never fail to be choked up with mud."

It is possible that it was this same configuration upon the land to which Shakespeare referred in his A Midsummer Night's Dream:

The nine men's morris is fill'd up with mud,
And the quaint mazes in the wanton green
For lack of tread are indistinguishable.

The "quaint mazes" that Shakespeare refers to are the large scale labyrinths that were still relatively common in his time, some of which were laid out in the Bronze Age. In the Middle Ages they were associated with May-day rites and such seasonal jollities as Robin Hood's Dance, or Robin Hood's race were performed on them, often

An Ancient Game

by morris or sword dancers.

In his book Mazes and Labyrinths, Nigel Pennick quotes one account of such a maze from the 18th century:

"Shepherd's, or Robin Hood's Race, was a curious labyrinth or maze, cut in the ground, on Snenton Common, about a mile from Nottingham, and within a quarter of a mile of Robin Hood's, or St. Ann's Well. This maze, though only occupying a piece of ground about eighteen yards square, is, owing to its intricate windings, five hundred and thirty-five yards in length; at the four angles were oval projections intersecting the four cardinal points."

The maze was sadly ploughed up in 1797 when a local farmer planted a field of potatoes. The well itself suffered a not dissimilar fate in 1887 when it was buried beneath a railway embankment, though the spring, apparently still flows underground and causes flooding from time to time.

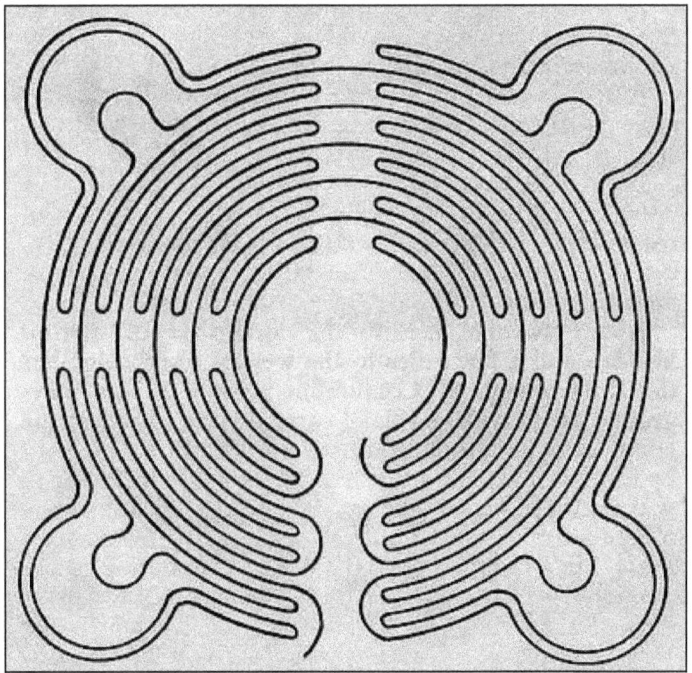

Plan of the turf maze, or labyrinth at Saffron Walden

The close association between the two types of turf-cut features that Shakespeare makes is interesting, and perhaps links the playing of the out-door version of Nine Men's Morris with May-day traditions. Appropriately, a modern large-scale outdoor version of the design has been created in the Shakespeare memorial gardens in Stratford-upon-Avon. The description of the maze at Snenton sounds similar to the existing labyrinth at Saffron Walden, which is traditionally ancient, and the largest in the country, but can only be reliably dated to the seventeenth century. Other historic labyrinths exist at Somerton, in Oxfordshire, Hilton in Cambridgeshire and at Wing, in Rutland.

It would appear, that by playing the game, we may be participating not only in a contest of skill, but also connecting to something that at one time our ancestors associated with the turning of the year, and which may have been a part of seasonal rites which pre-date the coming of Christianity to these shores.

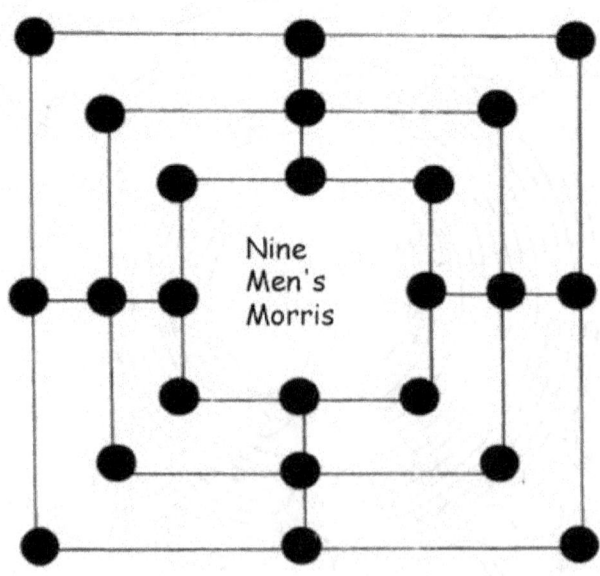

An Ancient Game

Playing the Game:

1. Equipment:

The game of Nine Mens Morris or Mill is played on a board consisting of three concentric squares connected by lines from the middle of each of the inner square's sides to the middle of the corresponding outer square's side. Pieces are played on the corner points and on the points where lines intersect so there are 24 playable points. Accompanying the board, there should be 9 black pieces and 9 white pieces usually in the form of round counters

2. Preparation and Objective

The basic aim of the game is to make "mills" - vertical or horizontal lines of three in a row. Every time this is achieved, an opponent's piece is removed, the overall objective being to reduce the number of opponent's pieces to less than three or to render the opponent unable to play. To begin with the board is empty.

3. Basic Play

Player's toss a coin to decide who will play white - white moves first and has a slight advantage as a result. Play is in two phases. To begin with, players take turns to play a piece of their own colour on any unoccupied point until all eighteen pieces have been played. After that, play continues alternately but each turn consists of a player moving one piece along a line to an adjacent point.

During both of these phases, whenever a player achieves a mill, that player immediately removes from the board one piece belonging to the opponent that does not form part of a mill. If all the opponents pieces form mills then an exception is made and the player is allowed to remove any piece. It is only upon the formation of a mill that a piece is captured but a player will often break a mill by moving a piece out of it and then, in a subsequent turn, play the piece back again, thus forming a new mill and capturing another piece.

Captured pieces are never replayed onto the board and remain captured for the remainder of the game. The game is finished when a player loses either by being reduced to two pieces or by being unable to move.

4. Variations

Sometimes a wild rule is played for when a player is reduced to only three pieces. In this case, any player with only three pieces remaining is allowed to move from any point to any other point on the board regardless of lines or whether the destination point is adjacent.

Alternative board layouts have been used over the centuries. One common pattern adds four extra diagonal lines to the basic board outlined above, the lines being drawn from the corners of the inner square to the corners of the outer square. Pieces can be moved and mills made along these extra lines in the usual way

(Instructional text Copyright © 1999 Masters Games, used with permission)

Map References:

Canterbury Cathedral: TR151579
Chester Cathedral: SJ405664
Norwich Cathedral: TG235089
Saffron Walden Labyrinth: TL543385
Shakespeare Memorial Gardens: SP200543
Singleton Church: SU877130
The Mary Rose: SU 627006
Winchester Cathedral: SU482292

MAGICAL FOLK

The modern Pagan 'movement', if such it can be termed, in re-imagining and re-inventing a religious tradition in the latter half of the twentieth century has drawn on many strands of native British culture, some of which, like paganism itself were in danger of disappearing completely in a post-war, strongly Christian society which looked largely to America as the source of everything 'great and good' after the horrors of the Second World War.

By the early 1960s folk music and dance were very much in the doldrums, largely ignored by mainstream culture as something practised by died-in-the-wool, Arran-sweater wearing finger-in-the-ear types, represented by the earnest anthropological endeavours of song-collectors like Allan Lomax and politically motivated singers such as Ewan Maccoll, or reduced to self parody in the case of popular folk entertainers such as the Spinners, the Searchers or Val Doonican. Ironically, in America itself, Bob Dylan, Joni Mitchell, the Byrds and the Band were forging a distinctively American style of folk music with its roots in the traditional music of the early European settlers and the country-blues and protest songs of later American troubadors such as Woody Guthrie. English performers such as Martin Carthy, Maddy Prior and Shirley Collins, while respected among the cognoscenti remained virtually unknown to the general public at that time.

Oddly enough it was a band who originally sought to emulate the popular American bands the Byrds and the Band who were to change the situation and open up English folk song and dance music to a far wider audience by creating almost overnight that most quintessentially English of musical genres, 'Folk-Rock'.

Liege and Lief 1969

In 1968 Fairport Convention were a modestly successful rock band playing the college circuit. They appeared at the first Isle of Wight Festival on the same bill as Arthur Brown, Jefferson Airplane, the Move and Tyrannosaurus Rex, with recently recruited (folk) singer Sandy Denny. Even at this stage some of their material was nodding in the direction of traditional folk music, with versions of Nottamun Town and She Moved Through The Fair, while songs such as Ashley Hutchings and Richard Thompson's It's Alright Ma, it's Only Witchcraft and Thompson's Meet on the ledge hinted at an interest in things metaphysical. Denny, who came from a traditional folk background would entertain the rest of the band on long drives between gigs by singing traditional ballads, but it was only after the tragic and fatal van crash which killed their drummer Martin Lamble and Thompson's girlfriend, that the band acquired a new line-up and took a conscious decision to embrace traditional folk music as their principle inspiration.

The result was the epic album Liege and Leif, recorded in 1969. By now band leader and bass player Ashley Hutchings had become obsessed by traditional music and was spending more and more time researching songs and music at Cecil Sharp House (headquarters of the English Folk Dance and Song Society), while new band member fiddler Dave Swarbrick who had left his longstanding musical partner Martin Carthy brought his instrumental expertise and a strong writing ability which was to bear fruit in a classic collaboration with guitarist/songwriter Richard Thompson in Crazy Man Michael. The traditional material on the album includes several songs of a magical nature such as Reynardine and Tam Lin and is notable for not skimping on the darker side of the tradition, encompassing in Matty Groves adultery, violence, death, necrophilia and wife murder! This was English traditional song 'as she was wrote', not prettified for easy listening and at the same time given a fresh rock-driven backing treatment which had never been attempted in a serious way before.

Rising for the Moon 1975

England's Living Folklore

Liege and Lief was a critical and commercial success and introduced a whole new generation to native British folk music. The album sleeve contained old photographs of English traditions such as Morris dancing, the Padstow Obby Oss and the Burry Man, and its back cover was adorned by a photograph of a weird "totem object" that Swarb had apparently found mouldering away in some sacking, hidden in the corner of a churchyard. It is a strange phallic shaped carving with a face that appears to have lost some teeth, giving it a slightly quizzical expression. The whole concept and presentation of the album, produced by Joe Boyd's Witchseasons Productions, is steeped in folk tradition and magic. Sandy Denny influenced further Fairport albums, such as Rising for the Moon (1975). Sadly she died in 1978 of a brain haemorrhage after a tragic accident.

Sandy Denny 1947-1978

Shortly after Liege and Lief Ashley Hutchings left Fairport to form the hugely successful Steeleye Span, with Maddy Prior, and Gaye and Terry Woods (who years later played with the Pogues). They were joined later by Martin Carthy. Steeleye were slightly different in that they were folk musicians from the start, rather than rock musicians playing electric folk, as in Fairport Convention, but their repertoire was similar - a mix of English and Irish songs and tunes played with enormous skill and with a great love of the material. It was while he was with Steeleye Span that Hutchings conceived and recorded the album Morris On with his wife Shirley Collins, Richard Thompson, Dave Mattacks, Barry Dransfield and John Kirkpatrick. This was another unique project which sold in thousands and brought English folk material, this time the ancient weirdness and bawdiness that is the morris tradition, to a new audience. Hutchings was very aware of the ritual, pagan connotations of morris dancing:

"some of the movements of morris dancing were designed to draw a power from the atmosphere, and the ground beneath them, and their bodies. Some of the movements were specifically worked out, much as the mystical teacher Gurdjieff would instruct his followers. Our ancestors who did these dances, did these rituals, knew far more about what they were doing than we imagine."

Morris On 1972

Shortly afterwards Hutchings left Steeleye Span and formed the Albion Country Band, which toured alongside a morris side from Chingford, who called themselves The Albion Morris. Most of Hutchings' bands are still performing to this day, either regularly or for occasional concerts. The Cropredy festival in Oxfordshire (originally conceived as a fundraising effort for the local church roof) is an annual Fairport Convention reunion bash.

In the 1970s, the folk-rock genre was strong enough to have a considerable influence on more mainstream rock bands. This was especially true of Led Zeppelin who focused firmly on the mystical aspects of British folk music in their album Led Zeppelin III. In their next, untitled album of 1971 they embraced the folk spirit wholeheartedly, producing their most popular classic songs such as Stairway To Heaven, Rock & Roll and When The Levee Breaks. This became the band's biggest album, selling more than 16 million copies over the course of 25 years - the album has a grand sense of drama, deepened by Robert Plant's burgeoning obsession with mythology, religion, and the occult - notably the works of Aleister Crowley. Plant's mysticism comes to a head on the eerie folk song The Ballad of Evermore, a mandolin driven number with haunting vocals from none other than Sandy Denny. Of all Led Zeppelin's songs though, Stairway to Heaven is the most well known, and rightly so. Building up from a simple finger-picked acoustic guitar sequence to a storming torrent of guitar riffs and solos, it encapsulates the entire album in one song. It also has some of the most uncompromisingly Pagan lyrics of any of their songs, which includes the lines:

And it's whispered that soon, If we all call the tune
Then the piper will lead us to reason.
And a new day will dawn
For those who stand long
And the forests will echo with laughter.

Pink Floyd too, had their folky, mystical moments, particularly in their early work based around the vision of their founding singer/guitarist Syd Barrett, an art student whose world revolved around music, mysticism and large doses of hallucinogens. Piper at the Gates of Dawn (the title taken from a chapter in that most Pagan of books, Kenneth Grahame's Wind in the Willows) was an auspicious debut album, and proved to be a major influence on British pop music from David Bowie and Marc Bolan to XTC.

For a time, the Incredible String Band were a very successful act, and albums such as the Hangman's Beautiful Daughter were classics of the folk-rock genre. Songwriter Robin Williamson's lyrics were frequently very Pagan in content:

...I make a pact with you
you who are the liquidness of the waters
and the spark of the flame
I call upon you
you who make fertile the soft earth
and guard the growth of growing things
I make peace with you...

Robin Williamson has since been nominated an honorary bard by several Druid orders. Around the same time, Bob Stewart, musician, mystic and author produced the seminal study of traditional folk music Where is Saint George, a detailed analysis of several traditional English ballads, in which he found evidence of ancient Pagan practice and ritual. While his scholarship in folklore is probably as academically questionable as Margaret Murray's was in anthropology and the study of witchcraft, the book makes a good case based on a small number of songs, and is in itself a fascinating essay, indicative of a certain feeling prevalent at the time, that the English folk tradition was steeped in a mystical tradition which was almost lost to us, but had somehow survived centuries of proscriptive Christian culture (sounds familiar?). The book remains a Pagan classic, now long out of print and much sought-after.

In the late seventies and early eighties, Jethro Tull became the most prominent folk-rock band around, arguably with the most blatantly Pagan lyrics ever to make the UK popular music charts. It is rare to find a Pagan who doesn't enjoy their early music; band leader and lyricist Ian Anderson has become for many a sort of musical legend, who has helped define, or at least enhance the Pagan world view. Many a fan has probably wondered if he is in fact Pagan himself, with song titles like Ring Out Solstice Bells, Pan Dance, Beltane, and Cold Wind to Valhalla, to name but a few. Several of Jethro Tull's albums have become classics in the realm of Pagan music, most notably Songs From the Wood.

Have you seen Jack in the Green?
With his long tail hanging down?
He quietly sits under every tree
In the folds of his velvet gown.
He drinks from the empty acorn cup
The dew that dawn sweetly bestows.
And taps his cane upon the ground
Signals the snowdrops it's time to grow
(Jack in the Green, Ian Anderson 1977)

Songs from the Wood 1977

The revival of Celtic folk music, spearheaded firstly by the Chieftains and later Planxty and Christy Moore in Ireland came a little later than the English folk-rock scene, but it too contained a strongly magical content. Eventually a Celtic folk-rock genre emerged which was just as vibrant and inventive as the English version, and which also embraced its mystical roots. The Dublin band Horslips developed a whole cycle of songs based on Celtic Mythology, of which perhaps the best were The Tain (1973) and The Book of Invasions (1975), which to my mind is one of the finest albums ever produced in the genre. Clannad started off playing traditional folk in 1973 and had a major hit with The Theme from Harry's Game, after which they started to experiment with a more electric sound. The resulting album Magical Ring proved popular with a wide audience and as a result they were asked to record music for the TV series Robin of Sherwood. It was probably this more than anything that made them firm favourites with the Pagan community. Legend, the resulting album was also critically and popularly acclaimed.

Magical Ring 1983

In more recent years, folk has had far less of an influence on mainstream popular music and has tended to follow a relatively obscure (though no less artistically creative) path with its own ardent following. In this sense it has parallels with the modern Pagan movement, and there are certainly many points of contact between the two. Some are quite surprising. Folk singer and comedian Mike Harding (the 'Rochdale Cowboy') has produced a superb book on the Green Man, and his website proudly displays a Pagan Best of the Web award. Julie Felix (remember her?) performed a memorable sixtieth Birthday concert with the Avalonian Free State Choir in 1998 at the Royal Festival Hall. Her website proclaims:

"Julie sings from the heart, and her heart was filled with joy that so many of her Goddess sisters were able to come and help her sing in her emergence as a 60 year old Crone."

Damh the Bard

Martin Carthy, no less, has played at Pagan festivals and some folk-rock bands, notably The Morrigan and Shave the Monkey are hugely popular with Pagan audiences. The Hastings Jack-in-the-Green festival, while ostensibly a Morris Dance extravaganza is a Pagan celebration in all but name while the Eastbourne Lammas Festival merges folk music, dance and Paganism very successfully. A few folk bands and performers such as Dave Smith (Damh the Bard), Dragonsfly, The Dolmen, and the Morrigan, approach the folk scene with specifically Pagan or magical intent, and do so with aplomb, while the Wild Hunt, Wolf's Head and Vixen, Mythago and Hunters Moon Morris, among others have successfully forged a distinctively Pagan identity within the genre of traditional English dance.

There are certain constants you will find in the music collections of many music loving Pagans - among them albums by groups like Shaman, Solstice, Clannad, The Waterboys, The Levellers, Gabrielle Roth and the Mirrors, Praying for the Rain or The Cocteau Twins, along with the odd compilation tape containing pieces like Carl Orff's Carmina Burana, Kate Bush's Waking the Witch, Season of the Witch by Donovan, or almost anything by Loreena McKennitt.

Hunters Moon Morris dancing at Boscastle 2005

Not all of these are folk orientated by any means but a great many of them are. Perhaps it is the folk tradition's emphasis on the earthier aspects of life, love, and nature that chimes so happily with the Pagan world view that makes it attractive to us as a musical genre.

It may also be that folk music and Paganism have a mutuality born out of being minority interests, generally frowned upon and misunderstood by polite society, and often lampooned by the popular press as being eccentric and/or irrelevant. Those of us who know of the great beauty, depth, integrity and historic tradition inherent in both would beg to differ.

WESSEX

The land of the West Saxons became the most powerful kingdom in England, and under King Alfred it was strong enough to repulse the Viking onslaught. Its countryside contains some of the most famous ancient pagan sites in the world, such as Stonehenge and Avebury. Here we take a look at a few of its lesser known treasures: the mysterious henge at Knowlton in Dorset with a medieval church at its centre; another at Dorchester that was re-used by the Romans as an amphitheatre; the ancient settlement at Old Sarum that became a Norman Castle. The land of Wessex inspired some wonderful writing from the pens of the fiercely agnostic Thomas Hardy, and the proto-Pagan writer of occult landscape novels John Cowper Powys. As we travel through we learn the story of the first revival of paganism in a supposedly Christian Roman empire, and discover some surprising traditions from medieval times when giants walked the streets.

England's Living Folklore

I edged the ancient hill and wood
Beside the Ikling Way,
Nigh where the Pagan temple stood
In the world's earlier day.

Thomas Hardy
The Well-Beloved 1898

THE FIRST REVIVAL

Iron Age hill forts are perhaps Britain's greatest legacy from the Celtic tribes who occupied these islands in pre-Roman times. Some are spectacular, such as Maiden Castle in Dorset, Cadbury in Somerset and Hambledon Hill in Hampshire, while others are quite tiny by comparison, mere fortified homesteads. It was while reading the visitors' information panel at Poundbury hill fort near Dorchester that I was struck by the fact that in several cases, in the West Country at least, pagan temples had been constructed within ramparts such as these in the late 4th century CE.

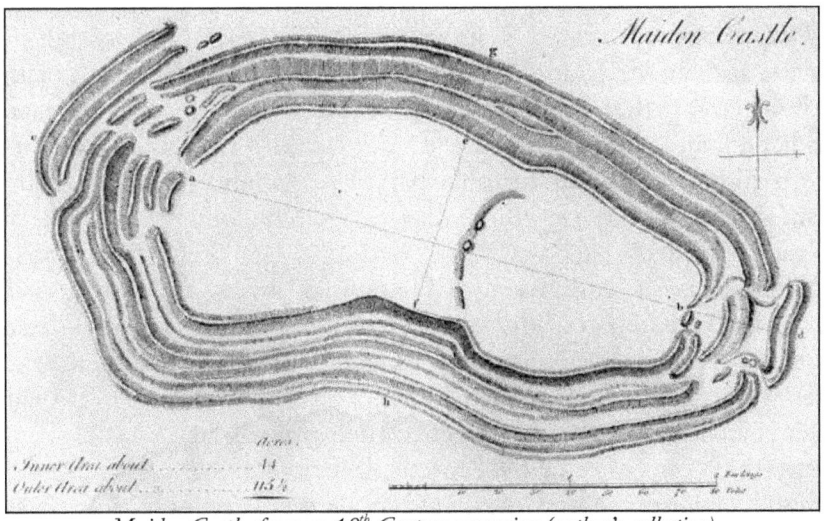

Maiden Castle, from an 18th Century engraving (author's collection)

It would appear on the face of it that Romanized Britons were constructing places in which to worship pagan gods not only at a time when the Roman Empire was supposed to have been Christianized, but also in places that had once been thriving communities but which had for centuries been abandoned in favour of walled towns on the Roman pattern. It seemed that my understanding of the Roman and early Christian history of Britain, based as it was on the schoolbooks of the 1960s was patently inadequate. Researching the subject with more modern texts revealed a far more complicated and interesting history than I had expected.

By the mid-4th century Britain had been under Roman rule for three hundred years. The myriad warlike tribes that had once claimed territories in these islands had been politically subdued and the country was divided into five provinces administered from Rome by provincial governors, occasionally with the help of large garrisons of soldiers.

Opinion is divided about how far the process of Romanization progressed throughout British society, but it would appear that the native aristocracy, at least, was quick to adopt the newly fashionable Roman way of life. As Tacitus described:

"[Agricola]...provided a liberal education for the sons of the chiefs, and showed such a preference for the natural powers of the Britons over the industry of the Gauls that they who lately disdained the tongue of Rome now coveted its eloquence. Hence, too, a liking sprang up for our style of dress, and the toga became fashionable. Step by step they were led to...the lounge, the bath, the elegant banquet."

Generally, the conquering Romans had always shown tolerance towards the religions of the conquered, though in Britain, the druids were regarded as a subversive influence and on Anglesey, at least, they were ruthlessly eliminated. This probably had more to do with their secular political influence than their priestly activities. It would seem that far from being repressed, British religious cults were actively encouraged and the native gods were frequently conflated with those of Rome, a process known as *syncretism*. The most famous example of this is of course Bath, known to the Romans as Aquae Sulis (the waters of Sulis). A massive temple was erected to the cult of Sulis-Minerva who presided over the hot springs that gushed forth from the earth as they still do today, and provided the *raison d'être* for a magnificent Roman spa town in the Avon valley.

Bronze head of Minerva from the temple at Bath (Aquae Sulis)

The majority of Britons continued to honour the genius loci of wells, springs and groves, and these were by no means overlooked. Professor Ronald Hutton, in his book Pagan Religions of the Ancient British Isles has described how Iron Age religious practice actually developed under Roman administration:

"It was a development rather than a break. Every known pre-Roman shrine in England was rebuilt as a Romano-British temple unless the settlement which it served was destroyed by conquest."

It is perhaps a sign of the individuality of the British pagan cults that these temples show great a variation of design. Most were certainly square or rectangular, which echoed the shapes of the old wooden shrines, and chimed happily with Roman practice, but many others were polygonal or round in plan. Archaeological investigations often unearth a host of figurines, bronze letters, and tablets inscribed with prayers, invocations and curses. British pagan religion in the first three centuries CE was certainly a blend of Celtic and Roman traditions and the evidence suggests that it became culturally Roman while remaining ethnically Celtic.

Altar to Sulis Minerva in the temple at Bath

There is some disagreement among scholars as to what extent the Romanization of religion in Britain took hold. Miranda Green points out that "many lower class rural Celts, at any rate in North and West Britain, were probably not Latin speakers…and one would expect their cults and beliefs to have been little altered by the presence of Rome." Professor Martin Henig tends to the opposite opinion "The Roman tradition provided a framework for the veneration of the gods, whether they were ancient deities from the east or Celtic nature spirits. All were 'Romanized', along with architecture and dress, even language."

Relief carving of the 'Three Matres' from Bath

It would appear that during this period the Iron Age cults flourished under a benevolent administration that encouraged all forms of pagan religion of whatever origin. Celtic deities were venerated alongside Roman ones at shrines which had been places of worship since the Bronze Age or earlier; while wealthy Romanized Britons might honour Minerva at the altar of Aquae Sulis, perhaps with a nod towards the Imperial cult, less 'cultured' citizens would bring offerings to the genius loci of the spring just as they had for generations. Many soldiers in the occupying army, whose ranks were drawn from across the empire were also Celts and it would seem that the cult of the Matres – the 'three mothers' was brought to Britain by soldiers from the Rhineland. Later more exotic eastern cults arrived from Persia and Egypt, so that Mithras and Isis were drawn into the Romano-British pantheon.

This happy state of affairs began to change in the fourth century, with the arrival of Christianity in Britain. No doubt the first arrivals in earlier centuries would have been a few individual converts in the army but by the late third century evangelical clergy were spreading their faith throughout the empire often using native languages rather than Latin. In 314 three bishops from Britain attended the Council of Arles, and evidence suggests that there were more than twenty by the end of the century. By 340 there is evidence that chapels and churches were replacing some pagan shrines, such as at Nettleton, Witham and Verulamium and Christian burials in east-west alignment and without grave goods started to become more and more common. At around this time, wealthy Romanized Britons started to incorporate Christian iconography into the mosaics in their luxurious villas; examples can be found at Hinton St Mary and Frampton in Dorset.

On the whole, the evidence suggests that the rise of Christianity and the decline of the pagan cults was slower in Britain than most other parts of the empire. Christianity had begun to flourish and co-exist with pagan religion in the atmosphere of toleration that Constantine had encouraged early in his reign. His sons, especially Constantius, took a harder line, with the banning of sacrifices and an implied official endorsement of the closing and destruction of urban temples. Despite this there is little evidence to show that this actually occurred to any great extent in Britain.

While it is tempting to believe that the pagan Britons were made of sterner stuff than their continental counterparts, the truth must be that Britain was something of an outpost of the empire and the extent of the implementation of proclamations from Rome did rather depend on the praetorian prefects of Gaul who were responsible for Britain at that time. As most of them were pagans during the time of Constantius' most viciously anti-pagan repression, who in any case generally had rather more pressing issues to deal with on their 'home patch' as it were, paganism continued relatively unscathed in Britain compared with Greece for example, where according to Libanius "no altar remained". Another

The First Revival

possible influence may have been Julian, who was Caesar of Gaul at the time, who while he had to pay lip service to Imperial policy, secretly harboured a great love of pagan religion and philosophy and was probably an initiate of the cult of Mithras. Julian was to become the last pagan Emperor of Rome (360-363) and while his attempts to restore temples and re-introduce religious tolerance (which of course earned him the derisory epithet 'Julian the Apostate' among Christian historians) undoubtedly halted some of the damage done to paganism, it was a case of too little too late, and with his tragic death on the battlefield by a Saracen's spear the floodgates were finally fully opened to the Christian onslaught.

Detail from the temple Pediment at Bath

Widespread destruction of pagan temples and shrines did not really begin in Britain until the middle of the 4th century, and this appears to have been due more to the acts of zealous Christian individuals rather than official policy, as no literary evidence for such policies in Britain exist. The fate of the Mithrea along the Scottish border and in London suggests such a situation, and of course by this time the Roman military presence was declining, as garrisons were withdrawn to defend Rome from incursions elsewhere in the empire, so that administrators in British towns could no longer always rely on a military solution to civil disorder.

Votive plaque from the 'Ashwell Hoard' found in Herefordshire (now in the British Museum)

With the decline of the Roman military presence in Britain, the economy also started to falter, and for decades no new temples were constructed. One of the reasons that Christianity spread so rapidly is that it was the wealthier classes who had money and political influence that converted first, and this period saw the conversion of some temples into churches. At Witham in Essex the

The First Revival

Romano-Celtic shrine had its sacred pool drained, sacred trees uprooted and a small oratory building and baptistry constructed in its place. At Nettleton Scrub in Wiltshire the octagonal temple to Apollo Cunomaglus was converted into a cruciform chapel. No doubt this happened in other places as well but ultimately, the collapse of the British economy was to affect paganism and Christianity alike, and a period of stagnation and even decay in both temple and church building seems to have occurred. Some, such as the temple at Chanctonbury Ring, Sussex, simply went out of use.

However, from around 360 onwards, there are clear signs of a pagan revival in Britain. For example after 367 the octagonal temple at Pagan's Hill near Chew Stoke in Somerset appears to have been in active pagan use once again, around thirty-five years after it had first been desecrated, and there seems to have been something of a revival generally in pagan burial practices. Dorothy Watts attributes this to the elevation of Julian as Augustus (Emperor) in 360 "...Julian's legacy was to slow down the spread of Christianity in Britain and weaken the church to the extent that it barely survived the following two centuries."

In Rome, Julian's pagan revival went some way to restoring the Christian/pagan equilibrium but it seems that Christianity had become too far entrenched within the state and those pagans who still remained in public positions were too conservative in their outlook for there to have been the complete restoration of pagan religion which Julian had so hoped for. Nevertheless, despite the shortness of his reign, for the next thirty years there was a new-found confidence in pagan Roman society and successive rulers showed a renewed religious tolerance. It was not until 391 that Theodosius re-introduced laws banning pagan cults and sacrifices, and prohibiting pagans from holding public office, writing wills or giving testimony. In 392 even domestic cults were prohibited; the temple burning began again.

In Britain, it may well be that Julian's anti-Christian stance was more important than his pro-paganism, and the tentative beginnings of a Christian Church were simply anomalous in a country where paganism had always been strong in any case. Henig refers to the restoration of pagan cults as a "return to normalcy". Philip Rahtz suggests that one factor was simply "a disillusionment with Christianity". This sounds entirely plausible given that the economy was collapsing, towns and cities decaying, and law and order generally in steep decline. In such a scenario the Christian policy of gaining converts among the political classes to spread their influence throughout the land was bound to backfire to some degree. Margaret Murray, while her seminal book The Witch-Cult in Western Europe is now often derided as an example of poor scholarship, may well have been correct in her theory that most Britons persisted with their pagan beliefs, even long after the mission of Augustine in 597, and that such beliefs lasted well into the Middle Ages. In other words the Christian Church, in the case of Britain, was on a hiding to nothing.

DORCM 1999.14: A model of the fourth century Maiden Castle temple, reconstructed (Woodward 1994) - Mr. J. Straw. Dorset County Museum

From around 360 when Julian became Emperor some temples were refurbished. As previously mentioned, the octagonal temple at Pagans Hill was restored and its cult statue replaced. The temple to

The First Revival

Nodens at Lydney was also restored, as was a shrine at Caerwent and the temple at Verulamium. At the same time churches were abandoned and some which had previously been pagan temples reverted to their former status, the aforementioned cases of Nettleton and Witham being prominent examples. In Bath, the desecrated temple to Sulis-Minerva was partially restored and pagan activity resumed, albeit now occupying a somewhat forlorn remnant of what had been one of the most magnificent classically styled temples in Britain. A *defixio*, or curse tablet from around this period confirms the presence of both Christians and pagans. Dorothy Watts lists thirty-seven known temple sites which survived to 360, many of which underwent refurbishment.

Slightly less easy to understand are the new temples constructed in rural locations at around this time. The best-known example is at Maiden Castle near Dorchester where a square Romano-Celtic temple building was constructed close to a more ancient circular shrine. Similarly positioned temples have been suggested at Poundbury hill fort, Cadbury Castle and at Old Sarum. It has been suggested that in some areas Christianity forced the pagan cults to locate new shrines away from the towns in more rural locations, but this was clearly not the case in most instances, and at Maiden Castle there is a suggested continuity of the use or re-use of a sacred site. Perhaps, as is so often the case with a 'revivalist' religion there was a fundamental desire to return to religious 'roots'. Mai Dun, the principle stronghold of the Durotriges had been comprehensively destroyed by the victorious Romans; it may be that the local pagan Celts took some pride in reinstating their native religion in their erstwhile tribal capital, turning their backs on the Roman settlement of Durnovaria (Dorchester) that had usurped it.

From archaeological evidence, funerary observances also appear to have undergone change at this period, with a resurgence in the practise of placing bodies in a prone position, the burial of animals along with humans – often horses or dogs, and of the pre-Roman practice of decapitated burials. This would certainly indicate that this new revival in pagan religion was along Celtic rather than Roman lines, the Celtic 'cult of the head' having been well documented. Interestingly, decapitated burials are also found in the 5th century and into the early Anglo-Saxon period, indicating that while the late 4th century temple building phase was short-lived, the religious observances continued for centuries to come, bearing out Margaret Murray's thesis. In almost all cases where the name of the deity associated with a late fourth century shrine is actually known, that name is Celtic, or a blend of Roman and Celtic. The one exception is that of the temple at Uley in Gloucestershire, which appears to have been dedicated to Mercury. The absence of Mithras, Bacchus and Isis may be partly because of the decline of the military presence among whom such deities were most popular, but may also indicate a disillusionment in salvation-type cults generally, perhaps tainted by a perceived similarity to the by now unpopular Christian religion.

Silver platter depicting Pan and his female companions, the Maenads. Part of the Thetford Hoard now in the British Museum.

Clearly in Britain Julian gave impetus to a pagan revival that was different to, and which outlasted that which occurred in the rest of the empire. Theodosius's decrees seem to have been blatantly ignored, and apart from some shrines at military centres such as at Richborough, there was no sudden or widespread compliance with the new Imperial endorsement of the Christian cult; where examples do occur, such as the burying of the Thetford hoard of treasure with its magnificent pagan iconography, or the dismantling of Coventina's Well at Carrawburgh such acts appear to have been deliberately and carefully carried out by pagans rather than being the result of Christian desecration.

The already tenuous hold that Christianity had in these Isles was now so weakened that it was unable to triumph here as it did in the rest of Europe. As the grip of Rome loosened politically, militarily and economically, the Celts reverted to their old ways. Many Roman towns were abandoned or shrank to a fraction of their original size. Many of the Romano-Celtic temples fell into disuse, or were desecrated by a new wave of pagan incomers who were not so tolerant of native cults as the invading Romans had been – the Anglo Saxons.

According to Dorothy Watts "In view of the failure of Christianity to organise and evangelize, and the twin disasters of the Saxon incursions and the Roman withdrawal, continuation of the native pagan cults into the fifth, sixth and seventh centuries, and even beyond, was inevitable." The British, who before the Romans arrived had had little use for grand religious monuments or buildings, went back to worshipping at springs and wells and in groves as they always had done, and after the ultimate success of Christianity following the mission of St Augustine in the sixth century CE their religious observances became folklore and magic: Their mythology became folk-tale, their sacred springs became holy wells, and their genius loci became local saints and guardian angels. Perhaps, in a sense, the first pagan revival never actually failed at all.

Maybe modern Pagans have more to thank Flavius Claudius Iulianus for than they generally recognize!

Map References:

Cadbury Castle: ST628251
Caerwent: ST469906
Chanctonbury: TQ139121
Coventina's Well, Carrawburgh: NY869708
Hambledon Hill: ST845126
London Mithreum: TQ319808
Lydney: SO615026
Maiden Castle: SY671884
Nettleton: ST819769
Old Sarum: SU137326
Pagans Hill, Somerset: ST555626
Poundbury Hill Fort: SY 681911
Roman Temple, Bath: ST750 646
Uley: ST789995
Verulamium: TL134072
Witham: TL809133

NINE STONES

Much is made these days of the contextual landscape of our ancient monuments. The recent fiasco over the Stonehenge plans which would have re-routed major roads away from the site is a case in point. Of course there are many lesser sites that suffer greatly from the proximity of busy roads. One such is the Nine Stones circle in Dorset, situated only a few feet away from the busy A35. Strangely, perhaps, the circle definitely has its own tranquil atmosphere and seems to welcome the visitor, who must cross the busy road and negotiate a small bridge over a ditch which leads into the enclosure, surrounded by iron railings.

The Nine Stones from the road, looking south

The circle is actually an ellipse, elongated along its SW- NE axis, and the stones appear to be arranged in alternate shapes and sizes, much like the Avebury stones, which Aubrey Burl has suggested indicates a sexual symbolism. The three largest stones seem to consist of some kind of flinty conglomerate which is actually rather colourful when wet, so don't rule out visiting in the rain. Its plan is identical in shape to the nearby Kingston Russell stone circle. It dates from the period 2200-1400 BCE and was much visited by antiquaries. John Aubrey visited it in the seventeenth century and included it in his illustrated Monumenta Britannica, although as is frequently the case with his engravings, the scale of the stones is greatly exaggerated. The tallest, most westerly stone stands seven feet high and weighs around eight tons, and the stones appear to be graded in size towards this impressive megalith. Burl has identified a low mound in the centre and two outlying rubble banks, but there have been no archaeological finds to indicate burials here.

The three largest stones

Nine Stones

About half a mile further along the main road to the west, adjacent to a road sign there lies a massive fallen megalith known as the Broad Stone, now partially hidden in the undergrowth. According to the English Heritage information board at the circle, the main road may follow the alignment of an ancient track-way. If this is the case the Broad Stone may have had some connection with the circle. A little further along the same road is the Poor Lot barrow cemetery.

Like other stone circles in the vicinity, the Nine Stones lie in a shallow valley, and the site therefore probably does not have an astronomical purpose, which has been suggested for many similar sites, although there may be a possible alignment to the summer solstice sunset. Barrows on the surrounding skyline may also have been markers for significant sunrises and sunsets. Peter Knight suggests the stones were erected at 'place of power' and claims that several important ley lines intersect here. Whatever you believe on that score the place does definitely have a powerful presence and is frequently used by local Pagans.

Looking north towards the A35

The Nine Stones have been regarded by local folklore to be the Devil, his wife and children, though another tale suggests that the stones were once children who where turned into stone by the Devil while playing five-stones on the sabbath. Another story is that they are the petrified figures of dancing maidens. As frequently occurs in such folklore, they are said to be uncountable. Westwood and Simpson suggest in their book Lore of the Land that an alternative name for these stones is "Lady Williams and her little dog Fido", which seems bizarre to say the least. Jeremy Harte states that this is "an allusion to the family at Bridehead." Bridehead House is an impressive manor house at nearby Little Bredy. Originally dating from the Tudor period it was rebuilt and enlarged in Victorian times.

The Broad Stone, lying next to the A35

A curious incident in 1985 involved a breakdown vehicle towing a Transit van. On passing the stones the engine cut out and the lights on both vehicles failed, only to burst into life again a few minutes later. At the same time a car on nearby Monkton Hill suffered a mysterious fault which caused its lights to flash on and off six or seven times before returning to normal. No explanation could be found for these phenomena and there was speculation in the press connecting the incidents with recent UFO sightings at Eggardon Hill, a large hill fort to the north of the stones.

The truncated beech tree still stands

Until 2007 the circle was shaded by a huge beech tree, but sadly this has now been severely lopped, presumably due to disease, and it now resembles a rather surreal sculpture, about thirty feet tall. At least one Druid group uses the site on a regular basis, as do many individual Pagans. It is not unusual to find the stones adorned with 'offerings', which can sometimes visually detract from the feeling of serenity encountered within the circle. On my most recent visit I found a plastic bag full of incense left in a hollow in one of the stones. Recently, the circle received attention of a more hostile kind when the stones were daubed with painted slogans by criminally irresponsible supporters of the so-called 'Fathers for Justice' campaign, and despite the best efforts of English Heritage and local Pagan groups, slight evidence of this vandalism still remains. Hopefully this will weather away in time, and perhaps in a few years time when the old beech tree has decayed somewhat the site will feel less as if it has suffered an assault, which in a sense I suppose, it has.

The site is easy to find, being about a quarter of a mile outside the village of Winterbourne Abbas in the Bridport direction, and is visible from a passing car if you know where lo look. You can either park in the village, or if there is space you may be able to park in the entrance of the Grange Farm Dairy (look for the big grey barn) just to the east on the opposite side of the road. Either way you will have to negotiate a fast and dangerous stretch of road, with no footpath and a deep drainage gully between you and the fence, so beware. Sadly this makes access for the disabled very difficult. There is a lay-by close to the Broad Stone, but once again there is no footpath to the stone itself. The Broad Stone, which remains unprotected from traffic on the main road, is on English Heritage's list of scheduled monuments "at risk".

Map References:

The Broad Stone: SY595903
Bridehead House: SY590887
Eggardon Hill Fort: SY542947
The Nine Stones: SY610904
Kingston Russell Stone Circle: SY577878
Poor Lot Barrows: SY589907

A FORGOTTEN PAGAN WRITER

About twenty-five years ago in a bookshop in Bath I picked up a copy of a large novel with the title A Glastonbury Romance, published in a new paperback edition by Picador. It turned out to be the most extraordinary book I had ever read, and before long I had amassed a large collection of books by the same author whose name I had hitherto never encountered. There was an indefinable 'something' about his writing which years later I recognize as being strongly pagan.

John Cowper Powys (pronounced 'cooper poe-iss') has been called the forgotten genius of English Literature. He is still widely unread in his native country despite the fact that his novels stand as literary landmarks in the development of the twentieth century novel. As a writer he has been compared to Hardy and Dostoievsky, and in 2000 George Steiner wrote in the Times Literary Review that Powys should be considered alongside Melville and Lawrence as one of "the three greatest writers in our language." Academic debate over his genius, or lack of it has raged controversially ever since his death in 1963. The debate has been fuelled by his individuality both as a writer and as a man, which has made him impossible for critics and academics to pigeon-hole neatly.

Born in 1872, the son of a vicar, he had a typical middle-class upbringing that took him almost inevitably from his father's Somerset vicarage to Sherborne School, and on to Cambridge University. He settled in Sussex and lived for several years in Court House at

Offham near Lewes. He taught literature in various girls' schools in Brighton and Eastbourne and produced some short and largely unexceptional volumes of poetry in the late nineteenth century; his first ever public lectures took place at Eastbourne and Hove Town Halls in the late 1890s.

JCP in the 1920s (author's collection)

Later on employment by the Oxford Union (a sort of Open University of its day) led to a public lecturing career that was to take him across Europe and North America where he found fame, if not fortune, regularly packing vast lecture halls. His lectures on literary figures must have been remarkable. "With almost an erotic emotion, as if I were indulging myself in some kind of perverted love affair," he wrote in his Autobiography, "I entered the nerves of Dickens or ... Henry James or Dostoievsky." At the same time, he never ceased to be John Cowper Powys, the highly-strung, perpetually dishevelled, eccentric Englishman. Once, when he was getting ready before a lecture, his hostess whispered to him that his fly-buttons were undone. "Madam," he replied, "I wear them that way."

Ill health forced him to curtail his lecturing career and he settled in a rural corner of New York State and began writing full time, completing three of the four books known as his 'Wessex Novels', namely Wolf Solent, A Glastonbury Romance, and Weymouth Sands. Having shunned literary London for several decades he returned to Dorset where he wrote some of his best work including Maiden Castle, the fourth of the West Country novels. His writing is marked by a unique personal philosophy that invests the landscape and inanimate nature with souls. Both the man and his writing are suffused with an inherent pantheism and a sense of the magical and otherworldly immanent in the here-and-now.

His many philosophical works, of which the best known are In Defence of Sensuality and The Meaning of Culture propound a vivid sense of Man's belonging to, and being a part of nature, and the connection of the individual's psyche to something universal and creative in the life force which, borrowing a phrase from Nietzsche he terms the 'First Cause'. This connection, according to Powys can only be made through "indulging our 'sensual' rather than our intellectual side" ('sensual' in the sense of 'sensations'). The following extracts are from his Autobiography.

"What I am revealing to you now is the deepest and most essential secret of my life. My thoughts were lost in my sensations; and my sensations were of a kind so difficult to describe that I could write a volume upon them and still not really have put them down. But the field-dung upon my boots, the ditch-mud plastered thick, with little bits of dead grass in it, against the turned-up ends of my trousers, the feel of my oak-stick 'Sacred' whose every indentation and corrugation and curve I knew as well as those on my hand, the salty taste of half-dried sweat upon my lips, the delicious swollenness of my fingers, the sullen sweet weariness of my legs, the indescribable happiness of my calm, dazed, lulled, wind-drugged, air-drunk spirit, were all, after their kind, a sort of thinking, though of exactly what, it would be very hard for me to explain."

"I touch here upon what is to me one of the profoundest philosophical mysteries: I mean the power of the individual mind to create its own world, not in complete independence of what is called 'the objective world,' but in a steadily growing independent attitude of other minds towards this world. ... The point is that we have the power of re-creating the universe from the depths of ourselves. In doing so we share the creative force that started the whole process."

In 1935 Powys moved to North Wales, to his namesake county, and was delighted to be made a Bard of the Powys Gorsedd at the Corwen Eisteddfod the following year. Wales was the land of his distant ancestors and home to the sixth-century magician-cum-bard Taliessin, who had been a sort of role model for Powys since childhood. In fact, he had sometimes referred to himself as a "tatterdemalion Taliessin." Powys was at heart a primitivist, for whom virtually every modern invention was anathema. He never drove a car or used a typewriter. He thought television was pernicious and hated talking on the telephone because he didn't want his words violated by a tangle of wires. Thus it is not surprising that after his move to Wales he looked to the past, especially the Welsh past, for inspiration. His next major works were historical fiction, although calling Owen Glendower and Porius historical novels is a bit like calling Moby-Dick a sea story. Porius particularly is a masterpiece. At times it reads like an extended study of what Powys called "the three incomprehensibles": sex, religion, and nature. At other times it reads like a magical mystery adventure. In one chapter an owl metamorphoses into a bird-maiden; in another the hero, Prince Porius, makes love with an aboriginal giantess while her father is plucking corpses from a battlefield with cannibalistic intent; in another the bard Taliessin (Powys's mouthpiece) chants verses such as "The ending forever of the Guilt-sense and God-sense, The ending forever of the Sin-sense and Shame-sense...."

Most of Powys' novels suffered unsympathetic editing at the hands of his publishers, and only now are unexpurgated versions of some of his books becoming available. Porius particularly is a very different book now from the version originally published and is much more pagan in feel, with a lot of alchemical symbolism mixed in with Dark Age magic and Celtic mythology. One might well imagine the horror with which the publishers, Simon and Shuster, received the original 1,589 page manuscript from its author who claimed to be an organ of communication for the departed spirits of the sixth century!

Bronze sculpture of JCP by Oloff de Wett, 1963 (author's collection)

By the time Porius was published in 1951 Powys was close to eighty, and enjoying an eccentric old age in his tiny cottage in Blaenau Festiniog. He maintained a strongly theatrical sense of the absurd, and would sometimes entertain astonished visitors by acting out the stoning of Saint Stephen. On getting up in the morning, he would pray to a host of deities, including Demeter, Greek goddess of agriculture, and Cybele, Phrygian goddess of nature.

His last books are weird, free-form fantasies in which anything can, and often does, happen. Odysseus in his old age can travel to the lost continent of Atlantis and surface in Manhattan, for example, or 'Time' can suddenly materialize as "an enormous black slug." In his final work, All or Nothing, a strange, almost childlike science-fiction story, someone called the King of the Milky Way wanders the solar system with his penis slung over his shoulder. Essentially daft maybe, but then Powys had always railed against the stifling effects of both social and literary convention and perhaps in his last years he felt able to give his bizarre imagination free rein.

Portrait by his sister, Gertrude Mary Powys, 1935

A Forgotten Pagan Writer

Was Powys a Pagan? Certainly from his writing one feels he would have embraced the modern Pagan movement wholeheartedly. He honoured the Old Gods with everyday rituals and incantations of his own devising, he believed in a "First Cause", a super-human force dualistic in nature, being "both beneficent and malefic", he was an exceptional scholar of both Classical and Celtic mythology, he delighted in immersing himself in nature, and he was a passionate anti-vivisectionist. The conventional Christianity of his upbringing was cast off at a very early age, although he admired and later wrote about the Bible as a work of literature. At times he studied Taoism, although the plurality of his world vision, and his political and spiritual anarchism would have made acceptance of any single religious system anathema; he often wrote about the "multiverse" rather than the universe. He was a contemporary of Dion Fortune, but unfortunately there is no evidence that they ever corresponded. Dion Fortune in fact wrote rather disparagingly about A Glastonbury Romance in her book Glastonbury: Avalon of the Heart.

In his Dark Age fantasy The Brazen Head, the giant Peleg's prayer to the moon expresses a deeply pagan frustration with imposed orthodox religion that sounds very much like a cry from the heart which any modern Pagan might express:

"Heal us...O Goddess, of the hurts and wounds in our souls that ache and bleed today because of the false doctrines about gods and men that have been inflicted upon us, false doctrines about all things in heaven and earth.

Have they not taken on themselves, these priests of pain, these ministers of blood, to invent signs and tokens and symbols and sacraments out of privation and deprivation, out of suppression and frustration, out of denial and negation? Have they not deified the revelations made by thy blessed mystery, and turned to nothing the secret of thy holy rapture, of thy sacred madness, of thy entranced, thy transporting ecstasy? Make them give us back the pulse of our life, great Goddess, give us back the beat of our heart, give us back the dance of our blood."

He certainly studied magical philosophy and at times referred to himself, perhaps only half-jokingly, as a magician; he also wrote some articles in the 1920s for a magazine called The Occult Review. He knew Kenneth Grant, and his friend and literary agent, Louis 'Marlowe' Wilkinson, was a practising occultist who wrote for Aleister Crowley's Equinox magazine. Wilkinson was also Crowley's literary agent, and it is known that Crowley and Powys read each others books and exchanged letters, but sadly (if the rumours are true) in what must be termed one of the great occult literary disasters of all time, their correspondence found its way into the library of the Solar Lodge of the O.T.O. in California, and was destroyed in a fire at their temple in 1969, an incident that led to a scandal involving the alleged physical abuse of the child arsonist, and uncovered the past involvement of Charles Manson with the lodge.

In letters to Louis Wilkinson dated in 1917, Crowley expresses an interest in Powys' philosophy and asks after him, mentioning that he had performed some "geomancy" for Powys' benefit, as the latter was about to undergo a serious operation on his stomach ulcers. He later wrote to say that he was very glad to hear of his recovery. As both men were in New York at that period it is possible, or even likely that Crowley may have attended one or more of Powys' public lectures. Wilkinson, incidentally, also claimed to have known members of the 'New Forest Coven' which Gardner discovered, and was present (allegedly) at the now legendary ritual to repel Hitler's invasion of 1940.

Powys wrote in his Autobiography (1932) that he met Crowley only once: "The only time I met Aleister Crowley was when I had to be the Speaker at a Foyle's Literary Lunch and I had him at my side and I treated him to a bottle of wine which he had finished before my speech was over!"

His possession of shamanic qualities, one might even say powers, is hard to deny. His biographer G. Wilson Knight wrote: "those who have incurred his anger have so invariably incurred misfortune that he has, as it were, been forced into a life of almost neurotic benevolence . . . Powys' early ambition to become a magician was no idle dream . . ."

In his Autobiography Powys confirmed this, writing:

"The evidence of this - of my being able, I mean, and quite unconsciously too, to exercise some kind of "evil eye" on people who have injured me - has so piled up all my life that it has become a habit with me to pray to my Gods anxiously and hurriedly for each new enemy." He also referred to ". . . that formidable daimon which, as I have hinted to you before, can be reached somewhere in my nature, and which when it is reached has the Devil's own force . . ."

That this 'daimon' was neither purely imaginary nor imperceptible to others is suggested by two anecdotes about Powys which Colin Wilson mentions in his book The Occult.

The American novelist Theodore Dreiser told the story of how after a social call to Dreiser's New York home one evening, Powys promised to return later "as a spirit or in some other astral form". About two hours later, Dreiser looked up from his book to see the apparition of Powys by the door, a pale white glow coming from it. The ghost vanished when Dreiser strode up to it, and when Dreiser phoned Powys' country home, "I told you I'd be there, and you oughtn't to be surprised," was all he had to say. It may be that he had no idea how he had done it, or that the apparition was in Dreiser's own mind. "I used to be aware," Powys wrote, "of surging waves of magnetic attraction between Dreiser and myself."

Powys' assertion ". . . that when I die it is the complete and absolute end of me . . ." was perhaps less than accurate. A month after he died in 1963 a medium, Miss Francis Horsfield, was standing by Wilson Knight in Exeter cathedral when she sensed the presence of a man and proceeded to describe Powys (whom she had never met): "He has rather gaunt features, with high cheekbones and unruly hair. He is a personality. He is nearly controlling me, but I do not want that. He himself was an occultist . . . He wrote didn't he?" Knight confirmed this. "He is close to you," she went on. "His power is so strong that you may well see him yourself sometime." She added that he had a "wide gleaming mouth" and a "beak-like nose". When Knight said Powys had latterly become a sceptic about 'survival', she said: "Anyway, he knows all about it now."

I have in my 'Powys collection' a copy of his 1950s 'philosophical pot-boiler' (his description) The Art of Growing Old, with a dedication in his own hand to his sister Marian which he signs off with "yours to the end, or ends"!

Powys is still a sadly neglected figure in his own country, though very popular in France and America. Most of his major novels are still in print, at least in American editions, and bookshops should be able to order them:

Wolf Solent (1929)

Wolf Solent describes one man's journey back to his roots, in his native Dorset. It is also a spiritual journey, as Wolf struggles with his subconscious ego to do battle with the evil of his Faustian employer, Squire Urquhart, in order to save his own personal life-illusion. One of the great psychological novels of all time, Wolf Solent is a good introduction to Powys' exuberant and spectacular writing style.

A Glastonbury Romance (1932)

A Glastonbury Romance is a magnificent tour-de-force of a novel, derided and admired in equal measure by critics when it was first published in 1932. It concerns the lives, loves and obsessions of a Glastonbury undergoing the pain of transition from a traditional rural way of life to a modern industrial based economy. It also portrays the nascent 'new-age scene' of Glastonbury between the wars (those of you who thought it was a more recent phenomenon should read The Avalonians by Patrick Benham). 'Glastonbury' is a massive book of nigh on half a million words and provides a rich tapestry of plot and sub-plot with human strengths, weaknesses and endeavours richly painted on a canvas woven from myriad strands of mythology, magic and folklore. The town itself, steeped in Arthurian lore and legend is certainly the most important character in the book, and the reader is left in awe at the author's magnificent vision in attempting such a deep analysis of the mythology of place in a novel.

Weymouth Sands (1934)

The third of Powys' great Wessex novels is much shorter than A Glastonbury Romance, but is equally vital and arresting. It was issued originally under the title of Jobber Skald the name of the boatman who is one of the principle characters. It is darker and more mysterious than 'Glastonbury' and has a character very much its own, reflecting the author's feeling for this small seaside town at the eastern end of Chesil Beach in Dorset, where his ashes were eventually scattered according to his wishes.

Maiden Castle (1936)

This, the most 'Hardyesque' of Powys' novels is the fourth in the 'Wessex' series. Maiden Castle, the ancient fortress of the Celtic or pre-Celtic past, exerts its strange but powerful pagan influence over the lives and loves of the protagonist Dud No-man and Wizzie Ravelson, a young woman Dud rescues from a travelling circus. This is probably the most profoundly pagan of the series, and the most strongly evocative of the landscape. It was the first novel Powys completed on his return from America and a lot of the book was written in his flat in High East Street, Dorchester and in the secluded Rat's Barn near the village of Chaldon Herring in one of the remotest parts of Dorset.

Owen Glendower (1940)

Powys' most straightforward historical novel, and one of his most commercially successful. It begins with a young Oxford scholar Rhisiart who presents himself at Glendower's court and becomes his secretary. The action takes place against the majestic backdrop of Castell Dinas Bran, an Iron Age hill fort, refortified in medieval times near Llangollen, with the "sacred river winding through its sun-illumined valley". Powys' portrayal of medieval Wales is spectacular, exciting and scholarly, and there are innumerable touches that show he had researched the period thoroughly. Idiosyncratically he eventually has Owen disappear into caverns below Mynydd-y-Gaer a mountain near Bridgend often supposed to be the final resting place of King Arthur. In an extensive and extraordinarily blatant case of plagiarism the novel was shamelessly plundered by Martha Rofheart for her 1973 novel Cry God For Harry.

Porius (1951)

The novel which Powys himself regarded as his masterpiece was ruthlessly cut by the publishers, and only now after years of painstaking scholarly research and with reference to several original drafts of the text is it available in anything like its intended form. The action starts in the location at which Owen Glendower ends, Mynydd-y-Gaer, with Porius, son of Einion, reigning prince and client king to the Romans of the province of Edyrnion looking out over his lands. The vast sprawling novel of Dark Age Britain, with some forty-nine major characters is sometimes difficult to follow, but is always impressive. The setting of the novel is the landscape around Powys then home in Corwen, North Wales. For Pagan readers there is the added enjoyment of spotting the alchemical and magical symbolism in the text, as well as beautifully depicted characters from Arthurian legend such as Merlin, who appears here as Myrddyn Wyllt, though Arthur himself tends to remain on the fringe of the story. If you were only given the option of reading one Dark Age fantasy novel in your lifetime, this should surely be the one.

The Brazen Head (1955)

A historical fantasy set in Wessex in the Middle Ages, in which the occultist Roger Bacon creates an oracular brazen head, and the lives of the populace are riven with religious and philosophical strife. Sexual magic is to the fore here, and an important theme of the book is the threat which theological dogma represents to human happiness.

The Powys Society exists to promote and discuss the works of the Powys family, particularly those of John Cowper and two of his brothers Llewellyn and Theodore Francis Powys.

www.powys-society.org

THE CHURCH IN THE HENGE

Few ancient monuments possess as much atmosphere as Knowlton Henge in Dorset. The ruin of a medieval church in the centre of a late neolithic ritual earthwork makes Knowlton unique. It may be found roughly two miles south of Cranborne just off the B3078 road to Wimborne in North Dorset. Knowlton village was once a thriving capital of a Saxon Hundred, able to hold a fair by royal appointment, no less. Today it can scarcely be called a hamlet in the parish of Woodlands. Its name simply means in Old English a town by or on a knoll.

Today it is a peaceful and mysterious place. The duality of Pagan and Christian sacred monuments adds pathos to this now desolate site, once the focus of so much human endeavour and worship. The ruined church seems somehow to be slightly uncomfortable in its surroundings, as if it recognizes somewhat sheepishly that it is really an intruder on the scene. The irregular shaped enclosure is surrounded by a ditch and bank, in places still over 3m high. The presence of two large yews on the bank provide a kind of portal (to what – who knows?) which it is almost impossible to resist the urge to pass through. The largest round barrow in Dorset is plainly visible from here, though it lies tantalisingly out of reach across a cornfield with no footpath access

The location of the Church within the central henge at Knowlton is perhaps the clearest physical evidence we have for the Christianization of an older pagan sacred site; definitive evidence is actually very rare in England despite the many speculative examples that antiquaries and earth mysteries enthusiasts have 'identified' over the years. Documentary evidence for the practice does, however, exist. In CE 601 Pope Gregory wrote of Britain:

"The temples of the idols in the said country ought not to be broken; but the idols alone which be in them . . . If the said temples be well built, it is needful that they be altered from the worshipping of devils into the service of the true God."

While possible examples of churches being built on ancient mounds or in sacred groves are not entirely uncommon in Britain and also Brittany, the actual demolition of a henge and the construction of a church at its centre is rare indeed. Earth mysteries writer Peter Knight has suggested that it may have been the revulsion of Church authorities to the festivities being carried on during the fair at the henge that caused them to have the church constructed.

The entrance from the north

The Church in the Henge

Jeremy Harte suggests that Neolithic settlers created the original religious complex of four henges in the Allen Valley. The site was respected by their Bronze Age successors who set up many burial mounds in the area including the Great Barrow. By the late Roman period the cult has been forgotten, and the monument was used as a convenient boundary marker by Christianized British farmers. In the seventh century the farm to the north is occupied by a pagan English settler who selects the Great Barrow as his burial place. The site then becomes recognized as a cemetery. After Dorset is annexed by the kings of Wessex around 700CE the place became known as Knowlton, after nearby Knoll Hill. In 961 a monastery was founded at nearby Horton and when the monks decided to build a church in the area the people at Knowlton requested that it be built among the earthworks.

The ruined church within the henge

Many alignments with other monuments have been suggested along with significant ley lines which are said to radiate from the henge like the spokes of a wheel. There are also interesting astronomical alignments to the Summer Solstice, Lammas and Beltane sunrises which Peter Knight outlines in his book The Ancient Stones of Dorset which is an excellent guidebook to this and many other sites in the area. Take a copy with you while visiting if you can.

Among archaeologists the monument is recognized as one of the five great Wessex enclosure sites, along with Stonehenge, Avebury, Durrington Walls and Marden. Just to the north, on Cranborne Chase is one of the largest concentrations of Neolithic remains in Europe, including the massive Pimperne long barrow and the six-mile long Dorset Cursus earthworks which would have been a focus for ritual activity along with probably hundreds of barrow graves most which sadly have been ploughed out over the years and are now only visible in aerial photographs.

The Great Barrow in the adjacent field

The henge surrounding the church is part of a larger ancient complex of Knowlton Rings, which consists of four earthworks: the North Circle, Church Circle, Southern Circle, and the Old Churchyard. In addition to these sites, to the east of the Church Circle is the Great Barrow, the largest round barrow in Dorset, and almost certainly directly related to the henge. Within a one-mile radius of these earthworks there are also a large number of barrows and ring-ditches. Excavations in 1994 by Bournemouth University designed to determine entrances and exits from the henge monuments and to investigate the North Circle and the Old Churchyard proved inconclusive. The dig did reveal that the ditches were originally around 5.7m deep, with almost sheer sides, which had been revetted at some point with wooden posts and wattle fencing, presumably to prevent collapse through erosion. Charcoal and bone fragments were found in the ditch along with a piece of carved chalk.

Interestingly in 2005 local dowsers seeking 'energy lines' discovered a large slab of stone hidden under a carpet of weeds that was hitherto unknown to historians or archaeologists, which might possibly be evidence that megaliths once formed part of the ritual complex.

Two smaller gritty heathstone slabs were reported to the Prehistoric Society in 2000 by the farmer at Knowle Hill Farm, who claimed they had originally been ploughed out of the Southern Circle at Knowlton. Intriguingly and almost unprecedented in this area, one of them contains an example of prehistoric artwork: four concentric rings engraved into the stone's surface. Megaliths with this type of carving are usually associated with tombs suggesting perhaps that the stones might originate from a neolithic grave either within the henge or in the immediate vicinity. However, the closest parallel in the region comes from the Bronze Age Winterborne Came barrow near Dorchester, in which two cairns were covered with stones decorated with three concentric circles. This may suggest that later burials were interred at the Neolithic site.

The nave and chancel of the church were built sometime in the twelfth century and had undergone several modifications by the fifteenth. It is widely believed that if megaliths (standing stones) were ever a feature of the surrounding henge they were broken up and used in the construction of the church building. Inside, the altar lying on the north side is of heathstone, and may have been a part of the original pagan complex.

The ruined church seen from between the yew trees

Although the area around the site is now rather isolated Knowlton was once a thriving community. In 1485 the village suffered the fate of so many other settlements and was virtually wiped out by the spread of the Black Death. All that remains of the villagers' dwellings today are vague traces of their foundations a few hundred yards to the west. Despite the epidemic the church itself continued in use and the fair continued to be held until the early part of the eighteenth century. In or around 1747 the church was given a new roof which promptly collapsed, after which it was abandoned and left to fall into ruin.

Unsurprisingly, there are folk traditions attached to Knowlton connected with the 'Devil' and involving oxen which are frequent motifs in tales relating to the erection of churches on pagan sacred sites. In this case however, perhaps because the church itself has become defunct, it is to the fate of the church bell that such tales have now become attached.

Local legend has it that the Devil stole the bell and threw it into the River Allen. When the villagers attempted to retrieve it they failed, being overcome by the Devil's strength as he held on to it. When a villager suggested they yoke a team of pure white oxen it seemed they were about to retrieve the precious bell. Pulling hard the oxen drew the bell close to the surface and the villagers cried, "Now we've got out the bell, in spite of all the devils in hell!" only to see the ropes part and release it. Their bell sank to the bottom once more and was never seen again.

A different story which has a slight ring of authenticity to it (pardon the pun!) is that thieves took the bell for scrap or to sell abroad. They were caught near the old bridge which crosses the River Stour, just downstream from White Mill. Realizing they could not escape the thieves heaved it into the river. According to legend every time the villagers secured it the ropes would snap, leaving the bell to rest in the river bed for ever. This story gave rise to the following rhyme:

Knowlton bell is stole
And thrown into White Mill hole,
Where all the devils in hell
could never pull up Knowlton Bell.

Other tales told that it ended up in the church tower either at nearby Shapwick or a little further away at Sturminster Marshall. Interestingly, according to Jaqueline Simpson the antiquarian and proto-Druid William Stukeley was told by local people that there had been seven churches here originally, but "six had disappeared entirely", though this of course may have been the locals winding him up rather than true folklore!

Knowlton Henge enjoys easy access by road, from Lumber Lane, just off the B3078, though parking is limited. Refreshments, including local ales are available at the Horton Inn, at the crossroads to the west of Knowlton. The Great Barrow is on private farm property.

Little now survives of the Dorset Cursus, its remains having been largely ploughed out over the years though along its route many other prehistoric remains do survive. It runs to the south of the A354 Blandford to Salisbury road. There is a car park at Wyke Down near Sixpenny Handley and the route of the cursus is marked on the OS map though it is not a public right of way.

The Pimperne Long Barrow, the most westerly of the Cranborne Chase barrows lies adjacent to a bridleway to the north of the A354 near the convenient lay-by close to the war memorial at a place named on the map as 'Collingwood Corner'.

Map References:

Knowlton Henge: SU023102
The Great Barrow: SU025102
The Horton Inn: SU016086
Pimperne Long Barrow: ST917105
The Dorset Cursus: SU017160

SAINTS AND DEMONS: AN INCOMPLETE HISTORY OF CARNIVAL GIANTS

"It appears that European processional giants and other figures were first known in Spain, arising from the conflict between Moors and Christians and possibly introduced from the east by the former". So writes Hugh Shortt in his introduction to the Salisbury Museum pamphlet The Giant and Hob-Nob (1972).

The Salisbury giant with attendants, Hob-Nob, the Whifflers and Beadle, photographed in 1887

In this country, where the tradition was halted by the Protestant reformation, evidence for 'gianting' is somewhat scanty, and there are possibly only three actual survivals from mediaeval times. The Salisbury giant, who represents St Christopher, is the only physically surviving English giant with any kind of real historical provenance. While he wore eighteenth century costume when last paraded, including a rather fetching tricorn hat, it is quite possible that his head dates from before 1500, though applying the principle of the 'philosopher's axe', the giant himself may have a much earlier history. He currently stands tewlve feet tall, having been lowered by two feet to fit into the museum when he was acquired from the local Guild of Merchant Taylors in 1869, along with his companion, the hobby-horse known as Hob-Nob. St Christopher is sometimes referred to as the patron saint of tailors, hence the connection with the Guild, presumably. Together they appeared at processions at mid-summer on the eve of St John the Baptist's day, June 23rd and on the 'Translation of St Osmund', July 15th.

The Giant and Hob-Nob now in retirement in Salisbury Museum

Saints and Demons

The legend of St Christopher, of which popular versions began to be written in the thirteenth Century states that he was twelve cubits tall (about eighteen feet). It is not surprising, therefore that processional giants used in religious celebrations throughout the Catholic world often depicted him. Other popular figures were St George or St Michael, inevitably accompanied by a dragon, and figures of this type were recorded in company with a St Christopher at Namur in Belgium as early as 1455. A dragon was also a part of the Salisbury procession as depicted in a woodcut of 1555. St George was often depicted in hobby-horse form, and 'Riding the Jorge' was the traditional term for parading the hobby-horse.

The Salisbury giant is the only surviving example of a religious processional giant in this country. More secular, though surviving in name only after a series of misfortunes, are Gog and Magog, the famous London Guildhall Giants, guardians of the City. Their origin and early history is obscure. Whatever their original provenance we know that by the reign of Henry V, they were resident at the Guildhall. Their names originate from Geoffrey of Monmouth's somewhat spurious medieval History of the Kings of Britain, first published in 1138. When they appeared in the Lord Mayor's Show in 1554, they were referred to as Gogmagog (the mythical Cornish Giant) and Corineus (the equally mythical Briton who slew him on behalf of the Trojan Brutus). By 1672, Thomas Jordan the then pageant master referred to them as "two exceeding rarities", and stated that "at the conclusion of the Show, they are to be set up in Guildhall, where they may be daily seen all year and I hope never to be demolished by such dismal violence as happened to their predecessors." He was referring to the destruction of much of the City by the great fire in 1666. Unfortunately however his giants only lasted a few years. Being made of wickerwork and pasteboard, they were eventually destroyed by mice and rats.

In 1708 they were replaced by a magnificent pair of wooden statues carved by Captain Richard Saunders. Interestingly by then the name Corineus had been forgotten, and the vanquished giant's name was shared between the two figures, as Gog and Magog, who were now regarded as mythical giant slayers themselves, and saviours of the British race from oppression. Charles Dickens related the story of how as a very small boy he resolved to set out on a journey to make his fortune. His first step on this epic adventure was to visit the guildhall giants, whereupon, exhausted by his expedition he fell asleep beneath Magog! These giants lasted for over two hundred years before their destruction in the blitz in 1940. They, in turn, were replaced by the pair that can now be seen in Guildhall, carved by sculptor David Evans in 1953 as a gift to the City by Alderman Sir George Wilkinson who had been Lord Mayor at the time of the destruction of their predecessors.

Gog, in the Guildhall London

The current Gog and Magog who take part in the Lord Mayor's procession are sponsored by a City firm who claim to have based their design on the 1708 statues. Unfortunately these large inflatables bear scant similarity to the elaborately dressed carnival

Saints and Demons

giants of folk tradition with wicker frames and ferocious faces. Appropriately enough though, given the fraught history of the Guildhall giants, they carry the symbol of the phoenix on their 'costumes'. Interestingly, according to the official Lord Mayor's website "These giants of pageantry that you will see today are the last vestiges of the pagan effigies" and "They are a part of a tradition in English pageantry which pre-dates Christianity".

Magog, in the Guildhall London

The third possible survival may not be a giant at all. The enigmatic Dorset Ooser is a part of that county's folklore, a massive wooden horned mask of fearsome and undoubtedly pagan appearance that was once the property of the Cave family who resided at Melbury Osmond. Presumably the intriguing coincidence of the village being named after St Osmund, and therefore connected somehow to the Salisbury giant is just that(?).

England's Living Folklore

*The Dorset Ooser, photographed between 1883 and 1891
by John W Chaffin & Sons of Yeovil*

Unfortunately its current whereabouts are unknown and it was more than likely destroyed a long time ago. It now exists only in an old photograph and in a slightly conjectural 'replica' which is on display in the Dorset County Museum in Dorchester, when it is not being paraded by the Wessex Morrismen, that is. The original mask was over two feet across and carved from a single block of wood, except for the jaw, which moved and was operated by pulling on a string. The wearer, who looked through the mouth, traditionally wore a calf-skin cloak. Its massive size and lack of eye holes for the wearer does make it markedly different from other 'guising' masks and it is possible that it was once paraded as the head of a giant, though on what occasions (presumably not church processions!) remains a mystery. It may possibly have been used in the tradition of 'skimmity riding', a rather brutal form of matrimonial vigilantism practiced in nineteenth century Dorset made famous by the episode

Saints and Demons

in Thomas Hardy's Mayor of Casterbridge. If in earlier times the mask had been placed on a wicker frame as the head of a processional giant, this might account for its strange name, the word 'osier' being used to describe a type of willow commonly used in basketwork.

The Dorset Ooser was well known in the nineteenth century even if its original function had been forgotten. The Dorset poet, antiquary and philologist, the Reverend William Barnes, included a definition of the term in his Glossary of the Dorset Dialect of 1863 as "a mask with grim jaws, put on with a cow's skin to frighten folk". By then, the mask, which had been with the Cave family for "time out of mind", was stored in a malt house where it performed the function of scaring away intruders. It is possible that the Ooser stayed in the building even after it had been converted into a chapel in 1875. Thomas Hardy certainly seems to indicate that that was the case in his writings. By 1897 the mask was in the hands of a Doctor Edward Cave who took it with him to Crewkerne when he moved. It made at least one appearance at Crewkerne Carnival, worn by the Doctor's coachman, but by this time it was in very poor condition with "hair coming out in tufts". Very soon after it was noted as missing, probably having been thrown away after succumbing to extreme woodworm infestation, though there are tantalising accounts of it having been sold to "a stranger".

Various modern versions of the Ooser have been made over the years, including one made for a medieval fair which still resides at Melbury Osmond, and a rather daft looking example adapted from an African tribal mask by Raymond Buckland for his 'Witchcraft and Folklore' collection, but the most true to the original is the afore-mentioned one in the Dorchester museum, constructed in 1975 by John Byfleet. The 'new' Wessex Ooser is not merely an object of curiosity however, as it accompanies the Wessex Morrismen to the top of Giant Hill above the Cerne Abbas Giant when they dance at dawn on Beltane morning. It then leads a procession through the village. It also makes an appearance on St George's Day. According to the Wessex Morrismen's website "It is said, by some, to be the Dorset manifestation of the Horned God;

also known as Herne the Hunter, Cerne, Cernnunos, etc".

The modern copy of the Dorset Ooser as used by the Wessex Morrismen

In Europe, the tradition of processional giants at religious and secular festivals is still widespread. There are fourteenth century references to giant St Christophers in Barcelona and Redondella (Spain), Aix-en-Provence (France), Roermond (Holland) and many Flemish towns. It is no coincidence that the references are contemporaneous with the popularization of the festival of Corpus Christi, which was designed to both formalize and supersede the celebration of the many local saints' and martyrs days celebrated throughout Europe, some of which had been criticized for their somewhat dubious theological provenance. Established by a Papal decree of 1264, the festival officially celebrates the belief that the eucharistic bread and wine contain the 'real presence of Christ'. In other words a kind of magical transformation, or 'transubstantiation' as it was officially termed. This perceived celebration of magic was taken up enthusiastically by the populace and as the date fell close to midsummer it is likely that just as had been the case with some of the 'saints' days', some of the revelry associated with festivals of the 'Old Religion' were soon incorporated into the outdoor part of the ceremonies, which by the fourteenth century had become the principle part of the event. By 1424 in Barcelona no less than one hundred and eight 'representations' were being carried through the streets behind the Eucharistic Host, including the creation of the World, the fall of Lucifer, the dragon of St Michael, and a swordfight between devils and angels. Old Testament characters included Adam and Eve, Noah and the Ark, David and Goliath, the twelve tribes of Israel and several prophets. There were also floats with nativity scenes, angels, the Virgin Mary and of course, Christ himself depicted as resurrected alone with his cross.

The pageantry and drama often lasted a whole day or more after the 'official' Church celebrations, and some clerical authorities began to express a distinct uneasiness as the Host with its escort of church dignitaries began to be eclipsed by portrayals of devils and demons, who being far more spectacular and vulgarly entertaining to a mediaeval audience than sweetly singing choirs of angels, soon became by far the most popular part of the festivities. By the sixteenth century, the Spanish clergy were objecting strongly to the 'disorder and confusion' caused by the intrusion of so many 'profane' elements into a procession devoted to the 'Holy Sacrament'. There were even accounts of masked figures and dancers invading sacred church space and interrupting the liturgy.

In northern Europe, of course, the Protestant reformation put an end to the Corpus Christi celebration altogether. In England it meant the death knell for 'gianting' as folk tradition, even after the festival had become somewhat secularised. At Chester in 1599, the appropriately named Henry Hardware, the Puritan mayor of the city "caused the giants in the Midsomer Show to be put downe and broken". Apparently the Chester 'Midsomer Show' had included four giants, as well as a unicorn, a camel, a dromedary, a luce (pike), an ass, a dragon, six hobby horses and six naked boys! In Coventry in 1565 the local Draper's guild paid a pyrotechnician fourpence for "setting the worlds on fire", three depictions of the World being consumed by fire during the performance of the city's Corpus Christi cycle, apparently. Similar celebrations were noted in Canterbury and Lincoln and it is certain that the traditions were followed enthusiastically in all the cathedral cities of England and many less auspicious places besides.

While in Britain such spectacles were by then to prove short-lived, in Catholic Spain the festival only grew in popularity, though not without official condemnation. Eventually, in the eighteenth century the Bourbon dynasty attempted to purge the festival of its perceived 'profanities'. In 1772 a royal decree banned giants and dragons from Madrid, and in 1780 the popular manifestations of the Corpus Christi celebrations were prohibited throughout Spain. However, many of the 'profane' elements simply attached themselves to other saints' days and celebrations, a testimony to the resilience of folk tradition and the popularity of 'Carnival'. After the civil war in Spain, Franco promoted the festival as an emblem of (Fascist) Spanish identity and Catholic triumphalism. Those cities, like Barcelona who were generally anti-Franco either played down the religious element or boycotted it altogether. The last appearance of the Host in Barcelona was in 1940, since when devils, fire breathing dragons and mules, giants, devils, Turks and hobby-horses have had free rein, and the festival is now known as the Patum, after the banging of the big tabal (bass drum).

Similar celebrations occur throughout many Catholic countries, including Puerto Rico, Mexico, Peru, Trinidad, Bolivia and Belgium, with varying degrees of riotous pageantry and anarchic good humour, and often infused with indigenous paganism. In many cases, as in Barcelona, a kind of folk-theology has overtaken the religious content, and the demons and devils are by no means always defeated by the saints and clerics in the folk dramas enacted in the street processions, just as the various characters of English mumming tradition can never really be categorized in a purely good versus evil context.

In some European towns and cities revived Carnival celebrations seem to hark back to pre-Christian practices, though this is probably due more to the influence of twentieth century folklorists than to any survival of folk-memory, however faint. In Nice, for example the culmination of the Carnival parade on Shrove Tuesday sees the papier-mâché giants dance their last dance as their Carnival King is taken down to the beach on his throne. There, he is ceremonially burned, bringing the proceedings to a close. Similar, more ancient traditions have been noted in Italy and Portugal.

In France, most giants were destroyed in the revolution of 1789, which was fiercely atheist and anti-church. However, Napoleon allowed more secular figures to be paraded and the tradition seems to have become fully revived after 1814. Nowadays many towns actively encourage the building of Carnival giants as a matter of civic pride, the figures generally representing local folk-heroes or legends. In Dunkerque there is a two month long Fisherman's Festival with weekly parades of giants from the Nord Pas-de-Calais region, of which there are anything up to two hundred, as well as visiting giants from other parts of France and from abroad. In Lille, in a 'tradition' dating from 1999, on 14 July all the region's giants gather in the city centre, along with some of their counterparts from as far afield as Mexico, China and Japan. In Belgium too the giant tradition is very strong. On 25 November 2005 UNESCO acknowledged the giant figures of the processions of Dendermonde, Mechelen and of the Meiboomstoet of Brussels as being part of "cultural world inheritance" The famous Ros Beiaard of Dendermonde was also recognized. The figures were nominated along with the processional giants and dragons of Flanders, the Walloon provinces and France.

In Britain, our religious history and continuing official hostility to any form of unregulated public exuberance has meant that in the main we do not really have much of a Carnival culture (Notting Hill being a somewhat different case, of course), and the stinginess and indifference towards our folk culture of public authorities have tended to hold back any form of revival in modern times. Nevertheless, BIGG, the British Isles Giant Guild does list over three-dozen active groups throughout the country, though this list does include some Jack-in-the-Greens and other figures slightly outside the genre. The North-west and the West-country seem to be particularly active giant-wise, although there are plenty of others in other parts of England (though not Scotland or Wales, it seems), including Salisbury where a new Salisbury Giant and Hobnob now appear accompanied once again by a dragon.

Some giants are attached to morris sides such as Sheffield City Morris who have been custodians of the giants named War and Peace ever since they were presented to the City by the Government of Catalonia at the time of the World Student Games in 1992. Some are specifically Pagan, a product of the post-war revival of the Old Religion. Prominent among these are The Morrigan, a notable part of the Pagan Pride Parade at the annual Beltane Bash in London, and the Eastbourne giants Herne and Andred, who were commissioned by and constructed for the organizers of the first Eastbourne Lammas Fayre in 2001.

The Morrigan, Lammas Festival, Eastbourne 2006

Saints and Demons

In the South-east the Hastings Jack-in-the Green parade, the Beltane Bash and the Lammas Festival all parade their blatantly Pagan giants with a degree of impunity, being popular events with the local community as a whole, as well as among their Pagan supporters. Having said that, in 2005 Herne and Andred fell foul of some evangelical Christian influenced Councillors in Hailsham (where they had regularly been invited to attend the town's 'mediaeval' Charter market) for one of whom sadly the giants represented tones of "inherent Satanism". "Giants Axed in Pagan Row – Political and religious groups all barred from Charter Market" ran the headline in the Sussex Express on 8 July. At least by implication the Council recognized the Pagan element as religious, which is some sort of progress at least, though it seems a shame that the traders and people of Hailsham now have a less colourful event as a result of the ban, even if the 'fundies' are barred as well!

The giants Herne and Andred were made by professional puppet maker Mel Myland for the organizers of the first lammas Fayre in 2001. Here they lead the procession along Eastbourne's seafront with the Pentacle drummers, in August 2004.

England's Living Folklore

Perhaps at some time in the future giants will once again be seen regularly on our streets at midsummer festivals and other events. Who knows? It would be nice to think so but with government interference and licensing and insurance implications at every stage of the game, without the active encouragement of arts financing organisations, local government and strong community support such as France and Belgium enjoy, sadly it does seem to be unlikely for the time being.

Map References:

Dorset County Museum: SY692907
Guildhall, London: TQ324813
Salisbury Museum: SU141294

OLD SARESBYRI

Just outside of present day Salisbury lie the large, oval earthworks of Old Sarum, one of the most ancient and interesting sites in southern England, which may have been occupied more-or-less continuously from at least the Bronze Age to its abandonment in the late Middle Ages.

The site as we see it today consists of the massive bank and ditch of the Iron Age enclosure, whose fortifications were probably first raised by the Belgae, the invading Celtic tribe from Europe who came to dominate the south central area of Britain. They are alleged to have named the fort Caer Saflog, or Citadel of the Service Tree, which is taken to be the whitebeam, a tree that thrives on chalky soil. After the Roman conquest it remained a military stronghold under the name of Sorviodunum, and continued in such use sporadically until the early medieval period. Cynric, Saxon King of Wessex is said to have captured the fort in 552CE and it became a flourishing population centre with important civic and ecclesiastical buildings. King Edgar assembled a National Council here to discuss a means of repelling the Danes in 960CE.

In 1070 William the conqueror raised his royal stronghold in the centre of the site, creating an inner set of fortifications with a new bank and ditch, while using the Iron Age ramparts as the outer enclosure or bailey. It was here that his conquering army was paid off and the oath of allegiance sworn in 1086. The town was then renamed Salisburie after the Earl who received the lands from the new King.

The church tried to establish a major presence in the town, intending to move the see from nearby Sherborne, but met with ill luck at almost every stage. The first cathedral was founded by Osmond (later Saint Osmund) a Norman nobleman appointed by William of Normandy. It was started around 1078 but not completed until 1092 only to be burned down in a violent thunderstorm only five days after its consecration, according to William of Malmesbury. Rebuilding continued in fits and starts over the next ninety or so years and was completed by Bishop Jocelyn de Bohun around 1180. Peter of Blois, writing later in that century described the site as "barren, dry, and solitary, exposed to the rage of the wind; and the church [stands] as a captive on the hill where it was built, like the ark of God shut up in the profane house of Baal."

An aerial postcard view from the 1950s (Author's collection)

The new cathedral was probably the most short-lived in England. A papal bull issued in 1218 listed many reasons for its abandonment. Apparently the building's fabric was already so ruinous as to be a danger to the congregation, there was a lack of accommodation for the Clergy, the water supply was erratic, and it was so windy that "those celebrating the divine offices can hardly hear each other speak"! In 1226 the demolition of the cathedral was begun, following the removal of graves to the new building, including the mortal remains of St Osmund. Much of the stone was re-used for the new cathedral outside the walls of Old Sarum. Almost the entire population moved to the new settlement by the River Avon, and Old Sarum once again became merely a military redoubt. It appears that the castle was finally abandoned in 1514 when Henry VIII effectively gave the site to one Thomas Compton to quarry the stones of the old walls. By 1540 the antiquary John Leland noted "Ther is not one house in Old Saresbyri or without inhabited".

Remnants of the Norman Stonework

Samuel Pepys recorded his visit to the site in 1668 and noted its somewhat spooky atmosphere: "I saw a great fortification, and there light, and to it and in it; and find it prodigious, so as to fright me to be in it all alone, it being dark. I understand it since to be that that is called Old Sarum.". Pepys owned a copy of the Missale ad usum Sarum, which contained the so-called Sarum Rite, which had been a common part of Church liturgy from Osmund's time until the Church of England separated from Rome and began to formalize its liturgy. While it has undergone something of a revival in twentieth century Anglicanism, in the anti-papist hysteria of 1679, Pepys was actually charged with treason, accused of "Popery and other chimeras" partly as a result of having books such as this in his library. The Sarum rite is known for the beauty of its melodies and it formed the basis for much of the sacred music in England in Tudor and Elizabethan times, regarded as the golden age of English polyphony. Strange, perhaps that something so beautiful could have its origins in so bleak and inhospitable a place.

'Remains of Old Sarum', engraving by Charles Knight 1845

After its abandonment the old city settled into a long slumber being used primarily as pasture, its only other value being its status as probably the most famous, or notorious of the 'rotten boroughs', that continued to support parliamentary candidates despite the fact that it they had virtually no population. Thomas Pitt bought himself Old Sarum in 1691 and the borough remained in the hands of the

Pitt family long enough for two William Pitts to attain Prime Ministership (The elder in 1766, and the younger in 1783 and 1804). Rotten boroughs were effectively abolished by the reform act of 1832. The old elm under which MPs were elected became known as the Parliament Tree. Fittingly perhaps it blew down in a gale shortly after the act was passed; today a plaque marks where it once stood.

Perhaps Pepys was affected by the same spirits of place that made the hill so inhospitable to the clergy that they had to demolish their church and move it elsewhere, a rare (though not unique) example of the genus loci getting their way. Interestingly, the site for the new cathedral was said to have been chosen by the shooting of an arrow from the ramparts of the old town, which apparently killed an ox in the pasture below. Oxen are a familiar feature of such folklore, such as at Alfriston in Sussex, where the so-called 'Cathedral of the Downs' is sited atop a large pre-Christian mound upon which four oxen were said to have sat rump to rump, forming the sign of a cross.

One of the massive yews that grow from the still impressively steep ramparts

In 1911 an unfinished medieval well was discovered, which

allowed archaeologists to reach the Iron Age levels of occupation below the central mound of the Norman earthworks. Intriguingly they found the corner of a Romano-British structure at the centre of the site with flint-cored walls and an internal pavement, which has been interpreted as a temple building. Further, if speculative, evidence for Old Sarum being a pre-Christian sacred site lies in its location, situated on one of the most famous ley lines in England, first noted by Norman Lockyer in 1906, and later discovered independently by Alfred Watkins. In a direct line from Stonehenge, it links Old Sarum with the 'new' Salisbury Cathedral and the Iron Age forts at Clearbury Rings and Frankenbury Camp, an alignment which is clearly visible from the castle ruins. This ley is renowned for the large number of crop circles and UFO phenomena which occur on or close to its alignment.

Today, the site is a national monument in the care of English Heritage. It is a good place to wander and contemplate our ancestors, their vast earthworks, now dotted with mature yew trees, being some of the most impressive in the south of England. There is a small charge to enter the Norman ruins. Unfortunately, on my last visit for some bizarre reason there was a group of First World War re-enactors recreating the trenches of the Battle of the Somme among the ruins of the Norman castle, which was both annoying and irrelevant, and made taking decent photographs difficult, while the sound of birdsong and the gentle rustle of the breeze was all too frequently interrupted by the buzzing of light aircraft from the local flying club. Old Sarum is certainly worth a visit but perhaps is best avoided at weekends.

Map References:

Salisbury Cathedral: SU142294
Old Sarum: SU13783266
Alfriston church: TQ521029
Clearbury Rings: SU152244
Frankenbury camp: SU167152

EVOLUTION OF A SACRED SITE

Dorchester, the county town of Dorset is rich in both Roman and pre-Roman remains. The Roman town of Durnovaria was built on the site of a vast Neolithic henge structure, which now lies below a shopping centre. Another large henge, at nearby Mount Pleasant is visible only from the air as marks in the grass, having been ploughed out. Other sites were more fortunate and today it is possible to view the spectacular remains of the country's biggest hill fort, Maiden Castle, just outside the town, complete with the foundations of its late-Roman era temple. Poundbury hill fort, which while much smaller is no less spectacular in its way lies within the boundary of the town while almost at the centre of modern Dorchester, now uncomfortably squeezed between railway lines and roads is Maumbury Rings, a neolithic henge monument with a fascinating history.

Before excavations were carried out in 1879, scholars were divided as to whether the site was a pre-Roman henge, or a Roman Amphitheatre. In the event, both schools of thought were proved to be correct. Excavations showed that the site was indeed built in the late Neolithic or early Bronze Age, c 2500 BCE, almost certainly with a ritual purpose, and that it was re-used by the Romans as an amphitheatre, during their colonization of the territory of the Durotriges. More extensive excavations were carried out in 1908-13 which confirmed previous findings and provided a detailed history of its construction and remodelling over the years.

The information boards at the site, written by former Dorset County Archaeologist Laurence Keen OBE give a potted history of the henge's construction and subsequent remodelling:

"A large circular bank was built of chalk rubble on open grassland, with an entrance in the N-E provided with a large standing stone. Inside the bank was a wide and deep ditch. Cut into the base of the ditch was a series of large tapering shafts about 10ft (3m) apart and with an average depth of 34ft (10.4m) below original ground level, 22ft (6.4m) from the base of the ditch. Eighteen shafts were located. The spacing suggests there were 45 in total. The shafts were dug using antler picks and spoil was raised in baskets by ropes. The archaeological evidence suggests that each was deliberately filled in with several separate deposits. Four shafts contained red deer skulls or skull fragments, of possible ritual importance. Carved chalk objects were also found.

The entrance to Maumbury Rings. The information panel is on the site of the former standing stone

After many hundreds of years of disuse the prehistoric earthwork was converted into an amphitheatre in the 1st century AD, probably by the Roman army. It was one of the largest in the country. The existing earthwork influenced the shape of the new one but colossal earth moving operations were carried out. The interior of the old enclosure was lowered by 10ft (3m) and the material dumped over the Neolithic bank. The entrance stayed in the same place but a ramp was constructed down to the arena which was spread with sand. Around the inside of the arena was a timber safety wall. Behind this was a passage two to three feet wide around the whole circuit with three changing or rest rooms on the main axes, perhaps with spectators' boxes above. The wall against the bank was constructed of timber also, with horizontal timbers laid in the bank, and providing structural support. The northern entrance had doors in the safety wall and side timber supports carried a bridge over the gateway onto the narrow platform which ran all the way around the inner edge of the viewing area.

The amphitheatre was not used for long, being out of use by AD150. A number of alterations had taken place notably the southern room being abandoned and a secondary access ramp constructed over it. Archaeological evidence shows that it was re-used from the mid 3rd to mid 4th century.

In more modern times parliamentary supporters remodelled the earthwork between July 1642 and June 1643 as an artillery fort guarding the southern approach to Dorchester. It was linked to another fort at the south gate by a covered way. The main elements of the remodelling consisted of a ramp in the south from the level of the arena to the top of the projecting promontory. On the west and east, further ramps were constructed."

The excavations of 1908-13 carried out by Harold St George Gray discovered around forty-five deep shafts in a rough circle inside the ramparts, shaped like long ice-cream cones. The Roman alterations had involved lowering the floor within the banks which had isolated these features from each other. It is likely that they were originally joined together in a continuous trench when the henge was first constructed. Various items including fragments of deer skulls, antlers, flint scrapers and a number of carved chalk objects were discovered in the infill. The latter included some shaped like phalluses. It seems these pits were only in use for a season before being filled in with chalk rubble. Perhaps this was a way of consecrating the site with offerings deposited by family groups in 'their' ritual shaft as a way of bringing a scattered community together for a common religious purpose.

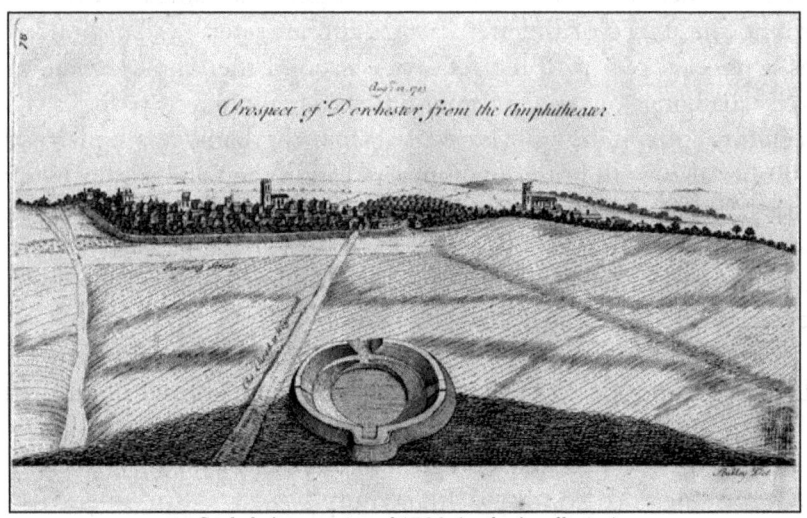

Stukeley's engraving of 1723 (author's collection)

The earliest published mention of the monument was by Christopher Wren who passed it regularly on his way to the stone quarries on the Isle of Portland which supplied materials for his London building projects. William Stukeley recorded in 1724 that 'the plough encroaches on the verge of the entrance every year'. It was ploughing that uncovered a large standing stone at the entrance in 1846. This stone was said to have been set deeply in the ground and was only fully exposed at a depth of thirteen feet. The stone was apparently buried again to avoid damage to agricultural equipment and all excavations since then have failed to identify its precise location. It is possible that it may have been blown up rather than reburied. According to Peter Knight, in his Ancient Stones of Dorset in the 17th century a stone used for bull-baiting was moved to Maumbury from the centre of Dorchester, and he suggests that it was this stone that was uncovered, and subsequently lost, having been taken from the henge in the first place. Peter Knight points out that two more stones are marked at Maumbury on the 1903 Ordnance Survey map of Dorchester. These are probably the boundary stones erected by the Duchy of Cornwall in the nineteenth century for which they were soundly castigated by one William Wallace Fyfe writing in The Historical Magazine of 1859:

To the south extends the great Roman way to Weymouth - straight as an arrow on the inequalities of the surface. On the left of it, on quitting the town, Malmbury, or Maumbury, rings (lately disfigured by two hideous municipal boundary-stones, which it is to be hoped the authorities of the Duchy of Cornwall, on whose estate the relic is situate, will, on seeing this epistle, utterly extirpate)…

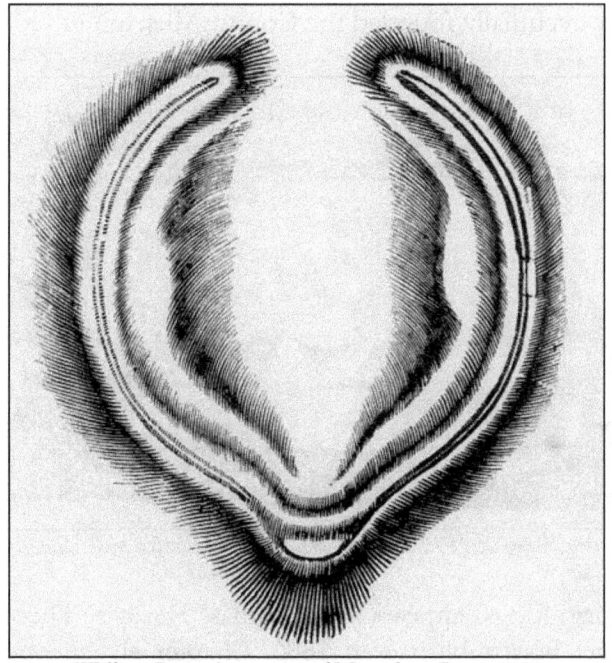

William Barnes' engraving of Maumbury Rings 1832

While Maumbury Rings was well known to antiquaries in the seventeenth century, it was the coming of the railways that almost destroyed it that led to renewed interest in the site and ultimately to the archaeological investigations which proved its origins. The two railway companies, the London and South Western Railway and the Great Western Railway opened their lines to Dorchester in 1847 and 1857 respectively. Local resident William Barnes, now best known for his poems in the Dorset dialect, was among the many local dignitaries concerned at the original proposals by the London & South Western Railway to remove a large part of the ancient earthworks at Maumbury and at the Great Western Railway's intention to put a deep cutting through the Roman aqueduct and the hill fort at Poundbury. Fortunately, his views were heeded and the railways (narrowly) avoided Maumbury Rings and tunnelled beneath Poundbury instead. As a result, Barnes became one of the founding members of the Dorset Natural History and Archaeological Society. The Society eventually founded the County Museum in Dorchester.

Maumbury Rings in 1832 before the arrival of the railways, by William Barnes

Maumbury Rings appears in Thomas Hardy's The Mayor of Casterbridge, first published in 1886. Chapter eleven opens with a reference to "The Ring at Casterbridge" and states that "this was merely the local name of one of the finest Roman Amphitheatres, if not the very finest, remaining in Britain." Maumbury was used by Hardy for a number of scenes in his novel, notably as the illicit trysting place of Henchard with Susan, and later Lucetta. The author

Evolution of a Sacred Site

was clearly fascinated by the site and in the same chapter he describes the rings and evokes some of the scenes that had taken place there since Roman times.

In John Cowper Powys' novel Maiden Castle published in 1936 Maumbury Rings plays an important role in the opening chapter. Here it is being used as an arena by the travelling show from which the historical novelist Dud Noman rescues the young orphan girl Wizzie Ravelston from her unpleasant adopted circus family, the Urgans. The anti-hero novelist is in Dorchester to research a novel about Mary Channing, a young woman accused of murder by poisoning who was burned at the stake here in 1706 and whose name he has a passionate desire to vindicate in his writing.

The entrance to the south

The henge's grim reputation as a place of execution seems to have already been established by 1685 when Judge Jeffries ordered eighty of Monmouth's rebels to be executed here. Public executions were a great spectacle of the time and thousands flocked to see justice take its macabre course. The execution of Mary Channing, which was almost certainly a miscarriage of justice was the most famous to be carried out here. This particular 'hanging fair' (or more accurately 'burning fair') attracted a crowd of ten thousand people. Thomas Hardy clearly believed the girl to have been innocent, and he used the event in his poem The Mock Wife.

According to Hardy, quoting a contemporary account:

"The girl was the wife of a grocer in the town, a handsome young woman of "good natural parts", and educated "to a proficiency suitable enough to one of her sex, to which likewise was added dancing". She was tried and condemned for poisoning her husband, a Mr Thomas Channing, to whom she had been married against her wish by the compulsion of her parents. The present writer has examined more than once a report of her trial, and can find no distinct evidence that the thoughtless, pleasure-loving creature committed the crime, while it contains much to suggest that she did not. Nor is any motive discoverable for such an act. She was allowed to have former lover or lovers about her by her indulgent and weak-minded husband, who permitted her to go her own ways, give parties, and supplied her with plenty of money. However at the assizes at the end of July, after a trial in which the testimony chiefly went to show her careless character before and after marriage. During the three days of its continuance, she, who was soon to become a mother, stood at the bar – then, as may be known, an actual bar of iron "by reason of which (runs the account) and her much talking, being quite spent, she moved the court for the liberty of a glass of water." She conducted her own defence with the greatest ability, and was complimented thereupon by Judge Price, who tried her, but did not extend his compliment to a merciful summing up. Maybe that he like Pontius Pilate, was influenced by the desire of the townsfolk to wreak vengeance upon somebody, right or wrong. When sentence was about to be passed, she pleaded her condition, and execution was postponed. While awaiting the birth of her child in the old, damp gaol by the river at the bottom of the town, near the White Hart Inn which stands there still [Now sadly derelict and recently sold for development] she was placed in the common room for women prisoners and no bed provided for her, no special payment having been made to her gaoler, Mr Knapton, for a separate cell. Someone obtained for her the old tilt of a wagon to screen her from surrounding eyes and under this she was delivered of a son, in December. After her lying-in, she was attacked by an intermittent fever of a violent and lasting kind, which preyed upon her until she was nearly wasted away. In this state, at the next assizes, the 8th of March following, the unhappy woman, who now said that she longed for death, yet still persisted in her innocence, was again brought to the bar, and her execution fixed for the 21st.

On that day two men were hanged before her turn came, and then "the under-sheriff having taken some refreshment," he proceeded to his biggest and last job with this girl not yet 19, and reduced to a skeleton by the long fever, and more dead than alive. She was conveyed from the gaol in a cart, "by her father's and husband's house", so that the course of the procession must have been up High-East Street as far as the Bow, thence down South-Street and up the straight old Roman Road to the ring beside it. "When fixed to the stake she justified her innocence to the very last, and left the world with a courage seldom found in her sex. She first being strangled the fire was kindled about five in the afternoon, and in the sight of many thousands she was consumed to ashes." There is nothing to show that she was dead before the burning began, and from the use of the word "strangled" and not "hanged", it would seem that she was merely rendered insensible before the fire was lit. An ancestor of the present writer, who witnessed the scene, has handed down the information that "her heart leapt out" during the burning, and other curious details that cannot be printed here. Was man ever "slaughtered by his fellow man" during the Roman or barbarian use of this place of games or of sacrifice in circumstances of greater atrocity?" [Thomas Hardy writing in The Times October 9th 1908.]

Maumbury Rings continued to be a place of public execution until 1766. Since then it has been used for rather more agreeable pursuits such as fairs, concerts, and as a place of public celebration. On 6th May 1935 thousands gathered to celebrate George V's Silver Jubilee with a procession, a service and a bonfire. In his idiosyncratic diaries, John Cowper Powys writes:

"Went up High West and met the Soldiers and their Band in the Old Red Uniform. The way the drummers waved their drumsticks was lovely to see. ….we all went to the service in the Amphitheatre or Maumbury Rings. The T.T. thought the Mayor was like Henchard. The daisies were lovely but it was impossible not to sit on them. The Wesleyan minister made the speech and he gloried over the Divine Right of Kings having now a new interpretation. He was the Mayor's chaplain…. Three fainted because of the heat & were revived except one who was carried out like one dead. We sat on the western slopes inside the Amphitheatre on my coat it was very hot sun…"

He is rather better at describing the fireworks later on at nearby Poundbury Hillfort:

"…And the fireworks were striking but the best thing was to see the crowds silhouetted against the sky. They actually were like the old Durotriges for you could not see their modern clothes as the Bonfire lit them up & they might have been the old Neolithics under the Crescent Moon & a single to me unknown star! The fireworks kept crossing the Crescent Moon. Balls of coloured fire floated far off changing colour as they flew."

The entrance to the north

Maumbury Rings is now a public park and used by dog-walkers and children playing. Its huge ramparts look like a massive green mound next to the police station as you approach it along Weymouth Avenue from the town marketplace. Once inside the rings it is like another world, far away from the hustle and bustle of the busy roads outside. Perhaps unsurprisingly given its history, it does have a slightly spooky atmosphere after dusk. There have occasionally been reports of ghostly Roman soldiers seen here.

During the annual Dorchester Festival many events are held at the rings, and the site is sometimes host to historical re-enactments. Recently, Maumbury was used by local witches and druids for an open ritual at which the memory of Mary Channing was honoured. Druid Chris Walsh said: "At the ritual we looked to recognise her fate and call for her spirit to pass by peacefully."

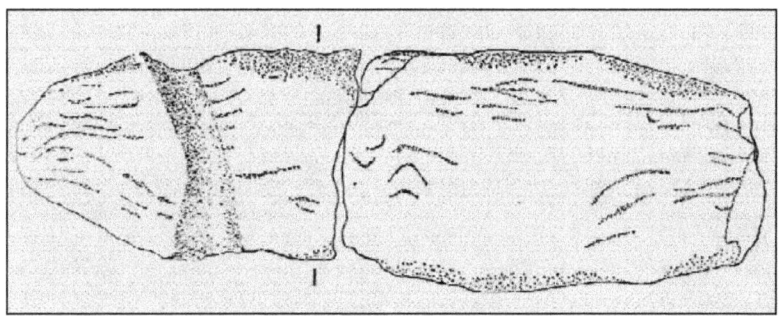

Drawing of the chalk phallus, found in 1908

Maumbury Rings is easily accessible and will soon have improved access for wheelchairs. There is no entrance fee and it is open throughout the year. It is situated in Dorchester off Weymouth Avenue close to Dorchester South Station. There is car-parking just across the road from the entrance. Items from the henge may be seen in the Dorset County Museum. They include a large carved chalk phallus and other ritual objects found in one of the ritual shafts discovered during the excavations of 1908-13.

Map References:

Dorset County Museum: SY692907
Maiden Castle: SY668884
Maumbury Rings: SY690899
Mount Pleasant: SY709899
Poundbury Hill Fort: SY681911

THE SOUTH WEST

The south west remains the most Celtic part of England. The ancient kingdom of Dumnonia resisted the westward advance of the Saxons and it still retains its own individual character. It is also probably the richest area in terms of the sheer number of megalithic monuments that remain from ancient times such as the huge stone circles at Stanton Drew in Somerset, immersed in folklore. As we journey through its forests and across its moors we encounter the smallest complete church in England, steeped in lore both Christian and pagan, stone circles and menhirs aplenty, a strange mystery concerning symbolic hares, and a Dark Age pagan artefact used as a church font. We consider the ritual slaying of John Barleycorn, and visit Boscastle in Cornwall, home of the finest collection in the world of historic items relating to magic and witchcraft, and hear the story of how it survived a near-total disaster. We also encounter controversy surrounding the first large-scale stone circle to be erected on a sacred site since ancient times.

Not idly fabled they the Bards inspired,
Who peopled Earth with Deities. They trod
The wood with reverence where the Dryads dwelt;
At day's dim dawn or evening's misty hour

Robert Southey
Hymn to the Penates 1797

POETS AND LEPERS

If you're ever in the vicinity of Porlock on the Exmoor coast in Somerset, the invigoratingly steep walk through the dense ancient woodland from sea level at Porlock Weir to Culbone Church, about 400ft above is well worth the effort. The path follows the coast for a short distance and then turns inland to join part of the spectacular toll road up through Worthy Wood that follows the fast-flowing stream. A short tunnel behind the toll house leads to the pathway to Culbone through Yearnor Wood. The path was once the packhorse road from Porlock to Lynton and clings perilously to a ledge on the steep wooded hillside; the roar of the sea hundreds of feet below a constant companion for the walker.

The woods here were once the site of a major charcoal burning industry. The original burners were reputed to be a colony of lepers who were forbidden from crossing to the Porlock side of Culbone Water. Stony ruins marking the site of the burners' huts and sawpits can still be seen and a network of paths connects them to the main track through the woods. It is a very atmospheric place, full of the ghosts of past travellers and inhabitants. Perhaps it is no coincidence that in 1797 while Samuel Taylor Coleridge was staying at Ash Farm, a little higher up the valley, he received (with the aid of a few grains of opium) the inspiration for his great poem Kubla Kahn. Could this perhaps be the place "where Alph the sacred river ran through caverns measureless to man down to a sunlit sea"? Certainly, the following lines from the poem could well refer to this dramatic and picturesque landscape:

**But oh! that deep romantic chasm which slanted
Down the green hill athwart a cedarn cover!
A savage place! as holy and enchanted
As e'er beneath a waning moon was haunted
By woman wailing for her demon-lover**
(Kubla Kahn, Samuel Taylor Coleridge 1798)

The tiny church seen from the path to Porlock

Coleridge introduced William and Dorothy Wordsworth to Culbone at around this time, taking them on the path from Porlock climbing up through the woodland which abounded in "wild deer, foxes, badgers and martin cats". They spent a great deal of time wandering around coastal Exmoor, and it is during this period that Coleridge wrote The Rime of the Ancient Mariner, and it is thought that he imagined the hermit character's cell to have been in the woodland around Culbone, which does seem to have inspired a good deal of his poetry at this period:

The hanging woods, that touched by Autumn seem'd
As they were blossoming hues of fire and gold,
The hanging woods, most lovely in decay,
The many clouds, the sea, the rock, the sands,
Lay in the silent moonshine - and the owl,
(Strange, very strange!) the Scritch-owl only wak'd,
Sole voice, sole eye of all that world of beauty!
(Osorio, Samuel Taylor Coleridge 1797)

The tiny, picturesque church is dedicated to St. Beuno, or Kil Beun, which is the derivation of the current name for the settlement. The saint was the son of a sixth century Welsh princess. He established a monastery at Clynnog on the Lleyn penninsula where he was buried in 640CE. It is likely that St Bueno arrived from Wales as a missionary to convert the inhabitants of Exmoor, the remnants of the Dumnonian tribes of pre-Roman Britain who at the time had remained stubbornly pagan and probably still spoke the Celtic language, having largely held their own against the Saxon invaders, who did not gain control until 938CE. A form of the Celtic language was still spoken on Exmoor as late as the eighteenth century. In legend he performed a miracle by saving his niece, Saint Winifred after her head was cut off by a furious King Caradog when she rejected his advances. Saints Beuno and Winifred have many sacred wells dedicated to them in their native Wales.

A little pamphlet is available in the church which indicates many points of interest: ancient oak pews, the Saxon windows including a strange impish face akin to, but not quite the same as a green man, the nineteenth century slate-covered deal spire and thirteenth century porch. The Domesday Book (in which it appears as Chetnore) and the Guinness Book of Records both make mention of this quaint building, which is regarded as the smallest parish church in England, as well as being the smallest complete medieval church in Britain, being just thirty five feet in its overall length. One amusing piece of folklore has it that the spire was originally the upper part of the strangely truncated spire at St Dubricius in Porlock which was blown off in a gale and transported here by the wind. According to legend, Dubricius was a close friend and advisor of King Arthur, and he officiated at the wedding between Arthur and Guinevere. Some historians are of the opinion that the spire at Porlock is so shaped because it was used as a lighthouse in medieval times. Further west along the coast in Cornwall St Nectan's Kieve, a tiny medieval monastic sanctuary once fulfilled a similar role in an almost identical setting to that of Culbone.

A postcard of the church, postmarked 1914 (author's collection)

Many of the tombstones in the churchyard at Culbone bear the surname Red, a variation on Ridd of R.D. Blackmore's Lorna Doone fame; the village of Oare, where the epic romantic novel is set lies within the same parish, just over the high ridge of the moors to the south west. It was apparently a custom in the late eighteenth century for unmarried women to scatter hempseed in the churchyard here at midsummer.

Also buried here is the American writer and Christian mystic Joan d'Arcy Cooper who lived in the hamlet for some years and played the church harmonium. She was of the opinion that the church window with the decorated mullion on the north side of the church was carved out of a single slab of stone which pre-dated the church and may have had pre-Christian religious significance. She certainly believed that the site was once of ancient spiritual importance and in her rather fanciful book Culbone - a Spiritual History, she claims that it had once been the home of an ancient Sumerian sage to whom wise men travelled from long distances to receive his wisdom. She considered Culbone to have been a "spiritual sanctuary" built on the "etheric plane" long before the arrival of Christianity. She also claims that Christ came to Culbone on the occasion of his legendary visit to Glastonbury.

One of the green men in the chancel

It would appear that its past history was not always as peaceful as the present. In the Assize rolls of 1280 it is recorded that Thomas, the local chaplain was indicted "for that he had struck Albert of Esshe [or Ash, the name of a prominent local family] on the head with a hatchet, and so killed him". By the sixteenth century the church and the local settlement (at that time known as Kytnore, and later, Kitnor) had been abandoned, but were re-established by a colony of lepers who lived by charcoal burning and trading in timber and the skins of feral goats, which still lived in the forest until very recently. Some of these goods were taken to the port at nearby Porlock Weir for export.

The curious carved face in the north window mullion

The community died out in 1622 upon which the site was abandoned once again until, according to Joan Cooper, a sort of commune was established in 1715 by a group of families from Somerset, who rebuilt some of the old stone dwellings which had become ruinous. In some accounts the settlers were actually a penal colony, dumped here by ship and left to their own devices, as the area was so remote there was no need to fence them in. They were eventually succeeded by Indian slaves who were allowed to work as charcoal burners in the forest for a period of twenty-one years in order to gain their freedom.

The churchyard, with Joan Cooper's gravestone at far right

The hamlet benefited by being close to the packhorse route from Porlock to Lynton, which was widened in the 1800s to allow the passage of carts, and for a time in the nineteenth century there was a small monthly market here and one of the cottages became a public house, known as the Fox and Hounds. A market cross was erected in the churchyard (replaced in 1966). According to the historian James Savage, writing in his History of the Hundred of Carhampton (1830) "A wake, or as it is called in this part of the country, a revel, used to be held annually in Culbone church-yard; but it has been discontinued many years". The church has been abandoned and restored several times over the years, according to the changing fortunes of the hamlet's occupants. The two green man roof bosses in the chancel ceiling probably date from around 1888, when that part of the roof was last rebuilt. It is possible they may have replaced earlier, medieval carvings.

According to an old Somerset saying: "Culbone, Oare and Stoke Pero" are "Three Churches Parsons seldom go", though the little church still has fortnightly services. Culbone is now an isolated sleepy place with just a handful of ancient looking dwellings clustered around the tiny church in a steep cleft of wooded hillside, untroubled except by the occasional group of ramblers passing through. Many of the latter will be Pagans and earth mysteries enthusiasts seeking the many stone rows, circles and megaliths which abound in this area.

The Culbone Stone

High above the church stands the Culbone stone. The information panel on the fence next to the style reads: "The Culbone Stone is an early medieaval standing stone approximately one metre in height, which was discovered in 1940. It lies in woodland close to the parish boundary, and features an incised wheeled cross, the style of which suggests it dates from 7th to 9th century. The stone is legally protected as a scheduled ancient monument."

I would tend to disagree with this dating. The incised wheel may have had one of its four spokes lengthened in the medieval period, maybe to Christianize a pagan symbol, or perhaps merely to provide a direction indicator for the settlement and church in the valley below. However, a nearby stone row with similar sized stones may indicate a more ancient, pre-Christian provenance for this small but interesting megalith, which is probably not in its original location, having been re-erected when it was re-discovered in 1940. There are also several cairns and barrows close by in the wood.

When I visited it last it certainly had a mysterious, somewhat magical air about it. The Culbone Stone is situated in a clearing amongst a grove of low-growing trees, stunted by the prevailing wind, and despite the rain and wind on that occasion, it had an impressive presence and stillness about it; a place of ancient spirits if ever there was one.

Culbone Church is about a five mile round walk from the very comfortable and ancient thatched pub in Porlock Wier, the Ship Inn where Robert Southey stayed on his way to Lynton and Lynmouth, and which was the starting point for several of Coleridge and Wordsworth's expeditions. On my last visit the route had become quite hard-going due to landslips which had resulted in rocks strewn across the path and several steep diversions. Culbone Church can also be reached from Silcombe Farm, further west. To find the stone go north from the A39 along the minor road opposite the Culbone Stables Inn for a couple of hundred yards. There is space enough to park a car or two next to the style from which the stone is well signposted. The inn itself claims to be the highest on Exmoor, and provides a welcome shelter from inclement weather, which, as I know from experience can be severe and sudden at this exposed place. The stone row, which starts close to the incised stone is largely buried in dense undergrowth, though a few of the stones can be spotted in the adjacent field and can be seen by walking a few hundred feet up the road marked 'Private, Luccombe Estate'.

Map References:

Culbone Stables Inn: SS830471
Culbone Stone: SS834474
Ship Inn, Porlock Wier: SS864478
St Beuno's Church: SS842403
Stone Row: SS834473

THE WEDDING PARTY

It is perhaps surprising that the stones of Stanton Drew have not received the same level of interest as their more famous counterparts at Stonehenge and Avebury. They are a little off the beaten track, but only slightly so, being no more than a couple of miles from the main A37 Bristol to Dorchester road, which has been a major thoroughfare for nigh on two millennia, and are plainly visible from the old turnpike road, now the B3130, which runs close to the village with its picturesque octagonal thatched tollhouse nearby. The name Stanton derives from the Anglo-Saxon 'stan' meaning stone, and 'tun' meaning farm. The stones are accessible along a short track signposted from the village centre.

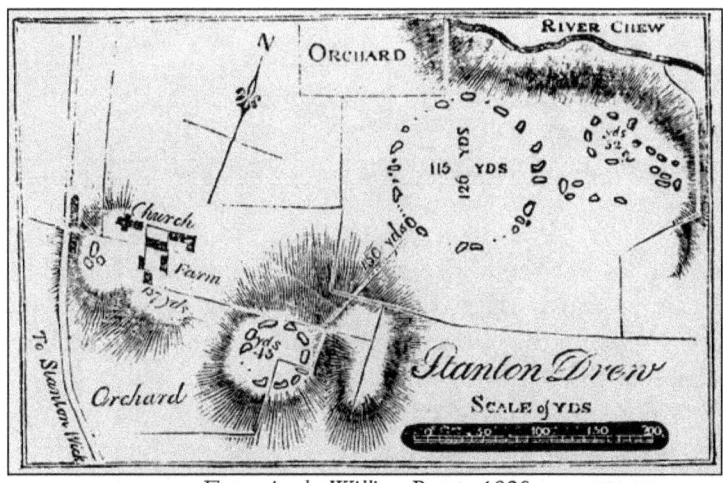

Engraving by William Barnes 1829

The circles, for there are three of them, along with their avenues and the outlying 'cove', were first noted by the famous antiquarian John Aubrey in 1664 and were surveyed by William Stukeley in 1723, with illustrations published in his Itinerarium Curiosum, a sort of gazetteer of interesting topographical and historical features of Britain. Surprisingly little has been published since, and the massive stones remain very much as they did in Stukeley's day, mostly fallen but undisturbed by early modern treasure seekers or modern archaeologists. No real archaeological investigation was made of the site at all until 1996 when a geophysical survey using magnetometry revealed some remarkable evidence that the circles are merely a ruin of what was a much more elaborate site than had hitherto been realised.

The stones as depicted by Stukeley in 1723

Stone circles such as those at Stanton Drew date broadly to the late Neolithic and early Bronze Age (approx 3000-2000 BC). In southern England the stone circles and avenues at Avebury and Stonehenge testify to a long and complex history within a landscape dense in other evidence of prehistoric activity. While there is little concrete archaeological evidence the circles are believed to have played an important part in contemporary social and religious life.

The Wedding Party

The three stone circles at Stanton Drew are quite a spectacle: the Great Circle with its 27 stones at 113m in diameter being one of the largest in the country. The other two, to the south-west and north-east respectively are much smaller. Both the Great Circle, as it is known, and the north-east circle were approached by short avenues of standing stones. While most of the stones have fallen, the few that still remain upright are impressive. Conveniently situated in the garden of the pub, The Druids Arms, is a group of three large stones (one fallen) known as The Cove, and to the north, across the river Chew, a small stone lies in a hedge, the rather sad remains of a dolmen known as Hautville's Quoit. Other outlying stones connected with the monument have sadly disappeared completely over the years.

The Cove, in the garden of the Druid's Arms

The proximity of these monuments to each other, and the obvious alignments between some of them, indicate that they once formed a single complex, and it is a fair to assume that Stanton Drew was a place of great significance during the later Stone Age. Sir Norman Lockyer postulated that in common with the great temples of Egypt, the Stanton Drew circles were erected to mark specific calendar dates, in this case the rising of the star Arcturus in May to start the season of growth and fertility. The observer for this event would have been situated in the Cove.

Looking between the stones towards the church

The 1996 survey revealed a highly elaborate pattern of buried pits below the pasture within the Great Circle. They are arranged in nine concentric rings with more at the centre. It appears that the pits are about a metre or more in diameter, spaced about a metre apart on the outer circle. This may indicate that the monument was once a massive wooden structure. Just as remarkable was the discovery that the Great Circle was itself contained within a large enclosure ditch (approximately 135m outer diameter). This was about 7 metres wide and had an entrance facing north-east. Such enclosures, or henges, are a well-known feature of the later Neolithic and are assumed to be the foci of ritual activity. Several henges enclose stone circles, the largest being at Avebury, though this one holds a respectable second place.

The sites that bear the closest resemblance to the patterns in the

The Wedding Party

survey are Woodhenge, near Stonehenge, and the Sanctuary, near Avebury, though at Stanton Drew the circles are larger. At these and other sites, the pits are known to have held timber uprights. It is likely that at least some of the circular pits once held massive posts, and it is a matter of lively debate and speculation whether these structures were roofed or not.

Stanton Drew is particularly well known for its folklore. There is the almost ubiquitous tale among stone circle lore that it is impossible to count the stones, but with, in this case, a rather more sinister twist. The antiquary and proto-Druid John Wood wrote in 1749 that:

"No one, say the Country People about Stantondrue, was ever able to reckon the number of these metamorphosed Stones, or to take a Draught of them, tho' several have attempted to do both, and proceeded till they were either struck dead on the Spot, or with such an illness as soon carried them off".

View of the NE circle

England's Living Folklore

Perhaps more interesting is the tale of the wedding party: One Saturday long ago a wedding in the village was followed by revelling which lasted well into the night. When midnight struck, the devout piper (or in some versions of the tale a harper) refused to play for fear of violating the Christian Sabbath. The bride was furious and swore she would find another musician if she had to go to Hell and back to fetch him. At that moment an old man appeared, a fiddler. His music was so exhilarating that the dancers found they could not stop. It seems that the fiddler was the Devil himself, and the faster he played the faster the party danced. When morning came the villagers found the revellers had been turned to stone, and the circles were hereafter known as the Devil's Wedding Party. The only survivor was the humble piper who had refused to play after midnight. A splendid tale, and one which may contain echoes from folk-memory of joyful pagan rites being carried out among the stones, much to the disapproval of the Church.

One of the massive fallen stones in the Great Circle

The Wedding Party

John Aubrey notes that the stones were locally referred to as The Wedding, while Stukeley writing in 1723 links specific characters in the legend to some of the stones in the circle: the two in the centre were the bride and groom, those in the circle were the wedding guests while the fiddlers were represented by one or two outliers "sunk into a ditch".

An engraving of 1864 (Illustrated London News - author's collection)

The association of an ancient pagan site with weddings is interesting. Until the Tudor period the Church's attitude to marriage ceremonies was ambivalent, and the wedding ceremony was not included among the seven 'sacraments' until the council of Trent in 1543. Up to then, there had been no requirement for a priest to solemnise a wedding, and marriages, or handfastings as they were popularly termed were essentially civil affairs. They were, nevertheless occasions for great celebration in the community, and a stone circle or similar monument in the parish would have been an obvious choice for a venue. When the Church finally did decide to make a church wedding the only official route to matrimonial union, no doubt such civil jollities, where they persisted, were frowned upon by the authorities, and any such rites that lingered would have been demonized in sermons throughout the land. It is also important to note that petrifaction as a punishment for committing sacrilege against God, or The Gods, is common in many cultures and is found not only in the Bible but also in Classical mythology. A similar tale to the Stanton Drew legend involving dancers breaking the Sabbath at Kolbeck in Germany was written down by the monk Lambert of Hersfield in 1075CE, and it is possible that the story spread throughout Europe picking up local colour as its association became transferred to individual sites. In recent years the story of the Stanton Drew wedding party has inspired at least two folk-songs – one by Colin Reece of the seventies folk-rock outfit Bully Wee, and one by Jim Parker and Muriel Holland which was recorded by the Yetties.

This engraving by William Barnes is believed to be of Hauteville's Quoit

Hautville's Quoit seems to have accumulated a wealth of folklore of its own. It stands in the neighbouring parish of Norton

The Wedding Party

Malreward. Writing in 1664 John Aubrey relates a tale which he was told when visiting the site:

"There lived anciently in these parts one Hakewell, a person of power and mighty strength; he lies buried in Chew church where he hath a monument... The common people tell this incredible story, that Hakewell stood upon the top of Norton Hill, about half a mile off where the coyte now lies, and coyted it down to this place."

For this amazing feat he was granted the manor of Norton. It seems he was less than overwhelmed by the gift, as he renamed it Norton Malreward. In actual fact the name Malreward was the surname of the man who held the manor in 1238. Another folk tale not only ascribes the hurling of the quoit to sir John Hauteville (Aubrey's Hakewell), but also credits him with making the earthwork known as Maes Knoll, to the north of Stanton Drew.

It is easy to see faces in the stones

The stones are well worth a visit with the north-east circle being the most complete and upright. They consist of a dark red sandstone conglomerate, and are mottled with lichens. Some of the stones are heavily weathered and it is quite easy to see faces in their rugged surfaces. The main circle has largely been felled while the SSW one is neglected and overgrown in an adjacent field. As previously mentioned, the cove is conveniently sited in the Druid Arms' beer garden, and it may be better in the summer to park in the car-park here if you are driving, as the car-park close to the stones only accommodates about three vehicles. If you do, make sure you sample the inn's hospitality while you are there or you may not be very popular with the landlord. Also, take your wellies as the site is grazed by cattle or sheep for most of the year. For this reason dogs are not allowed on the site. The circles are actually on private land and a small donation is asked for, in return for which a useful information pamphlet is provided.

Map References:

Hauteville's Quoit: ST602638
Maes Knoll: ST600660
Stanton Drew Stone Circles: ST599633
The Cove: ST597630

THE SACRIFICIAL KING

There were three men came out of the west,
Their fortunes for to try
And these three men made a solemn vow
John Barleycorn must die
They ploughed, they sowed,
They harrowed him in,
Threw clods upon his head
And these three men made a solemn vow
John Barleycorn was dead

They've let him lie for a very long time,
'Til the rain from heaven did fall
And little sir john sprung up his head
And so amazed them all
They let him stand 'til midsummer's day
'Til he looked both pale and wan
And little sir john grew a long long beard
And so become a man

They hired men with their scythes so sharp
To cut him off at the knee
They rolled him and tied him by the waist,
And served him barbarously

They hired men with sharp pitchforks
Who pricked him to the heart
But the loader he served him worse than that
For he bound him to a cart

They wheeled him around and around a field
'Til they came unto a barn
And there they made a solemn oath
On poor John Barleycorn
They hired men with their crabtree sticks
To cut him skin from bone
But the miller he served him worse than that
For he ground him between two stones

Here's little Sir John and the nut brown bowl,
Here's brandy in the glass
For little Sir John and the nut brown bowl
Proved the strongest man at last
For the huntsman he can't hunt the fox
Nor loudly blow his horn
And the tinker he can't mend kettles or pots
Without a little Barleycorn

 S. Baring Gould and Cecil Sharp are largely responsible for the widespread dissemination of John Barleycorn in the 20th century, having included the song in their publication English Folk Songs for Schools. It is certainly one of the few songs I remember from my earliest schooldays, and the strangest. Its relevance to modern Paganism is obvious, with the themes of death and rebirth - the ritual slaughter of the sacrificial Corn King which has been symbolically incorporated into many a modern Pagan Lammas celebration.

 The song has been recorded by many luminaries of the folk and folk-rock world: The Watersons; Steeleye Span; the English Country Blues Band; Martin Carthy; Jethro Tull; Traffic; Maddy Prior. The following are excerpts from the relevant album sleeve notes for three

The Sacrificial King

of these recordings. Between them they illustrate the various aspects of the song rather well:

"Sometimes called The Passion of the Corn. It's such an unusually coherent figuration of the old Frazerian myth of the Corn-King cut down and rising again, that the sceptical incline to think it may be an invention or refurbishing carried out by some educated antiquary. If so, he did his work long ago and successfully, for the ballad was already in print in the early years of the seventeenth century, and it has been widespread among folk singers in many parts of the English and Scottish countryside. Cecil Sharp obtained this version from Shepherd Haden of Bampton."
[Frost & Fire sleeve notes Watersons 1965].

"Adam, Cain and Abel staggered manfully across the field carrying a plough, a harrow and a grain of wheat ... John Barleycorn - mysterious intimations from above told them to dig three deep furrows and bury him - this done they returned home and started to

draw up plans for the first ale house."
[Below the Salt sleeve notes Steeleye Span 1972].

"Forget the academic stuff about death and rebirth, fertility symbols and corn gods! The reason that this is one of the best known and most popular of all ballads - and one which has crossed a great many musical thresholds -- is that it's actually about that other activity which most commonly accompanies the singing of traditional songs - drinking!"
[The Carthy Chronicles sleeve notes Martin Carthy 2002].

All of the above albums are still available as CDs. Steeleye Span's version, collected by Fred Hamer from Billy Bartle in Bedfordshire, is interesting as it contains a verse depicting the actual brewing process. This harks back to the earliest (16th century) Ballad. The 18th century broadsides to which most modern versions are related leave this part of the ballad out.

The Sacrificial King

Up to the last century, before the harvesting of crops became fully mechanized, rural communities invested the cutting of the corn, and particularly harvesting the last sheaf, with great ceremony. In Devon and Cornwall such harvest rites were known as 'crying the neck'. Broadly, for there were many local variations, the reapers would form a circle around the most senior of them (sometimes referred to as the Harvest Lord), carrying aloft the last ears of corn to be cut. He would shout "I havet, I havet, I havet", to which the response was "What havee, what havee, what havee?" The response would be "a neck, a neck, a neck, we have one" repeatedly, followed by much cheering from the assembled company. The last sheaf would be decorated with ribbons and borne home in great triumph. Sometimes an effigy, or corn dolly was created by weaving the stalks together. This would be present at the 'harvest home' celebrations which usually consisted of feasting and dancing; there are many different folk-dance tunes entitled Harvest Home. The corn dolly would often be kept either until the next year's harvest, or ploughed back into the ground with the next planting. It was from this, and similar customs throughout this country and elsewhere that Sir James Frazer formed his ideas about a 'sacrificial corn king' being an essential element of primitive religion.

It is this aspect of harvest traditions that has most strongly influenced modern Pagans in their re-invention of Lammas rites. The assumption that the last sheaf contains the spirit of the corn god or goddess is now taken as read in many such celebrations, and often John Barleycorn himself is seen as an aspect of the ubiquitous 'Green Man'. Lammas (the word itself meaning 'loaf mass' in Old English), while it was extremely important in the Middle Ages gradually disappeared from the Church calendar in early modern times, and seems to have been replaced by the more secular 'harvest home' celebrations which may have harked back to pre-Christian times. It was only in 1843 when the reverend R S Hawker, vicar of Morwenstowe invited his congregation to receive the sacrament "in bread of the new corn" that the modern 'harvest thanksgiving' services came into being. Lammas Fairs, however, do seem to have survived to some extent in Devon, and still take place at Exeter,

Chulmleigh and Honiton. Exeter city council claims the fair with its garlanded procession to be an unbroken tradition dating back over 900 years.

There was an excellent article by Peter Wood, entitled John Barleycorn: The Evolution of a Folk-song Family, in The Folk Music Journal, in 2004. It gives a picture of the way a whole group of related songs developed through a series of re-makings from the 16th century ballad. The 'original' barely mentions the death-and-resurrection theme, the bulk of which seems to be a rather later addition possibly in the 18th century, when the revival of Classical studies led to a growth of interest in such things. Robert Burns re-worked a version of the song in the 1780s, but according to Baring-Gould he "in no way improved it", and fortunately traditional versions prevailed among folksingers.

The earliest known version, dated from before 1568, is written in (to our ears) a strange Scots-Gaelic/Anglo-Norman-French dialect, and is called Allan O' Maut. The first known English version has the not very snappy title A pleasant New Ballad to Sing Evening and Morn, Of the Bloody Murder of John Barleycorn, and it ran to 32 verses! Other versions had the titles Three Knights North, or, Three Men West. Some versions have "Holly Clubs" instead of "Crabtree sticks". Unsurprisingly, the more popular versions of the 18th century were somewhat distilled (if you'll pardon the pun) down from the longer versions, and it is in this form that we know the song today as published in the Penguin Book of Folksongs from which Stevie Winwood, among many others took his inspiration.

At the first Eastbourne Lammas Fayre, Hunters Moon Morris (as they were later to be known) danced to a version of the song sung to the 19th century German hymn tune We Plough the Fields and Scatter, with the chorus:

Come put your wine into glasses,
Put your cider into old tin cans,
Put Barleycorn in the nut-brown bowl
And he'll prove the strongest man

This was roughly the version which the legendary Shropshire folksinger Fred Jordan sang. Interestingly his three men in the first verse "came out of Kent". Fred died in 2002 aged eighty. His version of the song was recorded by the Gloucestershire singing group, the Songwainers in the 1970s.

Cecil Sharp collected several versions of the song from singers in Devon and Somerset. Unfortunately Sharp sometimes had a habit of bowdlerising songs where lyrics, as he put it "would scarcely bear reproduction." Nevertheless he recorded a version from one John Trump of North Petherton which includes the following alternative lines:

John Barleycorn in a nut brown bowl
And brandy in a can
It will make any fair maid dance and sing
Stark naked as she was born

To my right fol the dol
To my right fol the dol
To my right fol the dol I die.

It is amazing to think that a song popular at Lammas celebrations today, and still sung in folk-clubs and pubs everywhere, has been around for perhaps five centuries, and that despite Burns' 'tinkering' has remained virtually unchanged for around 250 years. Almost inevitably, the earlier ballads tended to be more bawdy, as are one or two of the comic versions occasionally sung in folk clubs since the 1970s. A translation of the final verse of an early version of Allan O' Maut reads:

And whiskey never bore the stirrup cup
So boldly as Allan bore himself;
Neither did his pride get a fall
Until blokes pissed him at the wall

(fortunately it scans better in the original Scots!).

Illustrations are by Graham Higgins
www.pockettz.demon.co.uk

GHOSTS AMONG THE STONES

Fernworthy stone circle, or Foggymead as it is sometimes rather quaintly known is a twenty-yard diameter Bronze Age circle situated in a small clearing in a modern woodland plantation on the eastern edge of Dartmoor. The twenty-seven or so remaining stones appear fairly small, though in fact the largest stands four feet tall. It is quite easy to find. By car, follow the signs to Fernworthy Reservoir from Chagford and go all the way until it ends in the car park adjacent to the lake at Metheral. The reservoir drowned a number of other archaeological sites, no doubt some of them connected to the circle. From the car park follow the trail through the forest for about a third of a mile and you will find the clearing on your right.

The original function of the circle can never truly be known, but there is much archaeological evidence of funerary activity throughout the Bronze Age. In 1897 an excavation revealed that charcoal was to be found throughout the entire area within the circle. A number of burial cairns and cists exist in the immediate surroundings which have yielded cremated bones, a bronze knife, a flint knife, a lignite button and sherds of a decorated beaker (now displayed in Plymouth Museum). Thus, there is evidence of a change in burial practice over time (and perhaps different cultures?) from inhumation to cremation, and the introduction of grave goods by Bronze Age Beaker people. Flint arrowheads of the Wessex type have also been found in the locality, showing continued occupation of the area beyond the Beaker culture, and only yards from the site are to be found the remnants of granite walls and banks, the remains of Iron Age field systems.

Fernworthy Stone Circle

The stones appear to show some deliberate arrangement of height, which is rare for a circle in southern England, though more common in Wales. Aubrey Burl has noted Fernworthy's similarity to Gors Fawr circle in Dyfed and has suggested an early communication between west Wales and Dartmoor. There are also some interesting stone rows associated with the circle. Traces of the double row to the south can just be made out which led originally to a cairn near to the circumference of the circle, now lost. Unfortunately this has been cut through by the track and disappears into impenetrable undergrowth on the other side. Another row to the south east was not visible at all on my visit, being lost in the scrubby undergrowth and debris of the conifer plantation. I have since read that another to the north is much more plainly visible, but I was not aware of this and missed it. Damn! On my visit in December many stones were coated with various lichens and mosses, some of which bore exquisite, almost microscopically small bright red flowers. Beautiful!

Fernworthy seems to be the only known example on Dartmoor of a stone circle directly connected with stone rows. At Merrivale the complex contains a small circle, a tall monolith and two spectacular double stone rows but they do not seem to be related in any discernible way. Here, by contrast are monuments from different cultures which appear to form a sanctuary site akin, albeit on much a smaller physical scale, to Stanton Drew, Avebury and Stonehenge. It appears that Foggymead was a very important place for our Bronze Age ancestors.

Hut Circle, Fernworthy

While the wood that surrounds the stones today is a coniferous plantation very different from the broadleaf forest which would likely have surrounded the site in ancient times, it does give a better idea of how such sites may have appeared in their heyday than other more typically bleak, windswept circles on Dartmoor, such as the exceptionally desolate (though admittedly more spectacular) Grey Wether circles, just a mile or so away. Fernworthy circle, being enclosed by trees seems very welcoming, and the sounds of birds and other wildlife help to create the sense of a place dedicated to the sacredness of nature. The site is also associated with many cairns, stone rows, menhirs and cairn circles, and one wonders how much has been lost with modern forestry techniques, let alone the construction of the reservoir, which also drowned one of Dartmoor's most famous and picturesque clapper bridges. Perhaps one day the Forestry Commission will return the forest to native tree species, as they have often done elsewhere, and the site will once more appear truly glorious to future generations of visitors. It is, perhaps surprising to see the postcard view, reproduced below, that shows the circle completely bereft of surrounding forest, looking very much like other circles on Dartmoor such as Scorhill and the aforementioned Grey Wethers. Yet we must remember that the bleak deforested landscape of Dartmoor was essentially created by our distant ancestors' farming methods, just as post-WW2 government subsidies resulted in the huge forests of conifers that provide the backdrop to the Fernworthy circle today.

Postcard dated 1910 (author's collection)

Local, and evidently recent folklore would have it that the area has been cursed since the building of the dam and the flooding of the valley that created the reservoir. For many years Torquay Corporation had taken water from the river Teign, and with growing demand in 1928 a lease was signed with the Duchy of Cornwall. In 1934 an Act of Parliament empowered the Corporation to dam the river and build a new reservoir at Fernworthy. Work started in 1936, but in August 1938 a violent storm lashed across eastern Dartmoor so fiercely that floodwater swept a crane from the valley side into the river. Afterwards an estimated two million gallons of water and five hundred cubic yards of silt had to be cleared from the site. Despite the best efforts of such vengeful elemental spirits the dam was completed in 1942.

The Logan Stone, Thornworthy Tor

Piskies or Gnomes were also said to guard the outcrop of Granite on the moor overlooking Fernworthy known as Thornworthy Tor, (with its spectacular balancing, or 'logan stone'), and Fernworthy Farm, which was demolished during construction work on the dam, was said to have been cursed and a baby taken by way of recompense by the supernatural denizens of the enchanted hill after the farmer took stone from the Tor to rebuild the farmhouse. The residents of Fernworthy were also despised by the fictional Mr Frankland, a distinctly odd character in Arthur Conan Doyle's epic story The Hound of the Baskervilles. It is possible that Grimpen Mire, a few miles to the north-west was based on the nearby Cranmere pool, the source of no less than four Devon rivers. The pool, now little more than a muddy bog, is said to be haunted by the restless spirit of Benjamin Gayer (1640-1714), a wealthy ship owner brought to his knees by misfortune, who died with a guilty conscience after taking the money with which he had been entrusted to pay the ransoms of unfortunate sailors kidnapped by pirates. The ghost was said to have been banished to the pool by a priest until such time as he could empty its waters using only a sieve. The enterprising phantom apparently once found an abandoned sheepskin with which he lined the sieve. In bailing out the pool he caused disastrous floods which inundated the town of Okehampton, after which the priest re-appeared and this time demanded that the ghost should make trusses of grit bound with plaits made of sand, which Sysiphean task has occupied 'Cranmere Benjie' to this day, howling nocturnally at his misfortune. The ghost is sometimes said to take on the form of a black colt. Bizarrely Cranmere Pool, though at least eight miles from any habitation and 1,837 feet above sea level, had the first ever post box. This was originally provided in 1854 by James Perrot, a Dartmoor guide, for visiting hikers to leave their calling cards in recognition of their not inconsiderable feat in reaching so remote a spot. The current box, with its visitors' book (when it has not been stolen or vandalized) dates from the 1960s.

Also well worth a visit are the substantial hut circles to be found adjacent to the road that skirts Fernworthy Reservoir. In fact, there are so many significant remains in this area you could spend several days covering just a few square miles with map and compass and probably still not see everything. An excellent walk in good weather is across the moor northwards along Hurston Ridge to Chagford Common from the Warren House Inn on the B3212. I would recommend making it a circular walk, returning in time to sample the excellent game pie and the local ales at one of England's remotest (and cosiest) public houses.

Map References:

Cranmere Pool: SX602858
Fernworthy Stone Circle: SX655841
Grey Wether Circles: SX 639831
Hut Circles (illustrated): SX 668836
Merrivale Stone Circle: SX 553746
Scorhill Stone Circle: SX654873
Thornworthy Tor: SX665852
Warren House Inn: SX673809

TINNERS' HARES

A couple of years ago, holidaying in the West Country I was enchanted by a symbol crafted in a beautiful stained glass panel in the door of the sixteenth century Castle Inn at Lydford, a well known beauty spot in North Devon. It was a colourful depiction of three hares, chasing after each other in a circle and joined together by their ears, of which each had only one, but in being linked together appeared to have two each, forming two sides of a triangle between them. More recently I heard a delightful programme on BBC Radio 4 called Chasing Hares by writer and broadcaster James Crowden, which explored this mysterious symbol in some detail. This led me to the Three Hares Project website by photographer Chris Chapman who has been identifying and photographing the hares since 1989. It is this website and the radio programme which have provided much of the factual information for his article.

The county of Devon, and especially the Dartmoor area, has by far the largest incidence of triple hares, ranging from the highly stylized to the slightly cartoon-like and comical. There are seventeen parish churches in the county known to contain at least one roof boss depicting the symbol, with a total of twenty-nine bosses in all, of which nineteen are certainly medieval wood carvings. Broadclyst in East Devon has nine but many are early 19th century copies and mostly identical (this church is also well worth a visit to see the gargoyles on the tower). Kelly has two, one of which is modern, while Chagford, Sampford Courtenay and Spreyton have two medieval examples each. The bosses range in the county from Ashreigney in the north to Paignton in the south, and from Broadclyst in the east to Kelly in the west, although there does seem to be a concentration on the northern and eastern fringes of Dartmoor. There is a great variety of style, implying that they were created by different craftsmen. The bosses are often prominent in the church's architecture and several are associated by close proximity with Green Men. Other West Country examples can be found in churches at Cothele in Cornwall, and Corfe Mullen in Dorset. Most appear to date from the 14th and 15th centuries.

Window in the Castle Inn, Lydford, Devon

Examples of the design also appear in Devon in post-mediaeval plaster ceilings in private houses, and a beautiful modern example is the aforementioned window in Lydford (created in 1974). More recently the revived symbol has been taken up by artists and craftsmen in the area who have created many beautiful examples, such as the relief ceramic panel made by the Calstock Pottery, in the Tamar Valley. Perhaps eventually the triple hares will come to represent Devon much as the Celtic triple spiral, or triskell has come to represent Brittany. Elsewhere in the UK there are just a few examples known. These are at Long Melford, Suffolk (in a stained glass window), St Davids Cathedral, in Pembrokeshire, Wales (a stone roof boss), Selby Abbey, Yorkshire (a wooden boss), in a plaster ceiling in Scarborough, North Yorks, and on floor tiles from Chester Cathedral and the parish church in Long Crendon, Bucks.

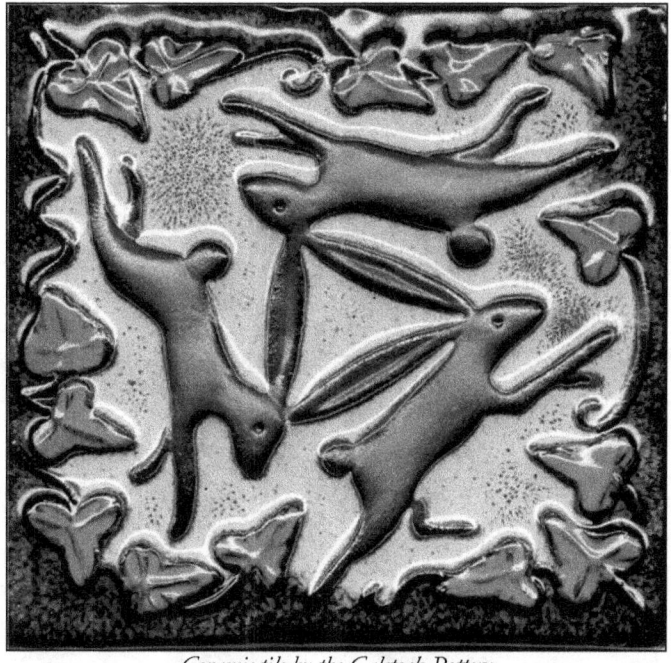

Ceramic tile by the Calstock Pottery

Academics have become intrigued at the motif's apparent prominence in Christian, Islamic and Buddhist holy contexts separated by 5,000 miles and almost 1,000 years. In Europe, the three hares appear widely in mediaeval ecclesiastical contexts in France, Germany and Switzerland. In eastern France, they cluster in churches in Alsace and the Vosges. There is a fine stone roof boss in the chapter house of the church of St Peter and St Paul in Wissembourg which dates to c.1300 CE. Another is carved in stone on an under-cill in the chapel of the Hotel de Cluny in Paris. In Germany, a well-known example is in the cloister window of Paderborn Cathedral. One of the most historically important is on a bell given to the Cistercian Abbey of Kloster Haina which can be dated reliably to 1224 CE. There is even a 19th century Dutch or Belgian carved wooden cake-mould featuring the motif, around which is incised the phrase "Voor Drie Hazen, Drie Ooren En Toch Is Ieder Met Twee Geboren," which translates into English as: "While Three Hares, Three Ears And Still Is Each Born With Two Ears". A fine modern representation can be found in the circular window on the west gable wall at St John's Malone, an Anglican Parish church in the heart of south Belfast. It was designed by Evie Hone and was considered by the late Sir John Betjeman to be one of the finest examples of 20th century stained glass in Europe.

Roof boss in Ashreigney Church, Devon

Tinners' Hares

The earliest known examples of the three hares motif are to be found on painted representations of textiles on the ceilings of Buddhist cave temples at Mogao, near Dunhuang, China. These date from the Sui Dynasty (581-618 CE) through to the end of the Tang Dynasty (618-907 CE). Dunhuang is situated at the western end of the Great Wall of China and was an important trading post on the Silk Road, the major conduit for the exchange of goods and ideas between east and west for many hundreds of years, and especially in the 13th and 14th centuries. It is thought that the design may have travelled from Persia in the sixth century, and back towards the west again in mediaeval times. Some of the Buddhist representations vary in number from three to four, and in at least one of the images the animals seem to have hooves, and may be deer, possibly representing the deer park in Sarnath where the Buddha reputedly first preached a sermon.

Roof boss at St Hubert, Corfe Mullen, Dorset

A Persian copper coin, minted in Urmiya in 1281CE, bears the three hares on its reverse side. The image is thought to reinforce the 'heavenly mandate' of the Mongol rulers. An earlier and very beautiful example is found on an Iranian brass and copper tray, dating from the 12th or 13th century. There is also a reliquary casket from Southern Russia, crafted during the period of Mongol rule in the late 13th or early 14th centuries, which is now preserved in the cathedral treasury of Trier, Germany. It displays Islamic iconography including sphinxes and griffins on its base-plate and originally featured two triple hare images, one of which has sadly been lost through damage. The reliquary was said once to have contained the head of St Lazarus. The motif may have travelled west along the Silk Road as a popular design woven into textiles. Sue Andrew, an art historian who is part of the Three Hares Research Project, said: "We don't know how for sure the symbol travelled to the West but the most likely explanation is they were on the valuable oriental silks brought to Western medieval churches to wrap holy relics, as altar cloths and in vestments". It is known that designs from these silks influenced medieval artists and church craftsmen. In Exeter Cathedral an oriental textile is depicted on the tomb of Bishop Walter Bronescombe, who died in 1280.

The three hares motif was clearly revered in all the contexts in which it is found, but, as yet no contemporary written record of its meaning has been found. One would expect that the symbol would have different meanings in different cultures, but as an archetype perhaps there is an element of meaning common to all. Hares are strongly represented in world mythology and from ancient times have had divine, and especially lunar associations. It is interesting to note that while in the West we see a 'man in the moon', many Asian cultures see a hare. It was said to have been the sacred animal of the Goddess Eostre, from whom the name of the Christian festival Easter is derived. Its elusiveness and largely nocturnal behaviour have reinforced its reputation as a magical creature and in folklore witches often take on the resemblance of hares to escape persecution. The Goddess Eostre with her springtime festival was after all revered as a fertility goddess (hence Easter bunnies, of course!). The goddess was

Tinners' Hares

believed to have mystical links to the female cycle (hence oestrogen) and to the moon that governed it. Perhaps therefore it is as a symbol of femininity and fertility that the motif may be best understood. The link with the Green Man, the symbol with which it is frequently found in the Devon churches may be significant here, perhaps in the context of symbolic male/female aspects of fertility. The British warrior Boudicca is said to have performed a ritual to Astarte that involved the symbolic releasing of a hare before she famously unleashed her avenging fury on the Romano-British settlements of St Albans and London. Hares often symbolized sexual promiscuity in medieval art and stories, yet it is hard to see how their appearance in church architecture might play a similar role as a warning against sexual incontinence as Sheela-na-Gigs are often proposed to have done. The imagery is surely too subtle and in many cases, simply too cute to carry such overtones.

Roof boss at St Michael the Archangel, Chagford, Devon

In Devon, of course, they are referred to as 'tinners' hares', or 'tinners' rabbits'. This may be because many of the churches in which they are found are in the so-called stannary towns, where tin was brought from the mines to be weighed and assayed, though in Devon the ore would have been just as likely to have been copper as tin. Interestingly, there are no triple hares to be found in the principle Cornish tin-mining areas, the only example in Cornwall yet discovered being in the Tamar Valley, very close to Devon.

An association has been made with an alchemical symbol for tin known as the 'Hunt of Venus' published in a book around 1600CE, but this appears to be based on a misreading of the symbol and in any case is probably a recent attempt to find an early explanation for the connection. The earliest reference linking the hares with tinners is actually a nineteenth century book about the church at Widecombe-in-the-Moor. The earliest known literary reference is from A Survey of the Cathedral of St Davids published in 1717 by Browne Willis. It appears that by then the meaning of the symbol had been lost: "In one key stone near the west end are three rabbits plac'd triangularly, with the backsides of their heads turn'd inwards, and so contriv'd that the three ears supply the place of six so that every head seems to have its full quota of ears. This is constantly shewn to strangers as a curiosity worth regarding."

It is tempting to suggest that the hares are perhaps symbolic of a lost pagan deity that hung on intractably enough in parts of Devon to be enshrined by local craftsmen in the Christian era. That, however, denies the circumstantial evidence of an oriental origin for the motif, unless the design appeared on some unwitting Bishop's imported robes and was seized upon eagerly by the aforementioned craftsmen as an acceptably subtle way of reintroducing a symbol of the 'Old Religion' into the new places of worship. Maybe the hares were not pagan at all but represented something, now forgotten, to the old Celtic Church that was held dear by the local population and was revived locally in the spate of new church building in mediaeval times. The church in Somerset and Devon remained stubbornly Celtic up until 768CE when these two counties were the last in England to accede to the domination of Rome. Attempts to explain the motif in terms of the Christian Trinity appear to be from a much later period than the time when the images were originally created. In Albrecht Durer's wood engraving Holy Family with Three Hares (1498) the hares are depicted in full, half and quarter view reinforcing the essentially lunar nature of the motif even in a Christian context. Interestingly the gestation period for hares is 28 days, which coincides with the length of a lunar cycle.

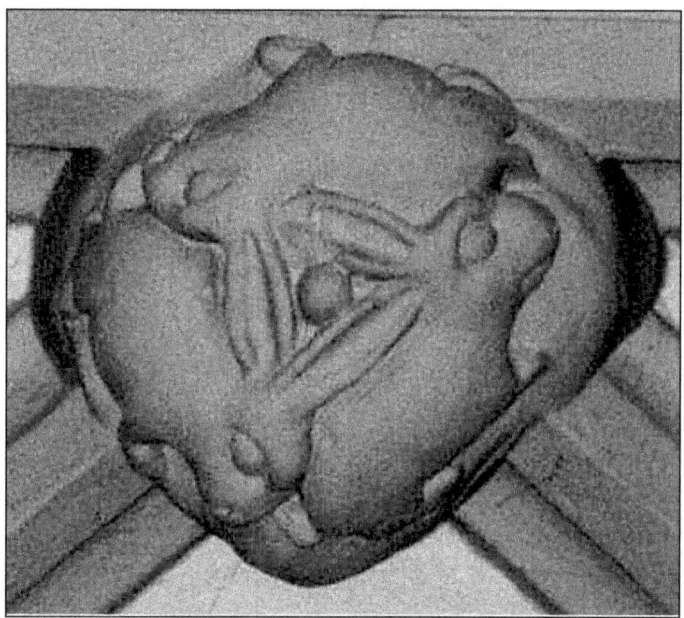

Roof boss in Broadclyst parish church, Devon

But why three hares? The symbol certainly fits as conveniently with the triple aspect of the Goddess popular in modern Pagan iconography as it does with the Christian Trinity, while the circular movement inherent in the image could be said to represent eternity. One Christian interpretation is that whilst hares are "wicked/lascivious/sinful" creatures (like human beings) even they can be "saved" if they use their long ears to listen to the "Word of God" (sounds a bit forced to me). Maybe it is simply a neat device for fitting three running animals into a circular space, but in that case why are there no similar depictions of other animals composed in the same manner? Like their frequent companions, green men, the hares remain an enigma for now, and unless some spectacular find amongst hitherto forgotten medieval church-builders' manuscripts is uncovered, they are likely to remain so for the foreseeable future. A splendid mystery!

Map References:

Lydford, The Castle Inn: SX510848
Churches:
Ashreigney: SS628136
Broadclyst: SX981972
Chagford: SX701875
Chester Cathedral: SJ405664
Corfe Mullen: SY976 983
Cothele: SX 422686
Kelly: SX395813
Long Crendon: SP698090
Long Melford: TL865467
Paignton: SX 886611
Sampford Courtenay: SS632013
Selby Abbey: SE615324
Spreyton: SX697967
St David's Cathedral: SM751253
Widecombe-in-the-Moor: SX718767

A HEATHEN PROMONTORY

Situated above the pretty village of Stoke-sub-Hamdon near Montacute in Somerset, Ham Hill is one of the more enigmatic Iron Age hill forts in the south of England. The entire 200 acre summit is enclosed by the remnants of its defences making it one of the the largest in Britain. It was very probably re-used by the Roman army after its capture around 43CE as a fortification within the territories of the Durotriges tribe. Archaeologically speaking, the site has yielded a number of finely-crafted pieces of Roman military equipment mostly identified as legionary in origin, and also pieces of a cuirass (leather breastplate) with possible auxiliary connotations. The quantity and quality of the finds coupled with the site's dominance over a large part of the surrounding countryside makes Roman occupancy very likely, with parallels at Hod Hill in Dorset and Brandon Hill in Worcestershire. Local folklore has it that there was a Roman amphitheatre within the fort on the northern side of the hill, where wretched British prisoners were forced to fight to the death or be thrown to wild animals for the entertainment of the occupying troops, but it is more likely that the 'amphitheatre', itself now destroyed by quarrying, was merely the physical evidence of earlier stone extraction on the site.

Another circular feature, often confused with the 'amphitheatre' is known as the Frying Pan. Ruth Tongue, writing in Somerset Folklore (1965) noted that it had once been the custom that every girl or woman who visited would sit down and slide from top to bottom of the bowl, adding "Surely here is a relic of pagan rites such as those embodied in the game of Trundles and others." The current guide to the site interprets this feature as a medieval livestock show ring. There is a tradition that an underground passage once linked Ham Hill and Montacute House, around a mile away, and there are tales of treasure buried here by monks from Glastonbury. The ghost of a Norman princess is said to haunt the hill, at the site of a former chapel, close to where the Prince of Wales pub now stands.

The new stone circle at the summit of the hill

The hill is most famous for its limestone, of course, and has supplied the surrounding towns and villages with its famous honey-coloured stone for well over five hundred years. A fine example of a Roman coffin, carved from Ham Hill stone is displayed in The Dorset County Museum in Dorchester and is widely taken as evidence of quarrying during the Roman occupation. As a result of stone extraction, a lot of the archaeology has been destroyed, with even some of the fort's bank and ditch defences succumbing to quarrying activity. Nevertheless there is much to see. Most of the site is accessible to the public, despite the fact that quarrying

A Heathen Promontory

continues to this day, and the quarry owner has thoughtfully provided a nature trail, sculpture trail and visitor centre. The owners also co-operate with Wessex Archaeology in advance of any new quarrying operations. The most recent resulting dig unearthed quantities of sling-shot, storage vessels and quern stones which are now in the care of the Somerset Museums Service.

Not only that, but there is also now a splendid new stone circle, referred to by the locals, I am told, as Ham Henge. This was erected as part of a Millennium project by the quarry to commemorate the men who worked the stone on the hill over the years. This caused a bit of fuss with the Parochial Parish Council. The controversy was reported in a local newspaper thus:

"A circle of standing stones on land owned by Prince Charles could be used for pagan worship, it is feared. Now councillors have demanded that the monument is destroyed.

It was created by quarry boss Richard England on Duchy of Cornwall-owned Ham Hill to celebrate the stonemasons who have worked in the area for more than 2,000 years. But the local parochial church council, at Stoke-sub-Hamdon, near Yeovil, fears the circle could become a focus for pagan and occult practices. It has now written to the Duchy asking for the stones to be removed. They claim picnic tables erected in the centre of the circle, created from large, flat stones, could make ad-hoc altars for sinister witchcraft rituals.

The Rev Peter Kerton-Johnson, 61, who served as a parish priest in South Africa for 20 years, said: "To put an altar in the centre of the circle is really inviting some sort of pagan practice. I have come from South Africa where these sort of things happen daily, even human sacrifice where children are killed and body parts taken by witch doctors. There has already been an instance recorded in Britain in which a mutilated child's body was found in the Thames. Now there is hearsay that some sort of wedding took place at the circle." He continued: "The flat stone may be intended as a picnic table but it also appears to be a mockery of the Lord's table." He said the book of Jeremiah refers to Israel's ancient pagan neighbours indulging in ritual sex at religious sites on hilltops in the belief that they would be put in touch with divine powers. A bemused Mr England said: "I can take it all away, but what will be next to go, Stonehenge?" [Western Daily Press 30/10/2002].

Fortunately, however, common sense prevailed and the circle still stands, its fifteen large golden coloured stones resplendent in the sunlight. There is also an outlier to the north, though whether this is intentional or not is unclear, given that there are large lumps of stone all over the site!

Fine views from the ramparts and splendid walkies for small doggies!

The essayist and nature writer, Llewellyn Powys writing some forty years on about the quarrying activity in the last quarter of Victoria's reign describes "rumbling carts bringing down skilfully moulded blocks cradled on beds of bracken, and with ill-paid men in dusty yellow-breeches – in breeches of gold ('Stoke Roughs', as the less generous landed gentry did not hesitate to call them) at the head of these horses, everyone of them hearty Sunday night drinkers and stout voters for Strachey. What toil those Ham Hill horses, with their defeated tragic heads, used to endure hauling wagons up the steep ways in the dust of summer and the mud of winter, and then coming down again with perilously heavy loads, skid pans on wheels, but even so with the old carts dangerously jolting and liable to get out of control". So great was the quantity of stone removed that there was a belief among the locals that the stone actually grew on the hill.

The hill was also the setting for political demonstrations with local labour activist George Mitchell hiring no less than seven brass bands on one occasion for a demonstration led by Joseph Arch in his fight to enfranchise the agricultural labourer. Their demands eventually led to the 1884 Parliamentary Reform Act, and Arch became a Liberal MP the year after. Mitchell unfortunately failed in his parliamentary endeavours and died a penniless and disappointed man in London.

Two contemporary sculptures, known as the 'Time Stones'

Llewellyn Powys was the brother of John Cowper Powys, the great writer of mystical landscape novels, who was to find literary fame (some would say notoriety) in this country with his rambling tales set in the Wessex of his youth: Wolf Solent, Maiden Castle, A Glastonbury Romance and Weymouth Sands. The brothers lived at nearby Montacute where their father was the local vicar, and during their schooldays at Sherborne School, Ham Hill was a frequent destination on their many rambles.

John Cowper set his first published novel, Wood and Stone (1917) in this landscape. The book is something of an apprentice work, but quite readable for all that, despite his tendency to give many of his characters outlandish names. The story is a romance set in the village of Nevilton (Stoke-sub-Hamdon) where two distinct powers, the mystical and the materialist, the world of the machine and that of nature are fighting for the soul of the town. The quarry and the stoneworks on 'Leo's Hill' (as he calls it in the novel) are owned by the sadistic Mortimer Romer who delights with his daughter Gladys in terrorising the gentle Lachrima Traffio and Maurice Quincunx. With forgivable hyperbole, the academic writer Morine Krisdottir has written of the novel:

"Against the Zarathustrean cry for consciousness, individuality, lifemastery, he sets the Hardyesque assertion that consciousness brings retribution and that only the passive ones who abandon themselves to the grace of the Mother Goddess, Nature, avoid being destroyed".

In the light of this, the erection of the stone circle against the wishes of the local church, who would have it destroyed, seems almost poetically appropriate! John Cowper's description in the novel reveals the arcane splendour, and also the ambivalent character of a hill which has such power over the lives and destinies of the inhabitants of the village which nestles in its flanks:

"Even in Pre-Celtic times those formidably dug trenches and frowning slopes must have looked down on the surrounding valley; and to this day it is the same suggestion of tyrannical military dominance, which, in spite of the quarries and cranes and fragrant yellow gorse, gives the place its prevailing character.

A Heathen Promontory

The rounded escarpments have for centuries been covered with pleasant turf and browsed upon by sheep; but patient antiquarian research constantly brings to light its coins, torques, urns, arrowheads, amulets; and rumour hints that yet more precious things lie concealed under those grassy mounds.

The aboriginal tribes have been succeeded by the Celt; the Celt by the Roman; the Roman by the Saxon; without any change in the place's inherent character, and without any lessening of its tyranny over the surrounding country. For though Leo's Hill dominates no longer by means of its external strength, it dominates, quite as completely, by means of its interior riches.

It is in fact, a huge rock-island, washed by the leafy waves of the encircling valleys, and containing, as its hid treasure, stone enough to rebuild Babylon.

In that particular corner of the West Country, so distinct and deep-rooted are the legendary survivals, it is hard not to feel as though some vast spiritual conflict were still proceeding between the two opposed Mythologies – the one drawing its strength from the impulse to Power, and the other from the impulse to Sacrifice."

St Michael's Hill

This area of Somerset is steeped in history and littered with ancient sites. Just to the east on the lower slopes of the hill lie the remains of the deserted medieval Hamlet of Lower Warren, while only half a mile away is St Michael's Hill, an isolated conical hill whish has obviously been sculpted in a similar manner to Glastonbury Tor and Burrow Mump on the nearby Somerset Levels. The hill was a motte-and-bailey fort in Saxon times and a Norman Castle was later built here. A tower, a folly erected in the eighteenth century by the Phelips family now stands on the site of a former Cluniac chapel. There is a legend of a 'miraculous cross' which was discovered through a vision on this hill which led to the founding of Waltham Abbey. This legend, and the dedication to St Michael may tend to suggest a pre-Christian sacred site. The National Trust which owns the hill is gradually thinning out the woodland to make the earthworks more visible.

"This heathen promontory" as Powys called Ham Hill is very much worth a visit, and is easily accessible, having been a country park since 1975. The road from Stoke leads sharply uphill to the car-park close to the visitors' centre. There are some fine walks and stunning views to be experienced, the perimeter walk around the ramparts being roughly three miles in length. The stone circle is very impressive, and besides that, this must be the only hill-fort in England to have a public house, The Prince of Wales, set within its ramparts, dispensing real ale straight from the cask. St Michael's Hill with its folly tower is open to the public, while the medieval village of Montacute must be one of the most unspoilt places in England. Montacute House, one of the finest late Elizabethan buildings and its gardens are in the care of the National Trust and are also open to the public.

Map References:

Ham Hill Stone Circle: ST477171
Montacute House: ST499169
St Michael's Hill: ST493169
The Prince of Wales public house: ST480166

A CIRCLE OF QUARTZ

Visiting stone circles is not always as rewarding as you might at first hope. Often a long trudge across muddy fields and over rusty barbed wire fences while keeping a wary eye out for curmudgeonly farmers on quad bikes wielding shotguns of dubious legality may reveal only a few broken scattered shards of rock barely visible in thigh high nettles and wet grass, or occasionally nothing at all (has anyone managed to find Porlock stone circle on Exmoor, or is it just a cruel joke perpetrated by the OS cartographers?).

The Duloe Stones

Duloe, however is outstanding in many respects. Firstly, it is one of the easiest to find and gain access to that I have yet encountered. It stands at the south end of the village close to the road leading from Liskeard to Looe, up a little lane opposite the churchyard (look for the small wooden signpost). Although on private land it seems that as long as visitors act sensibly anyone can enjoy this interesting site. As the field in which it stands often contains livestock it is wise to keep dogs on a lead. It is small by Cornish standards being roughly 39 x 37ft. However, the stones are impressive, the highest of the eight surviving standing about 8'6" tall at the south of the circle, weighing about twelve tons. At a distance, the stones look pale and grey, but close up they are quite spectacular, the quartz-laden rock gleaming white through the thin covering of lichens. The stones were probably quarried at Herodsfoot, around two miles away.

The stones are rich in quartz, making them gleam in the sunlight

Although 'Stonetown', the farm nearby obviously took its name from the site, and is recorded as long ago as 1329, the circle itself was not officially 'discovered' until 1801, perhaps because at the time it was bisected by a field boundary, and stood partly in a field and partly in an orchard. The hedge and bank were removed in 1858 by the Rev. T.A. Bewes of Plymouth, who re-erected several fallen stones. Unfortunately in the process the largest was broken and was left prostrate, and an urn, said to be full of bones was broken by a workman's pick and crumbled into dust on exposure to the air. The Duloe Torque, a late Bronze Age gold bracelet, was found in a nearby field and is now in the County Museum in Truro.

While most Cornish stone circles are of granite, Duloe is constructed of a quartz-rich rock containing the mineral ankerite. This suggests they were brought from an outcrop about two miles to the north west. It has been calculated that it would have required 30 to 35 people to move the stones. Although small in diameter, the circle is one of the most complete in Cornwall, and the rough, unhewn stones are aligned to the points of the compass, suggesting an astronomical significance. There is a low mound within the circle, but this may just be the remnants of the former bisecting hedge.

As the land around the circle has been cultivated for millennia there are few related monuments in the area, compared with say, Bodmin Moor where some fifteen circles remain surrounded by the remains of settlements, field systems and burial mounds. There is also, unusually for the West Country, hardly any folklore connected with this particular monument, possibly due to it having been forgotten and un-noticed for so many centuries. Fortunately, perhaps due to its obscurity it survived, and is certainly one of the finest stone circles I have encountered. Inside the circle it feels somehow intimate, warm and welcoming, and I would recommend it as a site worth visiting, especially as its easy access makes it so suitable for the less mobile.

A few hundred yards away in a field opposite the entrance to Westnorth Farm is St Cuby's Well. It has a fine well-house situated beneath a large tree, and adorned with an equal-armed Celtic cross. Inside there are stone benches and some very ancient looking steps which lead down through a low arch to the water. Inside there is a serene and calm atmosphere, worlds away from the busy road which is only a few yards away.

There was once a massive and beautifully decorated ancient stone basin here but in the 1820s vandals (or according to folklore 'piskies'!) took it and rolled it all the way down the steep road to Sandplace. It was rescued in 1959 and now acts as the font in the church, near the stone circle. The pamphlet in the church reads: "The stone bowl from the well originally had dolphins carved round the top but they were damaged when the bowl was stolen. On the sides are a snake facing a gryffin, which are not Christian images." It is certainly an impressive and incredibly rare piece of pre-Christian dark-age art which dates from the sixth century at the earliest. It is well worth a visit, though it is a pity that the dolphins on the rim were so badly damaged. It is interesting to speculate whether it was used for ritual purification rites in pagan times. If so, its present use as a church font would seem most appropriate.

The massive stone basin from the well, now in the church

Both church and well are dedicated to St Cuby. Saint Cybi or Kebius as he was also known was born in Cornwall at Callington in 480CE, the son of a Cornish Chieftain in a well-to-do Romano-British family that could claim Vortigern and Arthur as relatives. He declined to succeed his father and instead became a monk. He founded churches in Gaul and Wales, and spent some time in Ireland before returning to Cornwall. There is an inscribed stone built into the church at Tregony, further to the west, which is known as the Cuby Stone. A splendid local beverage, St Cuby's cider is brewed by Cornish Orchards at Westnorth Farm, near the well.

Postcard image c1930s (author's collection)

Duloe is a Celtic place name whose meaning is uncertain. It is popularly taken to mean 'Two Loos', as the village lies between the East and West Looe rivers. However Dhu-Loo in Cornish actually means black pool and until recent times there was a dark pool in the hollow near the village well. St Cuby's church at Duloe has a rather odd look about it, the thirteenth century tower leaning noticeably towards the rest of the building. According to local folklore this was caused by smugglers storing contraband there! When visiting the church don't miss the splendidly carved gargoyles and grotesque beasts. It has been suggested that the churchyard was the site of an

Iron Age fort because of its circular shape and the fact that the church is built on a low mound. Tredinnick, the neighbouring hamlet means 'the town of the fort'. There is often much confusion surrounding the attribution of a site as a 'fort'. Just as often such places were settlements or farmsteads, and often a circular enclosure can indicate a ceremonial site. If this was the case here then Duloe may represent the continuity in use of a sacred site over more than three thousand years.

The village is on the B3254 road between Liskeard and Looe. The nearest railway station is Causeland, about a mile away. St Cuby's cider is available at the Old Plough House Inn in the village.

Map References:

Duloe Stone Circle: SX235583
St Cuby's Well: SX240579
St Cuby's church: SX234581

AFTER THE DELUGE

My wife Diane and I were on holiday travelling around Shropshire and the Welsh Borders when we first heard on our van's radio that there had been severe weather in North Cornwall and that at least one popular holiday destination had been badly hit by flash floods. Our worst fears were confirmed when the village most badly affected was named in the next bulletin as Boscastle, personally just about my favourite place on the planet. Perhaps it is just as well that we had no television in the van and therefore missed the spectacular and horrifying footage of cars being tossed around like toys in a bath-tub and washed out to sea by a roof-level torrent of filthy water. The newspaper photographs the next morning were frightening enough. We bought several daily papers and read them in silence. Tantalisingly, in all the photographs our favourite museum was just out of sight, but an article in the Telegraph reported that the Christian gift shop had been completely destroyed while the Museum of Witchcraft 'stood firm'. "The Devil looks after his own" one local was reported to have said, attempting a kind of gallows humour. A few quick phone calls later we had established that the owner, our friend Graham King was okay and that he and his staff had escaped without injury, as, remarkably had everyone involved. Over the next few days, as the tales of heroism and amazing escapes unfolded, Graham found time to speak to the 'Today' programme on Radio Four despite being heavily involved in the rescue and clean-up operation with his coastguard colleagues.

While the museum building had indeed stood firm, it appeared that most of the exhibits, comprising the largest and most important collection of its kind anywhere, had been badly damaged.

Arriving home on the Wednesday, one week after the disaster we looked at the museum's website, on which were posted photographs of the devastation. What brought home to me the potential danger and the miraculous lack of human injury or fatality was the picture of Lucy, Graham's beloved Landrover, just dredged up from the harbour and looking as if she had been put through a giant mangle. Further photographs showed the devastation inside the building: There was a two foot deep layer of sewage infected silt throughout most of the ground floor. The party wall between the Museum's store area and the Cornish Goodies gift shop had partially collapsed and would have to be demolished and there was a tide mark around the walls where the flood level had settled at about five feet. Cases had been overturned and smashed by the force of the water and it looked as if very few of the exhibits could have survived.

My first instinct was to get back in the van and head west, to see if I could help in any way, but a more considered approach was obviously needed. Boscastle was still sealed off from the outside world while roads were being rebuilt, debris cleared, and vital services restored. Cars were still being retrieved from the sea and searched for bodies. There would in any case be nowhere for visitors to stay in a town where many of the local people had lost their homes and businesses. The building itself was unsafe, and Graham and his friends would have enough on their plate without having to meet and greet visitors, no matter how well-intentioned. Instead, I sat down and wrote a circular letter appealing for funds from Merry Meet subscribers. It was gratifying that the first three cheques which arrived in the next day or so were all for fifty pounds.

The next day it was time to pack up the bookstall and go off to Herstmonceux Castle for the annual Medieval Festival, where I was trading, and was also booked to play as part of the medieval band Fracta Modi. Our local Pagan Circle had no bric-a-brac stall this year so instead, we put a cauldron in the centre of the tent with a sign

After the Deluge

asking for donations for Boscastle, and when not busy with the bookstall or playing on stage I busked with my medieval fiddle and lute guitar. In this way another £125 was raised for Merry Meet Magazine's museum fund, which ultimately raised well over seven hundred pounds.

On returning home from Herstmonceux on the Tuesday there was a message on the telephone answering machine asking if I could possibly arrange transport back to Eastbourne for Alan Manktelow's faery automata, which was on loan to the museum and had stood in the room next to the mocked-up stone circle. It was now in a sorry state and needed a great deal of remedial work. As it was at my suggestion that the item was loaned in the first place, and I had transported it down there, there was nothing for it but to empty the van and go down there to pick it up. It needed to be removed quickly as there was no room to store it as other exhibits needed the space to dry out. I decided to leave the next morning as I had to be back on Thursday afternoon by 2.30pm for a hospital appointment, for dental surgery.

The area around the bridge over the river Valency showing the village green, the Riverside Hotel and the 'Welly' (top right)

From the front, writer Paul Broadhurst's property appeared relatively unscathed. This rear-view picture tells a different story.

I arrived in the upper town at about 4.30pm and gingerly negotiated the van around the 'Road Closed' signs near the Bottreaux Hotel and began the long descent to the harbour. I was appalled to see that even this high up, all the houses along the road had sandbags in front of their garden gates. It was not until the hairpin bend at the bottom of the hill that the scenes of devastation unfolded fully. Spread out before me was a vast building site. There were cones and bollards lining the river on either side; skips and JCBs were everywhere. A tangle of blue plastic water pipes and cables supplied temporary water and electrical supplies. portaloos, scaffold poles, electricity generators and halogen lamps were much in evidence, with heaps of muck and rubble disfiguring the once beautiful scene. A quick glance to my right reassured me that the dear old 'Welly' – the Wellington Hotel where I have enjoyed several great nights of good music, beer and good company was still standing, though looking rather forlorn with most of its ground and first-floor windows boarded up. The large skips full of furniture and fittings in the car-park told their own tale. Earth Mysteries writer Paul Broadhurst's house and shop 'The Otherworld' looked amazingly intact, considering it is sited just where the rivers Valency and Jordan meet, though later I was to discover that it too had suffered enormous damage.

Feeling very self-conscious, driving a conspicuously new looking camper van into a place where tourists would almost certainly not be welcome at that time, I crossed the main bridge, which now had ugly concrete barrier blocks for parapets, and passed the site of the Clovelly Clothing shop, where Diane had never failed to buy something every time we visited. There was absolutely nothing there save the back wall. The adjacent terraced houses were shored up with scaffolding and planks, with tarpaulins where roofs had been. I passed more no-entry signs and proceeded along the narrow road towards the harbour, now rather narrower than it used to be, with the river wider in several places where the stone-revetted banks had collapsed. The public toilets adjacent to the old lime-kiln had completely gone, and the restaurant close by was badly damaged. I could see a few people in wellington boots and overalls inside. Everywhere there was thick mud and the stench of raw untreated sewage. I tried, and failed to imagine how it was over a week ago just after the disaster. It didn't bear thinking about.

The view across the river to the site of the Clovelly Clothing shop which was completely destroyed. The JCB stands on the village green

I drove past the ice cream shop outside of which we had whiled away some pleasant moments at Easter, eating chips from a plastic tray and watching the birds on the river bank as the water splashed noisily over the pebbles. That wonderful weekend earlier this year spent Morris dancing around the town and the harbour now seemed a world away. All the windows of the Cornish Goodies shop were boarded up, with holes in the roof presumably caused by cars and trees as they were washed past. I was to find out later that the river, once the lower bridge by the museum had become blocked with debris, almost instantly silted up and changed its course, effectively running through the shop. Unfortunately, the Harbour Light was then directly in its path.

One of the museum display cases, wrecked in the flood, is seen propped up against a skip on the museum forecourt

I parked next to another VW camper outside the museum, which although it looked relatively undamaged, had been completely

After the Deluge

submerged and was an insurance write-off. I could hear Graham was busy with a contractor upstairs so I had a few moments to survey the scene. Freya (my terrier dog) sniffed the air, bewildered. She obviously recognised Graham's voice and seemed to know we had been here before, but it was all so different. Of the Harbour Light Christian Gift shop opposite the museum, not a single brick or stone appeared to be left standing. Its destruction was absolutely complete. Whatever one may feel about the redoubtable Trixie Webster's religious views the loss of this beautiful building, formerly known as the Pixie House, one of the most photographed in all of Cornwall is a tragedy, and one must hope that it may be possible to build something at least close to the original to replace it. Later, Graham expressed a wish that perhaps when rebuilt, it could stand as a monument and exhibition centre about the flood that destroyed it and the subsequent rescue and rebuilding of the town and its community.

The Youth Hostel and the site of the Harbour Light

Graham seemed composed but completely shattered as he showed me around the building by torchlight. Upstairs, the museum had escaped with a wet floor and 90% humidity. The exhibits there were all intact but would have to be moved carefully to avoid damage caused by the damp atmosphere – mould growth, rust etc. For now, the rescue effort was concentrated downstairs, where the filthy sludge, which had to be picked through by hand, had now been cleared. Many exhibits had been rescued and Graham was now optimistic that overall maybe nine out of ten of the artefacts could be saved. Many of these had been cleaned up and were drying out under relatively controlled condition in two lock-up garages close to Graham's cottage. These included the mummified cat, which was apparently as limp as a wet chamois leather when first removed from the silt, and Alex Saunder's ceremonial mask, which had escaped with a couple of broken feathers. Many objects were still attached to the walls or in relatively undamaged, though filthy and wet cases. The cases attached to the walls had come off best, apart from one that had collapsed when the block-work which supported it shifted during the flood. Graham's favourite display, the divination cabinet, was relatively undamaged, as was the case relating to Satanism and Devil Worship. The Witch's kitchen was filthy but still there, and 'Joan' the resident witch had survived intact. After giving some firemen (who at first thought she was a real body) a bit of a scare she had been cleaned up, and with her clothes washed, was now sitting serenely in a chair upstairs, as if she'd seen it all before. Other cases which were free standing and not fixed down had been tossed around in the water and upended. One still lay thus, its glass though remarkably unbroken, smeared with mud and obscured with condensation. The contents were an unrecognisable mess in the bottom. The only two major exhibits found to have been destroyed so far were the sorcerer's wooden chest, and the Gypsy fortune-teller's tambourine, both of which are beyond repair.

Amazingly, Alan's faery automata had survived complete with little physical damage apparent at first sight, partly because being tethered to the wall by its electrical flex limited the extent to which it was dashed against the walls and other exhibits. After it was hosed down and disinfected it was left in the sun for a day or two to dry, and to allow the ultra-violet light to kill off the bacteria from the sewage. While we did not try to plug it in, the mechanisms appeared intact, and by pulling the drive-chain the figures could still be made to

After the Deluge

move. Obviously it was completely filthy and poor Alan will have to asses the damage and cost involved for the insurance claim. Taking it apart, cleaning every piece and reassembling it will be a phenomenal task in terms of time and patience, but Graham is determined to re-open the museum next season and would dearly like to have it back for the re-opening. The library and archives have already been evacuated to the Maritime Museum in Falmouth, paintings are being looked after by the Royal Cornwall Gallery in Truro and the Cycling Museum near Camelford has made storage space available for Graham to collect new or second-hand fixtures and fittings ready for the refurbishment. The day I arrived, Graham had been to collect some cases donated by a medical museum north of Bristol which was closing down, and it seems there may be a possibility of some new exhibits coming his way from that source to replace those in the folk-medicine section of the museum - one of the most badly damaged displays.

The task of rebuilding will be enormous. The downstairs walls and floor will have to be stripped back to the bare stone and rebuilt where necessary. Various bits of plaster wall sagged inwards from the weight of the water which had got behind it, and the large mirrors behind the stone circle display bowed ominously, as their supporting frames behind had distorted in the wet conditions. Graham explained that he would be using local helpers to do the clearing and rebuilding, as not only is it impossible to accommodate outside volunteers at present, but it is a very important healing process for the community itself to be involved with rebuilding the key buildings and businesses in the village. While as Wiccans and Pagans, most of us feel a proprietorial interest in the museum and its well being, it is only right that those whose livelihoods have been so badly affected by the disaster should be the principle workforce to get the museum, Boscastle's biggest tourist draw, back on its feet. The time will come, hopefully before next Easter when outsiders will be welcome to help redecorate and redisplay items, but for now it has to be down to Graham and his supporters within the community of Boscastle. Thinking it a bit flippant at a time like this, I rather nervously asked if he thought it would be okay for Hunters Moon Morris to come and dance again next Easter, whether or not the museum was reopened by then. He smiled, "We'd all be absolutely delighted, and yes, we will be open again by then".

Graham King in the entrance to the wrecked museum.

After we had wrapped Alan's automata carefully with bubble-wrap and thick polythene sheet, I parked the van near Graham's cottage and walked Freya along the green path, back to the harbour, guiltily taking a few photographs, afraid of being seen as a 'catastrophe tourist'. It was a beautiful sunny evening, but the place was almost deserted. There was an eerie silence, with no cars arriving or departing from this once bustling, thriving tourist 'honeypot'. I crossed the now tame river Valency by the old bridge near the harbour entrance which now had plastic netting and metal fence panels for parapets.

After the Deluge

    I walked up the right hand side of the valley to the Wellington Hotel, where the traditional Wednesday night song session was about to take place, albeit in the road outside, the famous hotel (where Thomas Hardy once stayed) now being dangerous and cordoned off. I met Kerriann whose cottage narrowly escaped damage and was used as the coastguards' HQ during the rescue operation. She offered me a beer and we stood listening as a small group of people arrived and began to sing. I recognised several old favourites, and the scene was incredibly moving as more singers arrived in the gathering dusk, especially during the rousing chorus line of "Rise again". I felt a huge wave of affection for these brave people, determined to stick to their traditions and determined above all, to rebuild their town, their businesses, their buildings; their community. I heard of the narrow escape of the score or so of drinkers and diners who, warned by one of the locals that the waters were rising as never before, escaped minutes before the River Jordan, which normally runs in a culvert beneath the building, suddenly punched a sixteen foot hole through the back wall, and flowed instead through the famous 'Long Bar' and out through the front windows taking with it the ceiling and the floor above. I heard of the bravery of the hotel's chef, a keen surfer who donned his wetsuit and set about rescuing people from stranded cars. I heard about the heroism of Graham himself, who as auxiliary coastguard tirelessly played a huge part in the rescue operations. Even Freya seemed quite awed, and sat quietly listening to the singers.

    Onwards to the Cobweb Inn, the only pub (in fact by then the only business) to have re-opened in the lower part of the town. A massive clean-up operation had got the place looking as though the flooding had never happened. Most of the assembled company from outside the Welly had arrived for a drink, and were soon joined by the lads from Port Isaac a few miles along the coast who had come to sing sea-shanties with the local singers as the pot was passed round for the Boscastle Disaster Fund. After rousing versions of 'Bound for South Australia' and many other old favourites, the pub quietened as the crowd left to go and sing in the Napoleon, at the top of the town. As I had a horribly early start the next morning I said my goodbyes to Graham and stayed for one more pint of delicious Cornish 'Doom

Bar' ale (no irony intended!). Before heading back to the van with Freya, I chatted with a Pagan couple who had had the misfortune to have purchased a local B&B at the harbour just before the disaster occurred. Their premises were undamaged but there would be little prospect of a good season in this, their first summer. Far from being downhearted, they were celebrating the arrival of their very first guests, who were foreign tourists and had apparently not heard of the disaster beforehand. "If you bump into some rather bewildered Germans wandering about," they said, "tell them we're in here – we'll buy them a drink!"

This article appeared in Merry Meet and Quest magazine in 2004

POSTSCRIPT:

The Museum of Witchcraft re-opened the following year after much renovation and repair-work, with most of the exhibits cleaned and restored; Alan Manktelow's faery automata is back in place entertaining the visitors once more; the village of Boscastle suffered the disruption of building and flood prevention works for several years, and was finally back to normal in the summer of 2008. The Harbour Light has been rebuilt and is open again as a Christian café.

The Museum of Witchcraft is open daily from Easter to Halloween. www.museumofwitchcraft.com

BIBLIOGRAPHY

Aburrow, Yvonne, *Auguries & Omens* Capall Bann 1994
Adkins, Lesley & Roy, *Dictionary of Roman Religion* OUP 2000
Alexander, Marc, *British Folklore Myths & Legends* BCA 1982
Alexander, Marc, *Folklore, Myths & Customs of Britain* Sutton 2002
Armstrong, J R, *A History of Sussex* Darwen Finlayson 1961
Beckett, Arthur, *The Spirit of the Downs* Methuen 1930
Beer, Phil, Hutchings, Ashley & While, Chris *Ridgeriders* (CD) 1999
Boardman, John *Great God Pan, The Survival of an Image* Thames & Hudson 1997
Bord, Janet & Colin *Mysterious Britain* Granada 1978
Bowley, E L, *The Fortunate Isles* Bowley 1990
Burl, Aubrey, *Prehistoric Avebury* Yale 1979
Burl, Aubrey, *The Stone Circles of Britain Ireland and Brittany* Yale 2000
Castleden, Rodney, *The Wilmington Giant* Turnstone Press 1983
Childe, E G, *The Dawn of European Civilization* Harper-Collins 1973
Clark, Cumberland, *Shakespeare & The Supernatural* Williams & Northgate 1931
Cavaliero, Glen, *John Cowper Powys, Novelist* Clarendon Press 1973
Cobbett, William *Rural Rides* Penguin 2001
Cope, Julian, *The Modern Antiquarian* Thorsons 1998
Cummins, WA, *King Arthur's Place in Pre-History* Sutton 1992
Cunliffe, Barry, *The Ancient Celts* OUP 1997
Darrah, John, *The Real Camelot* Thames & Hudson 1981
Darvill, Timothy, *Prehistoric Britain* Batsford 1987

Darvill, TC *Long Barrows of the Cotswolds* Tempus 2004
Day, Brian, *A Chronicle of Folk Customs* Hamlyn 1998
Dewar, H S L, *Dorset Monographs No 4: Maumbury Rings* Dorset DNH&AS 1968
English Heritage, *Stanton Drew Stone Circles* EH 1997
Fitch, Eric, *In Search of Herne The Hunter* Capall Bann 1994
Fortune, Dion, *The Goat Foot God* Aquarian Press 1989
Frazer, James, *The Golden Bough* MacMillan 1941
Gardner, Gerald *The Meaning of Witchcraft* I-H-O Books 2000
Gardner, Gerald, 1954 *Witchcraft Today* Arrow Books 1970
Glover, Judith, *Sussex Place Names* Batsford 1986
Graham, Kenneth, *The Wind in the Willows* Bantam Classics 1983
Graves, Robert, *English & Scottish Ballads* Heinemann 1967
Graves, Robert, *The Greek Myths* Pelican 1972
Graves, Robert, *The White Goddess* Faber 1999
Grose, Francis, *The Antiquities of England & Wales* Kessinger 2008
Green marian, *A Harvest of Festivals* Longman 1980
Green, Miranda, *Celtic Goddesses* British Museum 1995
Green, Miranda, *The Gods of the Celts* Sutton 1986
Grinsell, LV, *Dorset barrows* DNH&AS 1959
Grinsell, LV, *Folklore of Prehistoric Sites in Britain* David & Charles 1976
Hall, Chris, *The Cauldron and the Cave* in *The Leyhunter* 1987
Hardy, Thomas, Ed H Orel *Thomas Hardy's Personal Writings* Macmillan 1966
Hardy, Thomas, *The Mayor of Casterbridge* Macmillan 1960
Harris, Max, *Carnival, and other Christian Festivals* University of Texas 2003
Harte, Jeremy, *Cuckoo Pounds & Singing Barrows* DNH&AS 1986
Harte, Jeremy, *Explore Fairy Traditions* Heart of Albion Press 2004
Hawkes, Jaquetta & Christopher *Prehistoric Britain* Chatto & Windus 1947
Henig, Martin, *Religion in Roman Britain* Palgrave Macmillan 1984
Hole, Christina, *A Dictionary of Folk Customs* Helicon 1976
Howard, Mike, *Angels & Goddesses* Capall Bann 1993
Hutton, Ronald, *Stations of the Sun* OUP 1996

Bibliography

Hutton, Ronald, *The Pagan Religions of the Ancient British Isles* Blackwell 1991
Hutton, Ronald, *The Rise and Fall of Merry England* OUP 1994
Hutton, Ronald, The *Triumph of the Moon* OUP 1997
Hutton, Ronald, *Witches Druids & King Arthur* Hambledon & London 2003
James MacKillop *Dictionary of Celtic Mythology* OUP 1988
Jennings, Pete, *Old Glory & The Cutty Wren* Gruff 2003
Kay-Robinson, Denys, *The Landscape of Thomas Hardy* Webb & Bower 1984
Kaye-Smith, Shiela, *Weald of Kent and Sussex* Hale 1973
Keen, Laurence, William Barnes, *The Somerset Engravings* Somerset CC Library Service 1989
Keen, Laurence & Lindgren, Charlotte, *William Barnes, The Dorset Engravings* DNH&AS 1989
Knight, Peter, *Ancient Stones of Dorset* Power Publications 1996
Knight, Peter, *Sacred Dorset* Capall Bann 1998
Knight, Wilson G, *The Saturnian Quest* Methuen 1964
Krisdottir, Morine, *John Cowper Powys and The Magical Quest* Macdonald & Janes 1980
Legg, Rodney, 1998 *Stanton Drew: Great Western Temple* Wincanton Press 1998
Lewis, M J T, *Temples in Roman Britain* Cambridge UP 1966
Lewis, Richard, *The Magic Spring* Atlantic Books 2005
Lucy, Margaret, *Shakespeare and The Supernatural* Kessinger 2006
Marples, Morris, *White Horses & Other Hill Figures* Sutton 1981
Martineau, *Mazes & Labyrinths in Great Britain Wooden* Books 2000
Matthews, John & Caitlin *Encyclopaedia of Celtic Myth & Legend* Lyons Press 2004
Matthews, John, *The Quest for the Green Man* Quest Books 2001
McCall, Andrew, *The Medieval Underworld* BCA 1979
Merrifield, Ralph, *The Archaeology of Ritual and Magic* Batsford 1987
Morrish, John, (Ed) *Working With the Folk Tradition* Backbeat Books 2007
Murdoch, Adrian, *The Last Pagan* Sutton 2003
Murray, Margaret, *The God of the Witches* Faber & Faber 1956

Murray, Margaret, *The Witch Cult in Western Europe* Clarendon Press 1962
Museum of Witchcraft, *Songs of Witchcraft and Magic* (CD) 2007
Newman, Paul, *Gods and Graven Images - The Chalk Hill Figures of Britain* Hale 1987
Newton, Toyne, *The Demonic Connection* Blandford 1987
North, John, *Stonehenge, Neolithic Man &The Cosmos* HarperCollins 1996
Oates, Caroline & Wood, Juliette *A Coven of Scholars* Folklore Society 1998
Partridge, JB *Cotswold Place Lore and Customs* in *Folklore no 4 vol 23* 1964
Pegg, Bob, *Rites and Riots* Blandford 1981
Powys, John Cowper, Ed Morine Krissdottir & Roger Peers *The Dorset Year* Powys Press 1998
Powys, John Cowper, *A Glastonbury Romance* MacDonald 1955
Powys, John Cowper, *Autobiography* The Bodley Head 1949
Powys, John Cowper, *Maiden Castle* University of Wales Press 1990
Powys, John Cowper, *Owen Glendower* The Bodley Head 1941
Powys, John Cowper, *Porius* Colgate University Press 1994
Powys, John Cowper, *Weymouth Sands* Rivers Press 1971
Powys, John Cowper, *Wolf Solent* Jonathan Cape 1929
Powys, John Cowper, *Wood And Stone* Heinemann 1917
Powys, Llewellyn, *Scenes from a Somerset Childhood* Redcliffe 1986
Powys, Llewellyn, *Somerset Essays* John Lane The Bodley Head 1937
Price, Simon & Kearns, Emily *The Oxford Dictionary of Classical Mythology* OUP 1984
Readers Digest, *Folklore Myths & Legends of Britain* 1973
Reeves, Compton, *Pleasures & Pastimes in Medieval England* Sutton 1995
Richards, Mark, *The Cotswold Way* Penguin 1984
Rolleston, T W, *Myth & Legends of the Celtic Race* CRW Publishing 2004
Ronald, Millar, *The Green Man Companion and Gazetteer* SB Publications 1997
Roud, Steve & Upton, Eddie, & Taylor, Malcolm *Still Growing* EFDSS 2003

Bibliography

Sapouna-Sakellarakis, Efi, *Cycladic Civilization* Appolo Editions 1971
Sauer, Eberhard, *The Archaeology of Religious Hatred* Tempus 2003
Seznec, Jean, *The Survival of the Pagan Gods* Princeton UP 1981
Shortt, Hugh, *The Giant and Hob-Nob* Salisbury Museum 1972
Simpson, Jaqueline & Roud, Steve, *Oxford Dictionary of English Folklore* OUP 2000
Simpson, Jaqueline, *The Folklore of Sussex* Batsford 1973
Society of Antiquaries, *Archaeologia Vol CV* SoA 1976
Stanier, Peter, *Dorset's Archaeology* Dorset Books 2004
Stewart, Bob, *Where is Saint George?* Moonraker Press 1977
Strong, Gordon, *The Sacred Stone Circles of Stanton Drew* 2005
Tacitus, *The Histories* Penguin Classics 1984
Valiente, Doreen, *An ABC of Witchcraft* Hale 1984
Valiente, Doreen, *Where Witchcraft Lives* Aquarian Press 1962
Valiente, Doreen, *Witchcraft for Tomorrow* Hale 1978
Vinci, Leo, *Pan, Great God of Nature* Neptune 1993
Watts, Dorothy, *Religion in Late Roman Britain* Routledge 1998
Westwood, Jennifer & Simpson, Jaqueline, *The Lore of the Land* Penguin 2005
Westwood, Jennifer, *Albion* Granada 1985
Whistler, Laurence, *The English Festivals* Heinemann 1947
Wood, Peter, *John Barleycorn: Evolution of a Folk-Song Family* in *Folk Music Journal Vol 8/4* EFDSS 2004
Woodward, Ann, *Shrines and Sacrifice* Batsford 1972

WEBSITES

curses.csad.ox.ac.uk/
hoopixart.com
www.archaeology.co.uk
www.battelbonfire.co.uk
www.britarch.ac.uk
www.castles.me.uk/roman-temples.htm
www.chrischapmanphotography.com
www.contemplator.com/child
www.dorsetooser.fsnet.co.uk
www.english-heritage.org.uk
www.everythingexmoor.co.uk
www.gaybogies.co.uk
www.geants-carnaval.org
www.giants.org.uk
www.gippeswic.demon.co.uk
www.hastingsjack.co.uk
www.historic-uk.com/CultureUK/OldGlory.htm
www.lammasfest.org
www.legendarydartmoor.co.uk
www.lordmayorsshow.org
www.megalithic.co.uk
www.megalithics.com
www.merrymeetmagazine.co.uk

Bibliography

www.minehead-online.co.uk
www.mudcat.org
www.museumoflondon.org.uk
www.museumofwitchcraft.com
www.powys-society.co.uk
www.roman-britain.org
www.sacredsites.com
www.sacredthreads.net/morris
www.sheffieldcitygiants.co.uk
www.sbbrit.org.uk
www.sussexcountry.co.uk/
www.thecompanyofthegreenman.co.uk
www.themodernantiquarian.com
www.theotherside.co.uk
www.wessexmorrismen.co.uk
www.woodland-trust.org.uk/
www2.prestel.co.uk/aspen/sussex/

With apologies to any authors or websites I may have missed out.

England's Living Folklore

MERRY MEET MAGAZINE

Merry Meet Magazine is an independent journal of folklore and Paganism published quarterly at the solstices and equinoxes in the UK. It is published and largely written by the author of this book. Most of the material here has been re-written from articles which have appeared in the magazine since its inception in 2002.

To find out more, or to subscribe to the magazine please visit www.merrymeetmagazine.co.uk

Or write to:

Jerry Bird
Editor, Merry Meet Magazine,
51 Prospect Road
Dorchester
Dorset
DT1 2PF
United Kingdom